Celebrating African-American Achievements

WHO'S WHO in BLACK Chicago

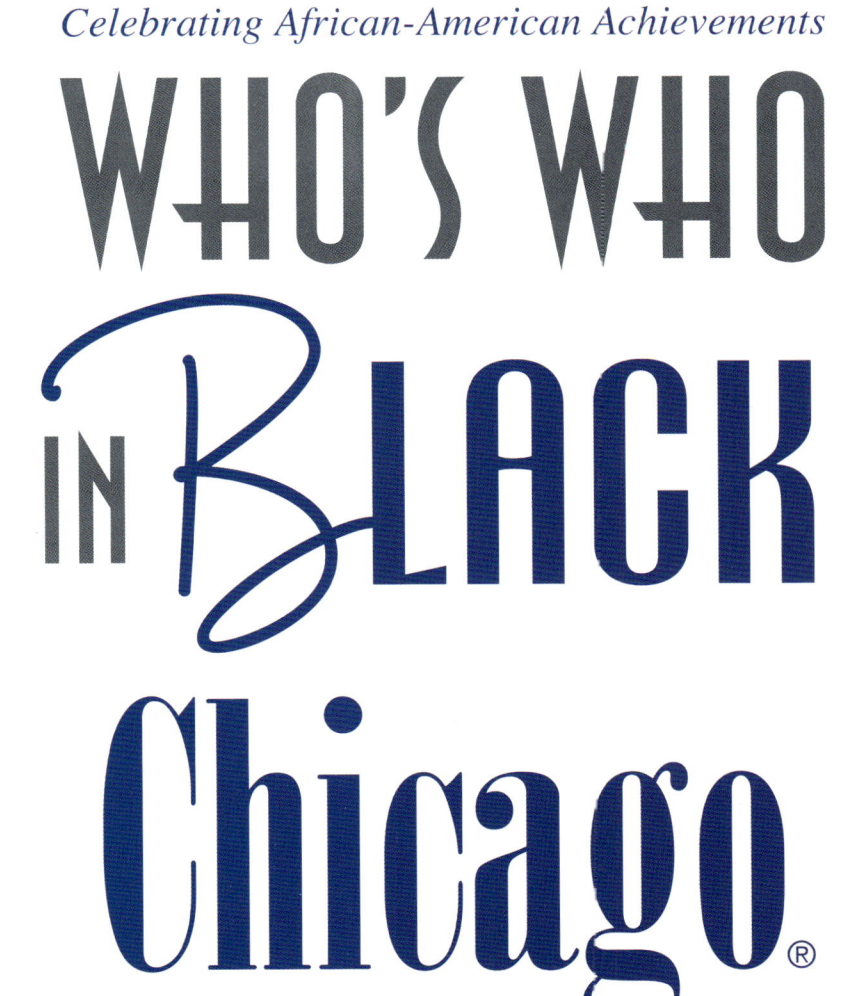

THE INAUGURAL EDITION

Celebrating African-American Achievements

WHO'S WHO IN BLACK Chicago®

THE INAUGURAL EDITION

Who's Who In Black Chicago®
is a registered trademark of
Briscoe Media Group, LLC

Purchase additional copies online @
www.whoswhopublishing.com

Corporate Headquarters
Who's Who Publishing Co., LLC
1650 Lake Shore Drive, Ste. 250
Columbus, Ohio 43204

All Credit Cards Accepted
Inquiries for Bulk Purchases for youth groups, schools, churches, civic or professional organizations, please call our office for volume discounts.

Corporate Headquarters
(614) 481-7300

Copyright © 2006 by C. Sunny Martin,
Briscoe Media Group, LLC

Library of Congress Control Number: 2006926762

All rights reserved. Printed in the United States of America. No part of this book may be used or reproduced in any manner whatsoever without the written permission from the Publisher, except in the case of brief quotations embodied in critical articles or reviews. For information, send request to address above.

Photo Credits
C. Sunny Martin
Steve Matteo, Getty Images
Powell Photography, Inc.
Billy Smith
Rodney Wright, Image Makers Photography
Dave Buston / AFP/ Getty Images
Tannen Maury / AFP/ Getty Images
Brad Barket / Getty Images

ISBN # 1-933879-01-7
$34.95 each-USA

THIS BOOK WAS MADE POSSIBLE BY THE GENEROUS SUPPORT OF OUR

Sponsors

Platinum Sponsor

HYATT Hotels & Resorts

Diamond Sponsors

U.S. Cellular   Exelon   Sara Lee

LaSalle Bank ABN AMRO   Boeing   Northern Trust

Emerald Sponsor

KRAFT

Unveiling Reception Sponsors

Cintas   Chicago Defender   Jones Lang LaSalle   Hewitt   Aon   Abbott

SIRVA relocation redefined   Peoples Energy   Macy's   Chicago Bears   N'DIGO   Harris

Houghton Mifflin   National City   Motorola   Columbia College Chicago

Proud to be part of the community.

National City is dedicated to strengthening the fabric of the communities we serve. With over $1,000,000 in local community support — including charitable gifts to civic, arts, education and human services groups — as well as economic initiatives, we're proud to help make Chicagoland a better place to live for everyone.

National City

Personal Banking • Business Banking • Investments • Mortgage Loans

First mortgage loans are products of National City Mortgage, a division of National City Bank of Indiana. NationalCity.com • Member FDIC • ©2006, National City Corporation®

CONTENTS

Letters of Greeting 8

Introduction 15

Foreword by John W. Rogers, Jr. 21

Founder & CEO 27

Criteria for Inclusion 28

Publisher's Page 29

Chicago's Legends 35

Hyatt Hotels & Resorts Corporate Spotlight 43

Chicago's Interesting Personalities 54

Boeing Corporate Spotlight 101

Exelon Corporate Spotlight 109

LaSalle Bank Corporate Spotlight 117

Northern Trust Corporate Spotlight 125

Sara Lee Salutes Corporate Spotlight 133

U.S. Cellular Corporate Spotlight 137

Chicago's Most Influential 145

Chicago Bears Spotlight 205

Chicago's Corporate Brass 213

Chicago's Counselors at Law 233

Chicago's Media Professionals 247

Chicago's Academia 261

Chicago's Spiritual Leaders 275

Chicago's Community Leaders 285

Chicago's Entrepreneurs 295

Chicago's Professionals 313

Biographical Index 321

Advertisers' Index 328

THE INAUGURAL EDITION *Who's Who In Black Chicago*®

Meet The Team At Who's Who Publishing Co., LLC

Beverly Coley-Morris
Chicago Publisher

Sheila Agnew
Accounts Manager

Yvette Moyo
Sales Consultant

Yulanda Thomas
Executive Assistant

C. Sunny Martin
Founder & CEO

Ernie Sullivan
Senior Partner

Carter Womack
Regional VP

Paula Gray
Columbus Publisher

Melanie Diggs
Senior Editor

Aaron Leslie
Production Manager

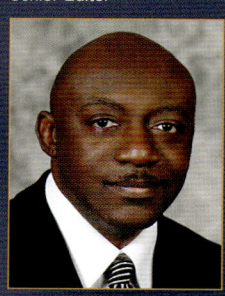

Ivory D. Payne
Senior Graphic Designer

Christina Llewellyn
Graphic Designer

Davina Jackson
Copy Editor

Nathan Wylder
Copy Editor

Ann Coffman
Executive Assistant

Sarah Waite
Webmaster

Corporate Office
1650 Lake Shore Drive, Ste. 250
Columbus, Ohio 43204

(614) 481-7300

Visit Our Web Site
www.whoswhopublishing.com

CHICAGO'S PREMIER HOTEL

EXPERIENCE THE ESSENCE OF THE CITY AT HYATT REGENCY CHICAGO

A vibrant hotel standing at the top of Chicago's Magnificent Mile, near world-class shopping, international cultural attractions, Navy Pier, Millennium Park, and so much more. The hotel features 2,019 guestrooms & suites and six restaurants & lounges. Wireless and high-speed Internet access is available in all guestrooms and suites. This is not your typical hotel story, this is the Hyatt Touch.™ To find out more or to book your next meeting, call our sales representative at 312 239 4540 or visit **chicagohyatt.com**.

HYATT
REGENCY
CHICAGO®
ON THE RIVERWALK

Celebrating African-American Achievements

OFFICE OF THE MAYOR
CITY OF CHICAGO
2006

GREETINGS

As Mayor and on behalf of the City of Chicago, I am pleased to welcome you to the inaugural edition of *Who's Who in Black Chicago*.

Who's Who in Black Chicago is a compilation of Chicago's African American entrepreneurs, business and community leaders, legendary musicians and other individuals who have helped make Chicago a better place to live, work and raise families. The publication will recognize and celebrate the contributions and achievements of African Americans and provide a valuable networking tool for our residents.

I commend *Who's Who in Black Chicago* for its efforts to pay tribute to the many who have made a difference in our community and offer you my best wishes for much continued success in the future.

Sincerely,

Mayor

Celebrating African-American Achievements

BARACK OBAMA

April 6, 2006

Who's Who Publishing
935 W. Chestnut Street, Suite 201
Chicago, Illinois 60622

To the Editors and Honorees of Who's Who in Black Chicago:

  I am pleased to congratulate Who's Who Publishing Company, LLC, the nation's largest African American directory publisher, on the inaugural edition of Who's Who in Black Chicago. For 17 years, this organization has highlighted the positive achievements of African Americans in cities across the country and I am happy that Chicago will pen the next exciting chapter in the history of this successful publishing giant.

  Who's Who in Black Chicago will provide an opportunity to celebrate and recognize some of our city's finest leaders and it is my privilege to acknowledge them for the fine work they have done to build Chicago into the cultural and economic force it is today. Each honoree serves as a living example of how hard work and strength of character leads to success.

  It is no secret that Chicago has a multitude of notable African Americans from politics to entertainment. However, I believe readers of this directory will be amazed at the diversity of career disciplines and experiences that have helped shape the character of our community and provided countless role models for our youth.

  I'd like to take this opportunity to thank the individuals on the following pages for serving as an inspiration to our city, our community and our youth – our city's future Who's Who in Black Chicago.

Sincerely,

Barack Obama
United States Senator

Celebrating African-American Achievements

OFFICE OF THE GOVERNOR
JRTC, 100 WEST RANDOLPH, SUITE 16
CHICAGO, ILLINOIS 60601

March 2006

GREETINGS

As Governor of the State of Illinois, I am pleased to congratulate the Who's Who Publishing Company on the release of Who's Who in Black Chicago.

Who's Who in Black Chicago celebrates and recognizes outstanding leaders whose contributions have made a significant impact in numerous communities. With that in mind, I extend my fondest congratulations and appreciation to each honoree in this publication. Your hard work has certainly made a lasting impact on the State of Illinois, and will undoubtedly continue to do so in the years to come. I am very proud to be a part of this wonderful book.

On behalf of the citizens of Illinois, I offer my best wishes for continued health, happiness and success in the years to come.

Sincerely,

Rod R. Blagojevich
Governor

Celebrating African-American Achievements

JESSE L. JACKSON, JR.
2D DISTRICT, ILLINOIS

Congress of the United States
House of Representatives
Washington, DC 20515-1302

March 20, 2006

Ms. Beverly Coley-Morris
Chicago Publisher
Almae Publisher's Representatives, Inc.
935 West Chestnut Street
Suite 201
Chicago, Illinois 60622

Dear Ms. Coley-Morris:

It is with great pleasure that I congratulate your company for producing the inaugural edition of *Who's Who in Black Chicago*. I know that this was a labor of love and will be a phenomenal success.

From late heroes like Emmett Till and Lorraine Hansberry to living legends such as Koko Taylor and Bernie Mac, African-American Chicagoans have a legacy of which everyone should be proud. In fact, one cannot talk about Black history without mentioning Chicagoans and one cannot talk about Chicago without mentioning Black Americans. I salute you for documenting the lives of a significant population in this magnificent city.

Once again, thanks for this publication! *Who's Who* will be an important resource for all people, in Chicago and throughout the nation.

Sincerely,

Jesse L. Jackson, Jr.
Member of Congress

JLJJr.:JM:jm

2419 RAYBURN HOUSE OFFICE BUILDING
WASHINGTON, DC 20515-1302
(202) 225-0773

2021 EAST 71ST STREET
CHICAGO, IL 60649
(773) 241-6500

17926 SOUTH HALSTED
HOMEWOOD, IL 60430
(708) 798-6000

THIS MAILING WAS PREPARED, PUBLISHED, AND MAILED AT TAXPAYER EXPENSE

Celebrating African-American Achievements

BOBBY L. RUSH
CONGRESS OF THE UNITED STATES
1ST DISTRICT, ILLINOIS

Washington Office:
2416 Rayburn HOB
Washington, D.C. 20515
(202) 225-4372
(202) 226-0333 (fax)

Chicago Office:
700-706 E. 79th Street
Chicago, Illinois 60619
(773) 224-6500
(773) 224-9624 (fax)

Midlothian Office:
3235 West 147th Street
Midlothian, Illinois 60445
(708) 385-9550
(708) 385-3860 (fax)

WEBSITE: http://www.house.gov/rush

April 10, 2006

Dear Friends:

I want to extend my deepest support and congratulations on the inaugural edition of **Who's Who in Black Chicago**. Finally, there's a comprehensive archive of Chicago's vast number of African American leaders who have achieved, transcended, overcome and beat the odds to become successful in their chosen fields. While history over time is subject to be rewritten, *Who's Who in Black Chicago* ensures the legacies of today's African American leaders remain intact.

This publication is a testament to the rich history of African Americans in our city, and will undoubtedly serve as a networking resource when searching for role models, potential contacts or a blueprint for success. While looking for inspiration, I am certain you will find valuable insight that will be instrumental in helping you to achieve your own personal and career goals.

Again, all the best and continued success.

Sincerely,

Bobby L. Rush

Bobby L. Rush
Member of Congress

Celebrating African-American Achievements

OFFICE OF THE SECRETARY OF STATE
Springfield, Illinois 62756

Jesse White
Secretary of State

April 2006

Almae Publisher's Representatives, Inc.
935 West Chestnut Street, Suite 201
Chicago, Illinois 60622

Greetings:

    As Illinois Secretary of State, I am honored to have this opportunity to thank Almae Publishers for making "Who's Who In Black Chicago" a reality.

    Chicago has been home to some of the most accomplished and celebrated African-Americans of our time. Bringing recognition to these individuals – the heroes and legends of our communities, is not only a great way to say "thanks for a job well done," but serves to inspire future generations.

    As you peruse the following pages, I hope that you find the information in this book to be enjoyable and enlightening.

Very truly yours,

Jesse White

JESSE WHITE
Secretary of State

LEADING THROUGH INSPIRATION

By leading through inspiration, we can affect education, economic development and community empowerment. From one dynamic organization to another, we congratulate your accomplishments and support your future.

www.uscellular.com

U.S. Cellular
We connect with you.

We are a drug-free workplace and an equal opportunity employer dedicated to DIVERSITY AND INCLUSION.

Celebrating African-American Achievements

Introduction

CHICAGO'S
EMERGING HISTORY

By Timuel D. Black, Jr.

When one has lived in Chicago as long as I have, and has been as active in the observation of the social, cultural, economical and political life of it as I have, it is very difficult to select three specific developments that have shaped the life of this city as we know it today.

To layout the framework for this introduction, I will say that during my lifetime in the city, the three most important developments have been the following. First, the first great African-American migration to Chicago that took place between 1915 and 1945. This includes the driving forces that made that migration necessary and possible, and the social, political and economic outcomes of that migration. The second development was the Great Depression of 1929-1940, and the impact of that depression on the life and population of Chicago. The third most important influence socially, politically and economically was World War II, with the beginning of a new great migration of African Americans from the south of the United States, and the increased migration of Hispanics from Puerto Rico, Cuba, Mexico and Central America. Also important were the increase of Asians, and particularly the re-settlement of many Japanese Americans from the West Coast to Chicago.

The first great migration of African Americans had its greatest momentum during and immediately after World War I, starting at approximately 59,000 in 1915, increasing to 109,000 in 1920 to 233,000 in 1930, to 275,000 by 1940, and finally to approximately 475,000 in 1950.

WWII advance twin engine pilot training, Chanute Field, Rantoul, IL, 1944

This relatively steady increase of African Americans came mostly from the South during this period of time. It was concentrated in a relatively small geographical area consisting of a narrow strip on the South Side of Chicago, and in small pockets of population on the near West Side and near North Side of the city.

Why did they come? They came from the South for basically the same reasons that the millions of immigrants left Europe before World War II. They came to better their economic conditions. However, they had an additional reason to leave the South. They were fleeing a Jim Crow system of racial prejudice, discrimination and segregation. They were fleeing social, political, economic oppression and physical terrorism.

They felt, as James Grossman had put it in his recent book, that at least they were going to a "Land of Hope." What they found was much less than they had hoped for, but it was much better than what they had fled from. What did they find? They found racial conditions, but they also found a political freedom and opportunity that they had never dreamed of having in the South and they took full advantage of it. It was in that process and flurry of activity that my family arrived in Chicago in October of 1919, right after the 1919 Chicago race riot, where many lives and much property were damaged and destroyed.

This sudden, somewhat massive arrival of African Americans from the South, created new tensions and problems for the old main line residents, as well as for the relatively recently arrived immigrants from various parts of Europe. The competition of jobs, housing and recreation space was agitated and intensified. Where would these newly arrived children and grandchildren of ex-slaves live, work and play? That problem still lives with us today.

16   *Who's Who In Black Chicago*®   THE INAUGURAL EDITION

Kitchenette (one room apartment) family, South Side Chicago, 1940

They were confined to a ghetto, popularized by *Chicago Defender* founder and publisher Robert S. Abbott, as the "Black Belt," a narrow strip of land stretching from 26th Street on the north to 43rd Street on the south; and from the Rock Island railroad tracks on the west to the west side of Cottage Grove Avenue on the east. They were concentrated at 81,000 people per square mile as compared to 19,000 people per square mile for the rest of the city. They worked generally in menial jobs in the Union Stockyards, the steel mills of South Chicago, International Harvester, similar industries and manufacturing plants, and small businesses inside the "Black Belt" itself. Inside this enclave, Chicago jazz, blues and gospel music as well as black businesses were born, nurtured, embraced and exported to places all over the world. There was fun, friendship, and a joyful noise all over the black ghettos of the South and West sides. But it was much too crowded for human health, and so there was constant pressure internally to move beyond its confines, and constant, oft-times violent resistance. There was resistance to physical, economic and social movement. Most of the time this resistance was supported by the white "establishment."

In labor, the trade union movement had its greatest impetus during this period and blacks, who were at first strike breakers, soon became a vital part of this important economic and social movement. The labor movement was to lay the basis for what later became the Chicago civil rights movement, which was a vital part of Dr. Martin Luther King's operation.

In October of 1929, the Great Depression came upon us and quickly engulfed the total economic, social and political life of this city. Plants closed or slowed down with a suddenness that shocked everyone and the uncertainty of the city and the nation's future caused unrest, tensions and havoc all over the city and the nation. There were breadlines, soup kitchens and temporary shelters everywhere. Agitation and radical social organizations were rampant and it was at that time that the Communist Party had its greatest success in Chicago and throughout the nation. The Party made its greatest impact on working class people of all races and creeds and on the young intellectuals. There were no social security benefits such as welfare, unemployment compensation, health insurance and retirement benefits. If you lost your job you were literally out in the cold, on all levels.

The president of the United States, Republican Herbert Hoover, kept reminding us that "prosperity was right around the corner."

Legendary jazz trumpeter, Miles Davis, at the Jumptown Club, Chicago, 1949

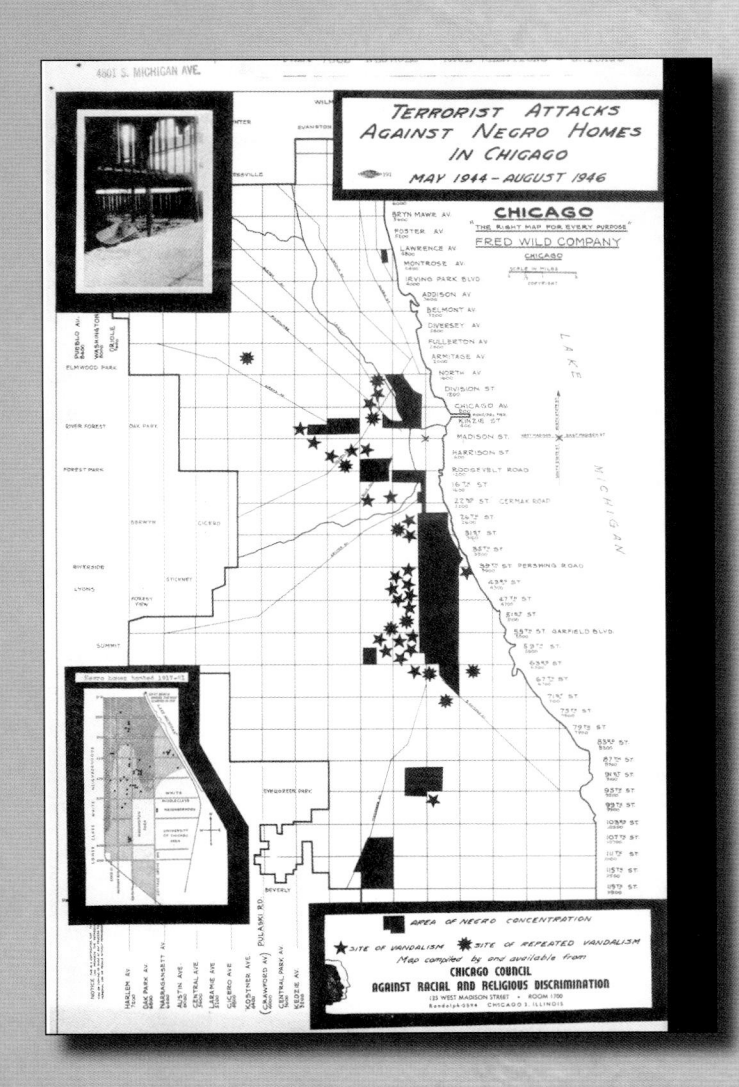

TOP: Picketer at Bowman's Dairy, Chicago, 1941

LEFT: Map of attacks against black homes in Chicago, May 1944 – Aug. 1946, Chicago Council Against Racial and Religious Discrimination

Those who were as young and as naïve as I kept looking around the corner, but all we saw were dark alleys, dark streets, and impoverished people. With few exceptions, we had been electing Republican presidents since Abraham Lincoln. In 1932 the National Democratic Party put up the governor of the state of New York, Franklin Delano Roosevelt, as their candidate. The convention was held here in Chicago.

Roosevelt won by a landslide in 1932, although blacks that could vote continued to vote Republican "because Lincoln freed the slaves." However, in 1936 under the mayoralty of Democratic Mayor Edward Kelley, and with the party switch of 2nd Ward Alderman William L. Dawson, blacks made the sudden and dramatic switch to the Democratic Party and have remained there since. Blacks have had the balance of power for either party since their advent into Chicago, but have not been accorded the benefits from either party commensurate to that support.

Franklin D. Roosevelt immediately created new social and economic programs that helped to renew and revitalize the social and economic life of this city. Such programs as the Public Works Administration (PWA), the Works Progress Administration (WPA), the National Youth Administration (NYA) and the Civilian Conservation Corps (CCC) (sometimes called "priming the pump") helped create a renewal of spirit for their city and industry slowly began to thrive again.

Because most people lived in racial, ethnic, or economic enclaves that were relatively stable, there was a general feeling of security and safety; we were in a very real sense "our brother's keeper." We drifted along this way until December 7, 1941. After that date our city and our world were never to be the same again.

Some of us had been predicting U.S. involvement in war since 1939, when Germany under Hitler had invaded the German-Czech Sudeten land and Poland. To many of us it seemed for many reasons undesirable but inevitable.

On December 7, 1941, my birthday, (as I was celebrating by imbibing) the word came by radio that the American naval fleet in Pearl Harbor had been bombed. The next day, at the recommendation of the president, Congress declared war on Japan and some days later on Germany and Italy. The U.S. immediately began to marshal all of its economic, military, social and human resources in war.

> "Blacks also sought relief from the tyranny and violence of Jim Crow and social injustice."

Dr. King about to be hit by a rock at a fair housing march through the Marquette Park and Chicago Lawn neighborhoods, August 5, 1966

We became the arsenal and the breadbasket of all of the Allied forces that were under siege, particularly Britain, France and the U.S.S.R.

Thus came the advent of the second great migration of blacks from the South. Needed for war labor and the armed services, hundreds of thousands of blacks and poor whites left the cotton and tobacco fields of the South for better paying jobs in the war industry. Blacks also sought relief from the tyranny and violence of Jim Crow and social injustice. Most of them were never to return south, not even to visit; Chicago's black population skyrocketed from 275,000 in 1940, to approximately 500,000 in 1950. This included the veterans as well. Improved highways and transportation made white flight to the suburbs easy, but expensive. The U.S. government helped in this flight through various subsidies to whites, which were unknown or unavailable to blacks. Schools began to deteriorate as the struggle for equal and quality education mounted; tensions increased and white flight accelerated. Industry and business, on the pretext of modernization and lower taxes, fled the cities claiming they needed more trained, disciplined and skilled workers, while withdrawing their resources that would have made this possible.

The result was a modernizing, fleeing industrial base, and a fleeing middle-class population, sometimes making their money in the city but taking that money and their taxes with them. Thus they left behind an increasingly unskilled and poor, black and Hispanic population to forage for themselves, while being deprived of the legitimate tools to forage with. This natural increase in disappointment, frustration, anger, confusion, poverty, violence and crime seems to be the natural outcome of these historical, economical, political, social and cultural changes.

At one point, some of us thought we had a partial answer or solution to these problems with the election of more state and local politicians to office, and certainly the election of Harold Washington was a crowning point of that effort. But we see what happened: Racism is so deeply imbedded in this city that the political and economic forces contrived to handicap and finally to work Harold Washington to death, while he strove mightily to bring unity, harmony and prosperity to this city.

However, we shall keep on keeping on. Because of Chicago's success story for literally hundreds of black men and women, there are several people, which due to space, cannot be noted at this time. They are all good examples of the possibilities in a city like Chicago.

Foreword

By John W. Rogers, Jr.

A City Rich in Black Leadership

I have always felt fortunate to be from Chicago. Even though many may refer to it as the second city, in my mind Chicago will always be first. The city boasts many charms—its beautiful lakefront, amazing architecture, numerous museums and cultural activities—not to mention unbelievable athletic teams—like the Bulls and the Bears. In terms of business, Chicago has become a hotbed of entrepreneurship and a nucleus of significant black leadership as underscored by this directory.

In my own career, I was fortunate to be influenced by the leadership of some of Chicago's quintessential entrepreneurs—legendary leaders like John Johnson and George Johnson—truly giants of a generation. In addition to building remarkable businesses, they made significant philanthropic contributions to our city. In doing so, they established an important legacy of leadership for others to follow and proved that black innovation and influence would be a force not a footnote in American history.

Giants of a Generation

Like many other black Chicagoans, their stories are awe-inspiring in terms of what they achieved and the obstacles they overcame. The late John Johnson built what would become the largest black-owned publishing company in the world. He marked an important milestone in 1971, when he moved Johnson Publishing to Michigan Avenue, becoming the first African American to open an office building in the Chicago Loop. George Johnson created Johnson Products, a titan in hair care, which became the first African-American company ever traded on a national stock exchange. They built incredible brands spanning multiple industries, which opened important job opportunities for thousands of blacks. Equally as important, their leadership and innovation were sought after by prestigious organizations, giving them multiple platforms to promote diversity and influence both thought and commerce. For example, John Johnson provided counsel to U.S. presidents and other political leaders.

THE INAUGURAL EDITION *Who's Who In Black Chicago*® 21

Celebrating African-American Achievements

He served on a number of boards including Chrysler and Twentieth Century Fox Film, as well as the advisory council at Harvard's Graduate School of Business. Additionally, he was a major supporter and contributor to the United Negro College Fund. Similarly, George Johnson was actively involved in the community. He became the first African American appointed to the board of Commonwealth Edison and accepted leadership roles in the Chicago Urban League, OperationPUSH, and Northwestern Memorial Hospital. In addition, he established his own foundation and educational fund.

From my perspective, their lives are special for many reasons. First, they succeeded without inherited wealth or a social network, and marked major firsts for the black community. Second, they serve as great examples to countless others on how to become strong and effective leaders. And far beyond their accumulation of individual wealth and recognition, they illustrated how giving back to the broader community could drive social change and help more African Americans rise to the forefront of Chicago business and society. Each became a tremendous inspiration, not only for black Americans, but for all people.

CREATING A COMMUNITY

In 1983, when I started Ariel Capital Management, it was the culmination of my dream to manage money professionally. The leadership and civic commitment of both John Johnson and George Johnson had a significant impact on my vision for Ariel—a vision which extended far beyond financial performance or assets under management. I hoped to build a successful business while fostering an ideal work environment that would effect positive change in the community. Today, our company remains committed to its original ambition to be the premier small and mid-cap value investment firm in the nation. In addition, I am inspired to work with a team of diverse and passionate people who are united in their pursuit of excellence, not only in business but also in life.

CARRYING THE TORCH

As a black Chicagoan, I am proud of the city's commitment to diversity and social reform. Chicago has been good to me and to Ariel. Yet I am aware that too many doors remain closed. I know how hard it can be to break in—to do business with institutions having many well-established relationships. Although unfairness still exists, each of us has a responsibility to change this. I believe we can create positive change by asking questions and creating awareness for a diversity agenda in the organizations and institutions we belong to or establish.

Looking to the future, I am inspired by the current generation of leaders emerging from the Chicago community. Take Oprah as just one example. She is at the top of everyone's *Who's Who* list. Oprah is a success story not only as a black woman, but as an incredible human being. She is one of the giants of our time, who like so many other Chicagoans, is doing her part to guide the torch of the past generation and inspire exemplary leaders for generations to follow.

As I reflect on the names in this book, I am reminded that the black community is making important contributions to every area of the Chicago community. These pages represent what a tremendous network of black leaders are living in our city, and when we work together we can make a world of change.

— *John W. Rogers, Jr.* —

Diversity
empowers us.

Exelon embraces the differences that make each of us unique, and enrich us all. Together we can build a world where our differences make us stronger.

That's our promise. That's our way.^{SM}

Exelon®

© 2006 Exelon

www.exeloncorp.com

"Understanding risk is one thing. Understanding our business is another. We need someone who does both."

You need an adviser who enables you to confidently secure the best risk management solutions for your company. Aon offers the kind of market presence that commands results. Our experts know your industry, understand the risks and have the resources needed to ensure that this objective becomes your accomplishment.

With 500 offices and 47,000 professionals in the United States and abroad, Aon is one of the world's leading providers of risk management, insurance and reinsurance brokerage, and human capital consulting services.

www.aon.com or +1.866.4AONNOW

AON

Risk Management • Insurance & Reinsurance Brokerage • Human Capital & Management Consulting • Outsourcing

www.boeing.com

SOME SEE A WALL. OTHERS, A BRIDGE.

It takes vision to empower a community and courage to enact change. We salute those who understand the passion of possibility. Boeing is proud to support individuals and organizations that inspire betterment for minority communities everywhere.

BOEING
Forever New Frontiers

Leaders.

Columbia College Chicago salutes our civic and business leaders, who contribute to the vibrancy and vitality of our dynamic city.

create... change

As the **largest arts and media college** in the nation and one of the most diverse colleges in the Midwest, Columbia is committed to **providing access and opportunity** to motivated young people who aspire to careers in creative fields. With a curriculum focused on the **leading edge of arts and culture,** and taught by faculty working in their disciplines, we provide an education that is relevant, experiential, and rigorous.

We invite you to engage with Columbia College Chicago. You can learn more about our academic programs, accomplished alumni, and public cultural events at www.colum.edu.

www.colum.edu

Columbia
COLLEGE CHICAGO

A MESSAGE FROM THE Founder & CEO

C. Sunny Martin

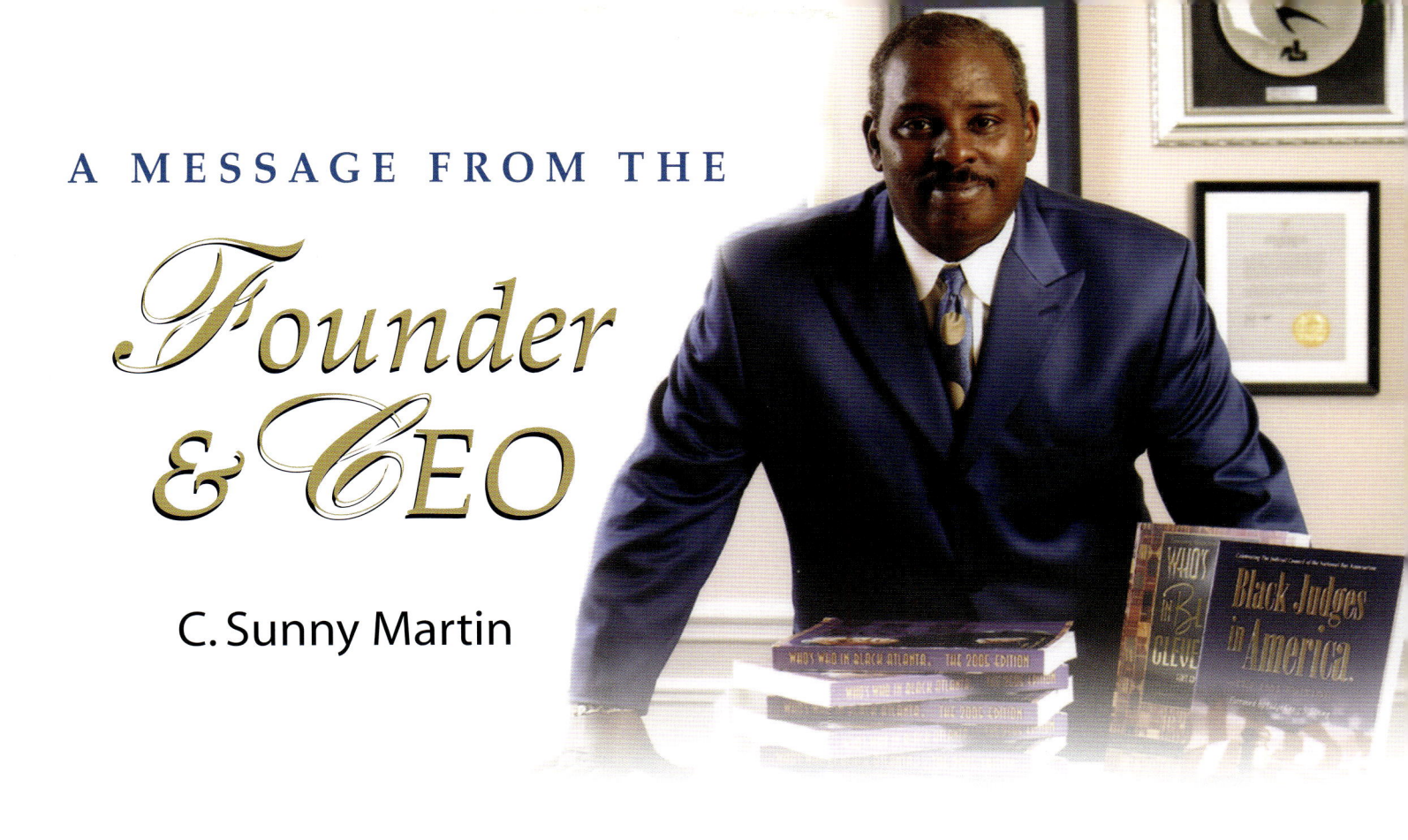

"If you fall in love with what you do, you never work again."
— JOHN H. JOHNSON

Welcome Chicago! We are truly honored to present this inaugural edition of **Who's Who In Black Chicago**® to the citizens of Chicago.

Since the 1940s, the Windy City had made its claim as the "Capital of Black America." Notables such as Congressman William Dawson, newspaper editor John Sengstacke, Mahalia Jackson, *Native Son* author Richard Wright, Joe Louis, *Ebony* magazine publisher John H. Johnson, and Nation of Islam leader Elijah Muhammad are all remarkable trailblazers who called Chicago home. And, who can ever forget "Sweetness," the great Chicago Bears hall of fame running back whose moves on the football field were as smooth as the soulful sounds of Lou Rawls, another legendary Chicagoan?

This is just the beginning of our commitment to annually present an upscale quality publication that celebrates the achievements of Chicago's most remarkable African-American citizens.

We are indeed thankful that Beverly Coley-Morris, our Chicago associate publisher, embraced our vision and has remained deeply passionate about telling your story and exposing the tremendous wealth of African-American history and talent that exists in this great city.

In closing, we sincerely hope you enjoy this quality edition and are perhaps motivated to share this publication with several young school age children. Be sure to tell them to keep dreaming big dreams because black Chicagoans have always represented the very best of the best!

Stay strong and remain blessed,

C. Sunny Martin
CEO & Founder

Criteria for Inclusion

Who's Who In Black Chicago® is an opportunity for us to afford a measure of recognition to the men and women who have made their mark in their specific occupations, professions, or in service to others in the Chicago community.

A sincere effort was made to include those whose positions or accomplishments in their chosen fields are significant and those whose contributions to community affairs, whether city-wide or on the neighborhood level, have improved the quality of life for all of us.

The names of those brief biographies included in this edition were compiled from customary sources of information. Lists of a wide variety were consulted and every effort was made to reach all whose stature or civic activities merited their inclusion.

In today's mobile society, no such publication could ever claim to be complete; some who should be included could not be reached or chose not to respond, and for that we offer our apologies. Constraints of time, space and awareness are thus responsible for other omissions, and not a lack of good intentions on the part of the publisher. Our goal was to document the accomplishments of many people from various occupational disciplines.

An invitation to participate in the publication was extended at the discretion of the publisher. Biographies were invited to contribute personal and professional data, with only the information freely submitted to be included. The editors have made a sincere effort to present an accurate distillation of the data, and to catch errors whenever possible. However, the publisher cannot assume any responsibility for the accuracy of the information submitted.

There was no charge for inclusion in this publication and inclusion was not guaranteed; an annual update is planned. Comments and other concerns should be addressed to:

C. Sunny Martin, CEO
Who's Who Publishing Co., LLC
1650 Lake Shore Drive, Suite 250
Columbus, Ohio 43204
Phone: (614) 481-7300

E-Mail: sunny@whoswhopublishing.com
www.whoswhopublishing.com

A MESSAGE FROM THE *Chicago Publisher*

Beverly Coley-Morris

"The tragedy of life doesn't lie in not reaching your goal. The tragedy lies in having no goal to reach." - DR. BENJAMIN MAYS

I bring greetings from all Chicagoans, well over three million strong, as we present our inaugural edition of **Who's Who In Black Chicago**. In this book, we present the nucleus of much that makes Chicago such a vital and vibrant American city in which to live, work, learn, play and prosper. I am grateful to the Who's Who staff for its invaluable assistance, especially the founder and CEO, C. Sunny Martin, for the opportunity to highlight many of the historical and contemporaneous experiences shared by African-American business leaders, educators, sports and entertainment personalities, fine arts promoters and performers, and just plain everyday ordinary hardworking people who call our city home.

Today, nearly 200 hundred years after Chicago's first settler—a black Haitian fur trapper named Jean Baptiste Pointe DuSable—became the city's first property owner, over one million African Americans live in Chicago and its suburbs. Throughout its history, Chicago has given rise to the massive growth of black businesses. The city once claimed the largest number of black-owned automobile dealerships, banks, and hair care companies. Today, Chicago provides even greater opportunities for successful business entrepreneurs and lays claim to significantly more black technically trained professionals than any other American city.

The world has benefited handsomely from the matchless contributions of great black Chicagoans, including legal giant Earl B. Dickerson, whose arguments before the U.S. Supreme Court ended legal housing discrimination for all Americans; Mayor Harold Washington; poet Gwendolyn Brooks; business leaders John H. Johnson, George Johnson, Fred Luster, Sr. and Edward Gardner; civil rights champion Jesse L. Jackson, Sr.; and the world renown television star, Oprah Winfrey. Chicago is also a gospel mecca that produced many great gospel singers and composers including Mahalia Jackson, Albertina Walker, Shirley Caesar and Thomas Dorsey. Other Chicago musical legends include Dinah Washington, Sam Cooke, Johnny Hartman, Lou Rawls, Quincy Jones, Nat King Cole, The Chi-Lites, the Dells and contemporary artists Kanye West and R. Kelly. Chicago was also the home of the great civil rights activist/historian and newspaper columnists Lu Palmer and Vernon Jarrett. Many immortal sports legends hail from Chicago, including Hall of Fame baseball star Ernie Banks and basketball legend Michael Jordan.

Our inaugural edition of **Who's Who In Black Chicago** makes it perfectly clear that Chicago continues to produce and to nurture more than its share of African-American men, women and children who have made us the "Most Diverse Northern City" in the United States.

As we prepare for our second edition we ask for your support in making it an even more inclusive and comprehensive resource guide that chronicles the achievements of African Americans who live in this great city of Chicago.

We thank you again for your continued support of our efforts.

Beverly Coley-Morris

CINTAS®
THE SERVICE PROFESSIONALS

Unique Perspectives.
Varied Cultures.
Innovative Ideas.

At Cintas, we're capitalizing on our greatest strength: **OUR PEOPLE**. As a leading provider of outsourced services, we embrace individuality in experience, age, appearance, physical ability, education, family status, and more. Our diversity has helped us to become one of the most successful companies in the country. It allows us to serve our customers better, which in turn, allows us to provide better opportunities for our employees.

For more information please visit our website at www.cintas.com.

THE ENERGY OF DIVERSITY

Peoples Energy proudly supports *Who's Who in Black Chicago*

PEOPLES ENERGY
www.PeoplesEnergy.com

THE INAUGURAL EDITION *Who's Who In Black Chicago* 31

You've made all the RIGHT MOVES

Make your next one at Hewitt. We take great pride in turning strong individuals into even stronger professionals. Through diversity, teamwork, and a positive working environment, we can help you become the kind of leader you strive to be. At work. At home. And in your community. Making the world a better place to work. For everyone.

A Global HR Outsourcing and Consulting Firm

Hewitt

www.hewitt.com/rightmove

©2005 Hewitt Associates LLC

COMMEMORATE YOUR APPEARANCE IN
WHO'S WHO IN BLACK Chicago®
THE INAUGURAL EDITION

With A Beautiful Handcrafted Plaque.

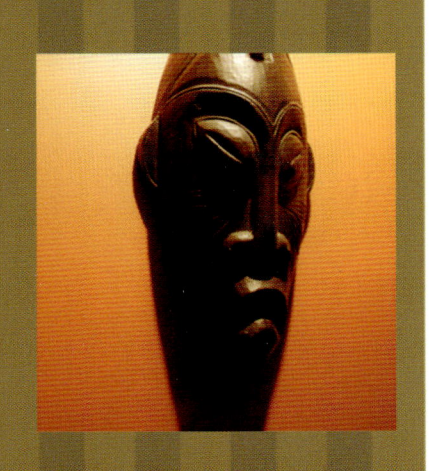

Your picture and biographical data will be mounted on a 16"x 20" rich, hand stained 3/4" birch wood plaque and sealed with a non-glare finish.

Order Your Commemorative Plaque Today!
Only $149.95
Plus Shipping & Handling

Call (614) 481-7300 Now!
www.whoswhopublishing.com

We Are Provocative, Informative, Sophisticated, Educational and Entertaining.

Inside: A Look At Who's Who In Publishing

N'DIGO®

www.ndigo.com

FREE WEEKLY

A MAGAPAPER FOR THE URBANE

Nation's Largest African-American Newspaper Circulation

**Get Your Subscription Or Advertise!!!
Call Today 312.822.0202**

Chicago's
LEGENDS

"We never stopped believing that we were part of something good that has never happened before."

Harold Washington, 1922-1987
Politician, Mayor of Chicago

CHICAGO'S LEGENDS

MILTON OLIVER DAVIS (1932-2005)

CO-FOUNDER AND CHAIRMAN EMERITUS • SHOREBANK

Born in Jasper, Alabama, Milton O. Davis was destined to be an agent of change. In the early 1960s, he joined south side Chicago's Congress on Racial Equality (CORE) and became its president in 1965. A self-described rabble rouser, Davis, along with countless others like himself, showed America its true face and called the country into accountability for its dark past and unfilled future.

Beginning in 1967, his energy was channeled from grassroots activism to commercial banking. From 1967 until 1973, he served as vice president of Hyde Park Bank and Trust Company in Chicago. In this role, he directed its urban development division, a model minority lending program. It was during this time in 1970 that he and his associates devised a plan to maintain South Shore National Bank's presence in the community. In what became a historic move, the four bankers purchased South Shore Bank with $800,000 and a $2.4 million bank loan. They attracted potential depositors, loan customers, and shareholders by various outreaches and even visiting their homes. Their efforts built the first and leading community development bank in the U.S. Now called ShoreBank, the institution began providing African Americans, low-income residents and businesses access to previously unavailable finances.

Davis' interests extended beyond the U.S. as he helped to create The Community Banking Project in South Africa. Likewise, he created an internship program at ShoreBank that trains black South Africans for positions in South African financial institutions.

His service on boards and commissions was endless, including Columbia College, the Chicago Housing Authority, the Field Foundation, Mayor Richard Daley's Blue Ribbon Committee, CORE, and the architect selection committee for Chicago's Harold Washington Library, to name a few.

Called the "ultimate family man," he is survived by his wife of 44 years, Gertrude, daughter, Shelley, son-in-law, Omar McRoberts, and granddaughter, Naima Davis McRoberts.

CHICAGO'S LEGENDS

JOHN H. JOHNSON (1918-2005)

PUBLISHER AND CHAIRMAN • JOHNSON PUBLISHING COMPANY, INC.

Born in Arkansas City, Arkansas, January 19, 1918, John H. Johnson forever changed the publishing world.

He began his publishing career in November of 1942 as editor and publisher of *Negro Digest*, later *Black World*. The company, founded by Johnson, has published *Ebony*, the number one African-American magazine in the world every consecutive year since its founding in 1945, and *Jet*, the world's number one African-American newsweekly magazine, founded in 1951. Johnson Publishing Company, Inc. has been the world's largest black-owned publishing company for 60 years. A true entrepreneurial venture, Johnson Publishing Company also publishes books exclusively by black authors and owns Fashion Fair Cosmetics, the largest black-owned cosmetics company in the world. Additionally, it produces television specials.

Johnson began his trailblazing career as an office boy at Supreme Life Insurance Company and eventually became chairman and chief executive officer.

He graduated with honors from DuSable High School and attended The University of Chicago and Northwestern University. During his lifetime, he received 31 honorary doctoral degrees.

Acknowledged for his influence, Johnson accompanied presidents Richard M. Nixon and John F. Kennedy on numerous goodwill tours. President Lyndon B. Johnson appointed him special United States ambassador to the Independence Ceremonies of Kenya and to the National Selective Service Commission; President Nixon appointed him to the President's Commission for the Observance of the 25th Anniversary of the United Nations.

His philanthropic, civic, and cultural activities and awards were numerous, including the Spingarn Medal awarded by the NAACP. As a credit to his legacy, Howard University honored him by establishing the John H. Johnson School of Communications, and he was inducted into several halls of fame.

Johnson is survived by his wife, Eunice, and daughter Linda Johnson Rice, president and CEO of Johnson Publishing Company.

CHICAGO'S LEGENDS

HAROLD WASHINGTON (1922-1987)

MAYOR • CITY OF CHICAGO

The first African-American mayor of Chicago, Harold Washington lived most of his early life on the city's South Side. His residence and upbringing by a politically, spiritually and civically active father proved to be a perfect combination for someone with Washington's leadership skills.

After dropping out of high school his junior year, he took a job at a meat packing company and then joined the Army in 1942. Decorated for bravery and receiving an honorable discharge, Washington received his high school diploma in 1946.

Elected class president in 1948, Washington graduated from Roosevelt College (now Roosevelt University) with a bachelor's degree in political science. He earned a juris doctorate degree from Northwestern University School of Law in 1952.

In addition to establishing a private law practice, Washington, who had been involved with the Democratic Party from the early 30s, succeeded his father as South Side Ward precinct captain in 1953. In 1964, he was elected to the Illinois House of Representatives, and he served in this capacity from 1965-1976. There, he sponsored anti-discrimination bills and played a key role in having Dr. King's birthday recognized as a holiday in the state of Illinois. Additionally, Washington was elected state senator in 1977, and was reelected as a state representative in 1980.

Chicago's black leadership persuaded Washington to run for mayor in a race where the odds were clearly not in his favor. With increased voter registration, he won the mayoral race in 1983. He is credited with increasing employment diversity for women and minorities within the City of Chicago's administration and ending city patronage. Further, he issued an executive order increasing minority business contracts and opened the city's process to the public.

Washington won an easy second term in 1987, but shortly thereafter he died of a massive heart attack at his City Hall desk on November 25, 1987.

RUSH UNIVERSITY MEDICAL CENTER PROUDLY SALUTES *WHO'S WHO IN BLACK CHICAGO.*

To build sustainable diversity, you need a strong foundation of inclusion. For more than three decades, health care professionals and students at RUSH University Medical Center have volunteered their time and skills to address the needs of Chicago's underserved communities. Community service is a vital part of RUSH education and employment.

Shaping the health care leaders of tomorrow. Recognizing diversity as the cornerstone of scientific discovery. Putting patients first in everything we do.

Quite simply, it's how medicine should be.

For more information about RUSH and its programs, visit our Web site at www.rush.edu or call (888) 352-RUSH.

RUSH UNIVERSITY MEDICAL CENTER

HOUGHTON MIFFLIN

Houghton Mifflin Company salutes Chicago Board of Education, President Michael Scott for his leadership in education for Chicago Public Schools

Solutions for Classrooms, Grades PreK–12

HOUGHTON MIFFLIN

Riverside Publishing — Edusoft — Great Source — earobics — McDougal Littell

For more information, visit www.hmco.com

© Houghton Mifflin Company. All rights reserved. 03/05 SS04065

MOTO SLVR

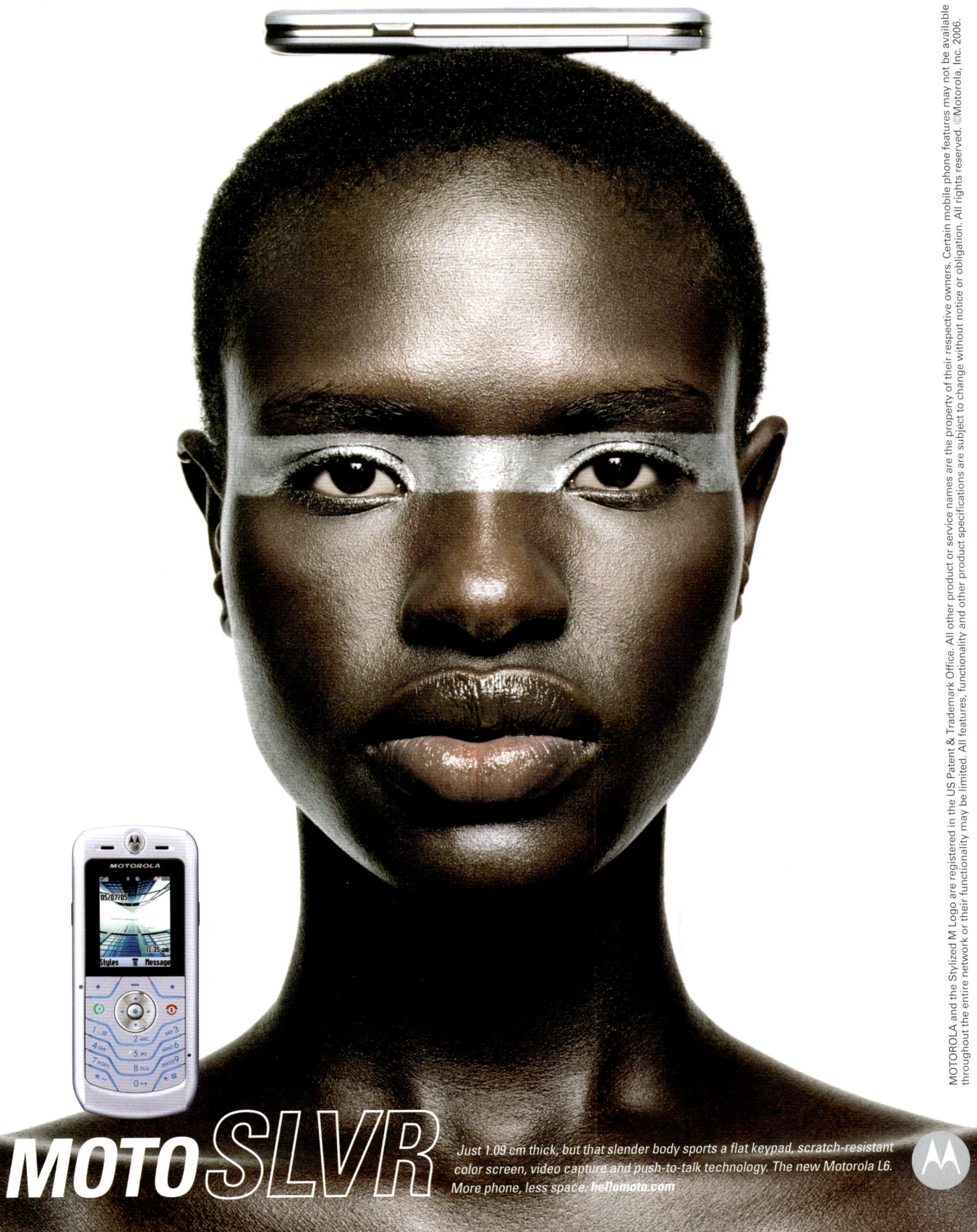

Just 1.09 cm thick, but that slender body sports a flat keypad, scratch-resistant color screen, video capture and push-to-talk technology. The new Motorola L6. More phone, less space. *hellomoto.com*

"The **MotoExperience** begins with our employees, a diverse workforce committed to developing exciting, innovative products. A breakthrough like the SLVR is an example of the way our employees anticipate and meet the needs of customers around the world. Exceptional products are an outgrowth of an inclusive culture where ideas are free to thrive, and my job is to ensure that Motorola continues to foster an inclusive environment."

Candi Castleberry-Singleton — Vice President, Global Inclusion and Diversity, Motorola, Inc.

MOTOROLA and the Stylized M Logo are registered in the US Patent & Trademark Office. All other product or service names are the property of their respective owners. Certain mobile phone features may not be available throughout the entire network or their functionality may be limited. All features, functionality and other product specifications are subject to change without notice or obligation. ©Motorola, Inc. 2006.

OUR BRANDS

IN ANY SETTING

SALUTE YOU.

Sara Lee®

CONGRATULATIONS
TO THE OUTSTANDING LEADERS
IN WHO'S WHO IN BLACK CHICAGO.

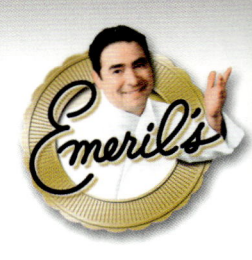

Sara Lee · Jimmy Dean · Hillshire Farm · State Fair · Ball Park · Bryan · Senseo · Emeril's

HYATT
HOTELS & RESORTS

CORPORATE SPOTLIGHT

Hyatt Hotels Corporation
Diversity Initiatives and Programs

Our commitment to Diversity is best evidenced by our focus on company-wide diversity initiatives. Our diversity initiatives, which fall into five key elements – Commitment, Accountability, Training, Measurement and Communication – maintain and enhance Hyatt's image as an Employer of Choice, Business Partner, and Community Ally throughout the communities we serve.

Hyatt Hotels & Resorts is an industry leader in the recruitment, retention, development and promotion of women and minorities. Hyatt's workforce of over 36,000 employees is 58 percent ethnic minority and 50 percent female. The management breakdown of Hyatt Hotels & Resorts is 36 percent female and 37 percent minority based. (Data derived from recent 2005 EEO-1 consolidated property report.)

Following is a brief list of national initiatives and programs sponsored and supported by Hyatt's commitment for Diversity:

- **Historically and Predominately Black Colleges and Universities**
  Over the last 10 years, Hyatt has sponsored outstanding junior and senior minority students, all who are pursuing bachelor's degrees in the hospitality industry to attend the Hotel/Motel Show held annually in New York. Hyatt's goal is to supplement each student's academic education with professional networking opportunities and development workshops given by some of Hyatt's minority general managers. In turn, Hyatt has the opportunity to acquaint students from around the country with our company culture, introduce students to members of our staff, and recruit students for internship and Corporate Management Trainee positions.

- **NAACP ACT-SO Program**
  In 1999 Hyatt Hotels Corporation joined the NAACP ACT-SO Program as an Advisory Council Member company. ACT-SO is an acronym for Afro-Academic, Cultural, Technological and Scientific Olympics. ACT-SO is a yearlong enrichment program designed to recruit, stimulate, improve and encourage high academic and cultural achievement among African-American high school students. The ACT-SO program encourages the dedication and commitment of community volunteers and business leaders to serve as mentors and coaches to promote academic and artistic excellence among African-American students.

- **Multicultural Foodservice and Hospitality Alliance**
  As an original founding member, Hyatt was instrumental in the developmental stages of the Alliance, an organization of foodservice suppliers, retailers and hospitality professionals created to encourage and enhance the image of minority development and career advancement opportunities.

- **National Society for Minorities in Hospitality (NSMH)**
  Hyatt has been a Board of Industry partner and sponsor for the NSMH Scholarship program and the annual national conference held in February since 1998. Hyatt is a sponsor of the H.I.R.E. (Hospitality Industry Recruitment Executives) scholarship given for building diversity in hospitality from NSMH.

AWARDS AND RECOGNITIONS

Hyatt continues to receive recognition as one of America's best companies for minorities in rankings based on information about recruiting and employment practices.

- The President's Roundtable and Black CEO Summit nominated Hyatt as a finalist in the category of Hotels/Marketing to receive the "2006 Diversity Trailblazer Award."
- *Essence* Magazine recognized Hyatt in their 2005 "Great Companies to Work" list.
- *Black Collegian* Magazine rated Hyatt number 49 in their 2005 "Top 100 Employers" list.
- *Savoy Professional* Magazine highlighted Hyatt as one of ten companies in their article: "Mixed Company: A Short, Hard Look At Corporate Diversity."

For a comprehensive list of diversity initiatives, programs, awards and recognition visit www.hyattdiversity.com or email Angela Johnson (angela.johnson@corphq.hyatt.com).

As a world class hospitality company, Hyatt – and its employees-have the opportunity to interact with guests and co-workers from all backgrounds. Embracing Diversity is a key element to our success. If you are ready to show your distinctive style in a career with Hyatt, visit carreers.hyatt.com.

HYATT HOTELS & RESORTS

Corporate Spotlight

Julie Coker
General Manager
Hyatt Lodge in Oak Brook

Charles A. Coleman, Jr.
Director of Labor Relations
Hyatt Hotels Corporation

Julie Coker serves as the general manager of the Hyatt Lodge at McDonald's Campus. In her executive role, she directs the entire operation and employees of the hotel, while managing the assets for the Hyatt Lodge's owners, McDonald's Corporation.

A 17-year Hyatt veteran, Coker began her Hyatt career in 1989 as a corporate management trainee at the Hyatt Regency Columbus. She also held full-time positions at the Hyatt Regency O'Hare. In 1994, she was promoted to her first rooms executive position at Hyatt Deerfield (Chicago), and held the same position at Hyatt Regency Cincinnati before being appointed to the opening team at Hyatt Regency McCormick Place in 1998. Her progressive career also led her to become general manager at the Hyatt on Printers Row (Chicago) in 2000.

A graduate of Johnson & Whales University in Providence, Rhode Island, Coker received a bachelor's degree in hospitality management. An alumni member with the National Society of Minorities in Hospitality, Coker was recently featured in *Fortune* where she was highlighted for her role in the key partnership between corporate powerhouses.

Charles Coleman, Jr. has worked for Hyatt Hotels & Resorts for 15 years. He is currently director of labor relations for Hyatt Hotels Corporation. Prior to joining the corporate office, Coleman was director of human resources at Hyatt Regency Chicago, Hyatt Regency Crown Center (Kansas City) and Hyatt Regency Savannah.

He is a graduate of Auburn University, earning a bachelor of science in criminal justice and a minor in political science. While in college, Coleman played point guard for the Auburn Tigers men's basketball team from 1982 through 1985.

Born in Reading, Pennsylvania, Coleman has spent his professional career dedicated to the human resource discipline. He is an active member of the Society of Human Resource Management, the Human Resource Association of Chicago, and the Chicago District Golf Association. Coleman is also a member of Kappa Alpha Psi Fraternity, Inc.

His personal interests include playing golf and listening to contemporary jazz.

Corporate Spotlight

Cecilia Cuff
BIG Bar Manager
Hyatt Regency Chicago

Cecilia Cuff is manager of the famous BIG Bar at Hyatt Regency Chicago – Hyatt and Chicago's largest hotel. BIG Bar is the longest free-standing bar in the U.S. and is a popular hangout for many Chicago visitors, as well as local residents.

In her position, Cecilia manages daily bar operations including special events, local marketing, and VIP services, as well as staff relations, motivation, and incentive programs. In addition to Cecilia's daily responsibilities, she serves as a facilitator for Hyatt Regency Chicago's associates Service Essentials training program. She is also a trainer in Hyatt's Train the Trainer program, and just recently was awarded an Excellence in Service Management Award.

Cecilia enjoys studying public relations and Spanish as a full-time student in the communications department at the University of Illinois at Chicago. She is also the founder of the C.Ras clothing company, which made its introduction to Chicago in spring of 2000.

In her spare time, Cecilia enjoys playing rugby, soccer, and taking Bikram Yoga classes.

Born in Philadelphia, Pennsylvania, Celcilia has been a Chicago resident for nine years.

Amy Jennetten
Hard Drive General Manager
Hyatt Regency Chicago

Amy Jennetten is the general manager of Hyatt Regency Chicago's Hard Drive, a weekday ultra-lounge and top nightclub in the city on weekends. She is responsible for managing all aspects of the Hard Drive lounge, restaurant, special events and nightclub.

Amy began her career with Hyatt in 2002 at the exclusive Park Hyatt Chicago, where she served as department head for the mini-bar, in-room dining and famous NoMi Gardens. She aggressively worked her way through the food and beverage division there, as well as at Hyatt Regency Chicago. Amy's future goal is to pursue her career with Hyatt and work towards becoming a director of food and beverage. She is well on her way.

Amy majored in fashion marketing and minored in visual design at Ray College of Design in Chicago. She enjoys downhill skiing in the Rocky Mountains, beach volleyball, and is a member of Hyatt Regency Chicago's softball team.

Amy was adopted at the age of four months by her parents Robert and Suzanne Jennetten, and raised in Peoria, Illinois. She was recently engaged to Ali C. Brown.

HYATT HOTELS & RESORTS

Corporate Spotlight

William L. Lumpkin
Executive Director
Hotel Accounting
Hyatt Hotels Corporation

William L. Lumpkin is the executive director of hotel accounting for Hyatt Hotels Corporation based in Chicago, Illinois. In his capacity, Lumpkin oversees the accounting operation for approximately 40 hotels located in the northeast, Washington D.C. area, Florida, and the Caribbean.

Lumpkin began his career with Hyatt 25 years ago at the Hyatt Regency Memphis, holding positions such as night auditor, night manager, payroll supervisor/chief accountant, and assistant controller. From there, he held positions as controller, regional controller, and manager of software development. Lumpkin also worked for four years as manager of software development for a major airline, and manager of business process design for a major consulting/accounting firm.

Lumpkin is a graduate of the University of Memphis with a bachelor of business administration degree in accounting. He is a certified public accountant and a certified hospitality technology professional.

A native of Memphis, Tennessee, Lumpkin currently resides in Carol Stream, Illinois and is married to Linda Lumpkin, vice president of human resources for the American Bottling Company.

Roosevelt Moncure
Catering Marketing Director
Hyatt Regency Chicago

Roosevelt Moncure is the catering marketing director at Hyatt Regency Chicago, Hyatt and Chicago's largest hotel. He is responsible for overseeing all aspects of catering functions, from sales and planning to execution and retention, with primary focus on the social market.

Roosevelt began working at Hyatt Regency Chicago in 1984. He has been named Hyatt Regency Chicago's Manager of the Year three times, and has received the prestigious honor of being named a Hyatt Master for the past seven years. Roosevelt achieved Hyatt's highest catering honor, being named Hyatt's Catering Manager of the Year in 2000 and again in 2005. His accomplishments, dedication, and service have set an entirely new standard at Hyatt Regency Chicago.

Roosevelt is an active member of 100 Black Men of Chicago, the Urban League, the RainbowPUSH Coalition, and the Chicago Assembly. In his spare time, he enjoys spending time with his wife, Shari, and daughter, Brooke.

Corporate Spotlight

Derrick Morrow
Executive Director of Sales
Central Division
Hyatt Hotels Corporation

Derrick Morrow joined Hyatt in 1991 as associate director of sales at Hyatt Regency Atlanta, moving on to Hyatt Regency Bethesda in the position of director of sales. He then served as director of sales at Hyatt Regency Baltimore for more than four years, followed by two years as director of marketing at Hyatt Regency O'Hare, and two years as director of marketing at Hyatt Regency Chicago.

Prior to his current position at Hyatt's corporate office in Chicago, Morrow was divisional director of sales for the central division office based out of Hyatt Regency O'Hare. As the current executive director of sales, Morrow is responsible for overseeing the sales operations of the central division, including 25 hotels in the central U.S. and Canada.

Originally from Washington D.C., Morrow now lives in suburban Chicago's Naperville community with his wife and two kids.

Connie Davis Powell
Corporate Counsel
Hyatt Hotels Corporation

Connie Davis Powell is a corporate counsel for Hyatt Hotels Corporation. Her current practice areas include global intellectual property, advertising and marketing, and e-commerce.

Powell holds a bachelor's degree in biology from the University of North Carolina at Chapel Hill, and a juris doctorate from the Indiana University School of Law in Bloomington, Indiana. She was admitted to the Illinois Bar in 2000, and to the District of Columbia and Minnesota Bar in 2002.

Prior to joining Hyatt, Powell was an associate in the intellectual property group at the law firm of Winston & Strawn. She was also a corporate counsel at Blockbuster, Inc.

HYATT HOTELS & RESORTS

Corporate Spotlight

Terry Witherspoon
Assistant Food & Beverage Director
Hyatt Regency Chicago

Jamila S. Woods
Guest Services Manager
Hyatt Regency Chicago

Terry Witherspoon is the assistant food and beverage director at Hyatt Regency Chicago, Chicago's largest hotel. He is responsible for overseeing operations of each department within the hotel's food and beverage division. This includes, three restaurants, three lounges, 24-hour room service, and the hotel's popular nightclub and banquets within 228,000 square feet of meeting space.

Prior to joining Hyatt Regency Chicago, Terry worked for Hyatt Regency Dearborn, where he was awarded Manager of the Year. He has also been a Stars of the Industry award recipient, as designated by the Michigan State Hotel and Restaurant Association. Terry is an active member of the NAACP and Urban League of Michigan, and he enjoys spending time as a volunteer coach at the Boys and Girls Club.

Terry has always had a strong love of basketball. He attended Whitman College in Washington State on a basketball scholarship, where he received a bachelor's degree in sociology. A family man, Terry and his wife, Sheila, devote their time to raising and keeping three daughters on the right path.

Jamila Woods is guest services manager at Hyatt Regency Chicago - Hyatt and Chicago's largest hotel. In this position, she manages the bell staff, door staff, and communications department at the 2,019-room hotel.

Jamila began her career with Hyatt in 2002. She has received promotions each year since, primarily throughout the communications department of the hotel. Jamila's latest promotion to guest services manager provides her with many new professional experiences in the hospitality industry. Her determination and entrepreneurial spirit has been recognized as she has received two Hyatt Regency Chicago management awards.

Jamila is currently working on her bachelor of fine arts degree in multimedia productions, with a concentration in graphic design. She is also a member of the Order of the Eastern Star and Faith Walk International Church.

A native to Chicago, Illinois, Jamila has established herself in and outside of the workplace. She enjoys art and art history, traveling, and any activity that nurtures her personal growth.

"Be the change you wish to see in the world."

– Mahatma Gandhi

Congratulations to all the leaders who grace this book. Your contributions inspire us all.

Making more possible **LaSalle Bank**
ABN AMRO

LaSalle Bank N.A. Member FDIC. ©2006 LaSalle Bank Corporation.

Harris

(part of BMO Financial Group) is driven by corporate values that foster a diverse workforce and an equitable, supportive workplace in which all employees are given the opportunity to meet their professional goals.

At the very heart of Harris' ongoing initiative towards a fully inclusive workplace is our unwavering commitment to create a high-performance culture for all employees. This determination energizes our company and allows us to reap the benefits of an engaged and diverse workforce.

It's called leading by example.

Please complete your online profile and enter your resume information at www.harrisbank.com while reviewing our career opportunities.

HARRIS

Global Presence. Local Expertise.

We are SIRVA, the world's largest global relocation services business. With offices in over 40 countries and Global Certified Providers in more than 175 countries, we're setting new industry standards for worldwide point-to-point control.

We're also setting new standards for customer satisfaction by providing your transferees with one-call assistance, single-source reporting and on-site expertise for any situation. At SIRVA, we're continually redefining relocation to make the process faster and easier than ever before.

700 Oakmont Lane
Westmont, IL 60559

1 800 215 9060
www.sirvarelocation.com

SIRVA is proud to be a sponsor of Who's Who In Black Chicago.

SIRVA
relocation redefined

Photo by Powell Photography, Inc.

Celebrating African-American Achievements

Chicago's
INTERESTING PERSONALITIES

A Legendary Cultural Anthropologist

TOM BURRELL

By Maureen Jenkins

It's hard to imagine a world without Tom Burrell and the creative genius spawned by the full-service advertising and communications agency, Burrell Communicatons, he founded in 1971.

Now chairman emeritus of his groundbreaking African-American firm, Burrell finally has time to reflect upon the influence he's had, not just upon the advertising industry or even black America, but upon the worldwide cultural landscape.

"The thing I have always tried to push is that since African-American culture is leading-edge culture, we should remember the emulative patterns that take place in this country," says Burrell, who assumed his current title in 2005 after co-CEOs Fay Ferguson and McGhee Williams Osse took over day-to-day duties. "One of the worst things we could do is go out trying to emulate *other* people and take our eye off the ball."

Today, with 130 employees in Chicago, Los Angeles and Atlanta, Burrell is a member of the Publicis Groupe, a Paris-based advertising and communications agency network. Billing nearly $200 million each year, the agency boasts a client roster that includes some of the biggest in the business—McDonald's, Procter & Gamble, Toyota, General Mills, and Allstate. It's ranked No. 3 in billings on *Black Enterprise* magazine's list of top black-owned advertising agencies.

"I grew up being aware of media, but being aware that media did not reflect me and my life or millions and millions of other black people in any realistic way," says Burrell, who cut his teeth at Leo Burnett, the London office of Foote Cone & Belding, and Needham, Harper & Steers. "What we did is something quite revolutionary but not very complex. We took pictures, snapshots of regular people doing regular things and projected that onto the screen and onto the page."

But timing is everything—and Burrell and then-business partner Emmett McBain were prescient. McDonald's became the agency's first powerhouse client in 1972, and Coca-Cola soon followed. Shortly after, Marlboro and Jack Daniels came aboard. Recognizing the need for an integrated marketing approach to the African-American consumer market, Burrell established a public relations arm in the mid-1980s.

And in today's world, where some try to pit the rapidly growing Hispanic market against the more established black one, Burrell says black agencies must "have people out there making a case for the African-American consumer market, not just quantitatively but qualitatively. We have to get the point across that it's essential."

These days, Burrell has "a very informal kind of consulting role with the company. I'm doing what I want to do for the first time in my life." That means writing jazz songs and a personally penned memoir.

"Marketing communications people have to be cultural anthropologists more than businesspeople or artists," says Burrell, who along with his agency has earned numerous awards from the local and national advertising industries.

Using a football analogy to explain, he says: "A quarterback is going to throw the ball to the wide receiver. You can't throw the ball to where that guy is running down the field, but where he's going to be and get under him. When you throw the ball, you've got to figure out where the consumer is *going* to be. That's what any marketer has to do."

Photo by Powell Photography, Inc.

Celebrating African-American Achievements

Chicago's
INTERESTING PERSONALITIES

Hooked on Finance

MELLODY HOBSON

By Maureen Jenkins

Money, and the understanding of it, is power. No one knows that more than Mellody Hobson, president of Ariel Capital Management, one of the largest such African-American-owned firms in the world. At just 37, this petite powerhouse oversees the downtown Chicago firm's non-investment management and strategic planning.

But beyond the title, beyond the impressive board memberships and corporate directorships she holds, Hobson has one major mission: "To make the stock market a topic of dinner conversation in the black community." That's why she flies to New York at least once a week, serving as a regular financial contributor to ABC's *Good Morning America* and *World News Tonight*. She considers it both an awesome honor and responsibility.

"There aren't any other (blacks) doing that on a national level, and it's a great way to narrow the wealth gap in this country," says Hobson, who was invited to join *GMA* by current co-host Diane Sawyer. Regular folks tell her "that they didn't know people like me existed. People tell me they do what I say. I always joke with them, 'Have I made you any money?'"

A woman who grew up in downtown Chicago and attended a public grade school and the prestigious St. Ignatius College Preparatory High School, went on to earn a bachelor of arts degree from Princeton University's Woodrow Wilson School of Public and International Affairs.

Although Hobson originally longed to be a broadcast news anchor, after meeting Ariel founder and Princeton alumnus John W. Rogers, Jr., she "got hooked" on the world of finance. Upon college graduation, she joined Ariel full-time and climbed the investment firm's ladder, becoming president in May 2000.

Ariel manages more than $19 billion in assets, and governs itself by the creed that "slow and steady wins the race," reflecting its commitment to realizing long-term investment value for its clients.

For Hobson, building for the long-term also involves community outreach. She's active on boards including the Chicago Public Education Fund, and Sundance Institute, and serves as a director for companies including The Estée Lauder Companies Inc. and Starbucks Corp. An avid world traveler, she's also a term member of the New York Council on Foreign Relations.

"I feel tremendous added responsibility as an African American. Race is the first thing people see," she says. "I'm always thinking, 'I'm representing no matter where I am. To the extent that all black businesses are successful, we make a bigger impact on our communities than white businesses do."

Take, for example, Ariel Community Academy, a charter school in Chicago's North Kenwood neighborhood that offers pre-kindergarten through eighth grade students a unique classroom focus on investment education and economics.

"I want to see as many Ariels as can be created in our community," says Hobson. More minority firms will lead to more minority wealth. And we'll be managing our 401(k)s better, saving to send our kids to college, and we will retire and go to Florida. No one in my family has ever retired and moved to Florida—we work until we die. If we'd learned about saving and investing 50 years ago, it might be a different story."

And if black consumers listen to Hobson and the national wealth-building mantra she preaches, it likely will.

Photo by Powell Photography, Inc.

Celebrating African-American Achievements

Chicago's
INTERESTING PERSONALITIES

Using Diversity to Drive Business Success

JAMES BELL

Contributed by The Boeing Company

James A. Bell is chief financial officer (CFO) and executive vice president of finance of The Boeing Company, the world's largest aerospace company and America's largest manufacturing exporter. From March through June 2005, in addition to his CFO duties, Bell served as Boeing president and chief executive officer on an interim basis.

One of the nation's highest-ranking African-American corporate executives, Bell oversees business and financial performance for a company that earns revenues of more than $1 billion per week, providing products and services that bring people together and protect the peace. As CFO, he is responsible for overall financial management of Boeing, its financial reporting and transparency, and for multiple corporate functions including treasury, investor relations, customer-financing activities and company-wide shared services. He oversees a team of nearly 20,000 people charged with safeguarding the integrity of Boeing's numbers and ensuring that the company returns value to shareholders.

Before being named CFO in 2003, Bell, 57, was Boeing's corporate controller. A 33-year Boeing veteran, he's also held leadership positions in auditing, program management, contracts and pricing, and finance, among other functions. He joined a heritage unit of Boeing fresh out of California State University at Los Angeles where he earned a bachelor's degree in accounting.

In addition to his fiduciary duties, Bell is a tireless advocate of diversity, ethics and career development for employees at all levels. Under his leadership, Boeing is striving to create a culture of inclusion that optimizes diversity to improve business performance, to grow next-generation leaders, and to drive change and social improvement in our communities.

"The key," he says, "is recognizing the power of diversity and integrity as business imperatives that provide a competitive advantage."

"As a business leader of color, I am personally committed to creating equitable opportunities and a high-performance, ethical culture in which all are free to compete and succeed, to have a seat at the table and contribute to company and community growth." That opportunity to excel based on performance-not-preference has been integral to his own professional success, which he describes as a "young black kid from South Central Los Angeles growing up to be the CFO of a Fortune 25 company."

It also communicates Bell's approach to business partnering. Under his leadership, Boeing established the Prime Opportunities Fund, a $1 billion pension investment program that targets emerging managers and provides minority-, women- and small, independently-owned investment firms greater opportunity to compete for assets in one of the nation's largest pension funds.

"Beyond ensuring equitable access to opportunity, business leaders also have a responsibility to use the power and prestige of their positions to give back to the community," Bell affirms. His membership on the boards of directors of Dow Chemical Company, Joffrey Ballet, the Chicago Urban League, World Business Chicago, The Chicago Economic Club and New Leaders for New Schools reflects his diverse commitment to supporting the arts, education, business and urban renewal.

Among Bell's many awards and recognitions are: *Black Enterprise* magazine's "75 Most Powerful Blacks in Corporate America" in 2005; Los Angeles Urban Leagues' 2006 Whitney M. Young award; Greater Los Angeles African American Chamber of Commerce's Executive of the Year in 2005; and Cal State Los Angeles' Distinguished Alumni award.

Married to the former Mary Howell, Bell has two grown children.

Photo by Powell Photography, Inc.

Celebrating African-American Achievements

Chicago's
INTERESTING PERSONALITIES

Helping Ideas and People Blossom and Grow

D. MICHELLE FLOWERS

By Maureen Jenkins

It's fitting that public relations executive D. Michelle Flowers, the daughter of a North Carolina horticulturist, bears the surname that she does. Since founding Flowers Communications Group 15 years ago, she's not only developed award-winning African-American-targeted programs for her Fortune 500 clients, but also cultivated young black talent. Flowers is all about helping both ideas and people blossom and grow.

"What I have created is an environment that allows us to nurture great ideas for our clients," says Flowers, her downtown Chicago office teeming with floral bouquets and green plants. "One of the things we also do is develop signature programs that create relationships, ownership and impact." Unlike some PR agencies that focus solely on getting media placements for their clients, "we truly are an integrated marketing firm."

"I wanted to be a pioneer and do in the public relations industry what Tom (Burrell) had done for African-American advertising." Flowers launched her own firm after helping establish the PR division for Burrell Communications Group.

With blue-chip clients like McDonald's, Unilever, Honda, and Miller Brewing Company on the FCG roster, Flowers is poised for continued growth.

Just this spring, her firm launched a Hispanic practice, one she says will "reach and respect" this burgeoning market while taking into account its complexities. She's hired three Hispanic communications professionals of Mexican, Chilean and Colombian heritage for her team.

At FCG, says Flowers, "We have already established and created a great reputation for impact programs, with African-American markets being our forte. It just makes perfect business sense to use that expertise against the Hispanic market. We've come up with this great model we call 'ethnic fusion' that really showcases the similarities" in how companies should reach out to African-American and Hispanic markets.

Recognizing the potential of this 40 million-strong market—Hispanics are now one of the nation's largest ethnic groups, and according to a University of Georgia report, possess buying power of more than $650 billion—Flowers has developed an aggressive business plan. This strategic thinker even hired a tutor to conduct weekly Spanish classes for her entire staff.

"We have immersed ourselves in our Hispanic practice with the same focus and passion in which we immerse our African-American clients," she says.

That passion is evident in the local and national honors that Flowers and her team have consistently won for their public relations and integrated communications programs. She has been honored by everyone from the National Council of Negro Women to Northwestern University's Medill School of Journalism Hall of Achievement, the school from which she earned a master's degree in advertising.

Now one of the largest African-American-owned PR agencies in the country, FCG is known for award-winning signature programs such as the "Pink Empowerment Tour," developed for black-owned and Chicago-based Luster Products Inc. Flowers is still just as thrilled about coming to work now as she was 25 years ago when she first entered the PR field. And the "Flower Shop," as her firm is often called, keeps blooming.

"On all these different levels," she says, "I impact people and help them grow; make an impact on the African-American and Hispanic communities. You really are honoring your Maker when you're able to do that."

Photo by Powell Photography, Inc.

Celebrating African-American Achievements

Chicago's
INTERESTING PERSONALITIES

A Classic Record of Community Service

HERB KENT

By Gregory J. Huskisson

Blinding smoke filled mid-day skies and hot blood flowed on urban streets as angry black Chicagoans – protesting the murder of Martin Luther King, Jr. – put the city in full riot mode. Fearing death and destruction, many black activists stepped forward to help stop the madness. One of them was a popular radio disc jockey nicknamed "The Cool Gent."

"When we had the riots and Chicago was burning, we went on the air and pled for sanity," smooth-talking deejay Herb Kent recalled during a recent interview. "We pleaded with people, 'Please, stop the burning; please.' We just kept saying, 'It's ridiculous to burn your own stuff down.'"

"This went on for a couple of days; not playing any music, just talking with the people," Kent said. "And they do credit us for helping to cool things down."

Kent, arguably the city's most popular radio personality over the last 50 years, is best known for owning the coolest nickname, advancing the careers of several Motown performers, and coining the phrase "dusty" – meaning a classic record. Less known is his use of the medium to fight for civil rights, keep kids in school, and promote community service.

"That's the way I think a radio station in the community should be used. Radio is a powerful tool and I've always figured it should be used to the betterment of mankind," Kent said. "And I still think we don't do as much as we could."

Over the years, however, he's certainly done his share:

- In the 1960s and 1970s, he dedicated a segment of his show to a Stay in School campaign – even broadcasting from some schools. The campaign was widely credited for helping to lower the city's dropout rate.

- When gang violence escalated, he helped launch a campaign to stop the violence, even putting some gang members on the air to share their views.

- He's accepted countless invitations to appear at career day programs; he recently helped promote a gift giveaway at a halfway house; and accepted a new challenge in 2001: teaching an advanced radio course at Chicago State.

Though he has served quietly, Kent has not gone unrecognized. Named honorary mayor of Bronzeville – the nickname for black Chicago, he has a ten-block strip of Stony Island named after him, and he has been inducted into the Radio Hall of Fame.

And although he recently celebrated his 77th birthday, Kent shows no signs of slowing down. He formed a band called "Herbie Babies" in which he plays guitar, hosts radio shows on V103 and Oldies 1690, and recently returned from China where he explored his newest hobby – taking photos.

So, what's next for the "Cool Gent?"

"I'd like to get back on TV and do another stepping show," he said of the popular dance show he once hosted. "Of course, I'd probably find some way to work community service into that."

"I used to say that James Brown probably could stop a gang fight back in the day," he said, half-jokingly. "I'm really interested in seeing if we can't help these young black brothers out here. And I think music is one key to it. You can get their ear and if they look up to you, you can talk to them. And that's where it starts."

Photo by Powell Photography, Inc.

Celebrating African-American Achievements

Chicago's
INTERESTING PERSONALITIES

A Focus Beyond the Numbers

JANICE FENN

By Lisa Lenoir

Janice Fenn hits a steady drumbeat about the importance of diversity in corporate America. She has reinforced its value while on staff at Sara Lee Corp. and Kraft Foods. And did so as founder of Professional Resources Organization, Inc., a consulting firm that assisted organizations such as American Express, Microsoft, McDonald's, and Time Warner.

She spreads her message with finesse, peppered with sound business principles and life experiences, some of which have become fodder for the book, *Do You See What I See?: A Diversity Tale for Retaining People of Color* (Pfeiffer, $35), co-authored with Chandra G. Irvin. While the diversity field is broad, Fenn and Irvin focus on retention of people of color.

What Fenn finds stimulating is simplifying the complexities of why people of color feel disenfranchised in corporations, and offering practical solutions to help organizational leaders create an environment where people of color will want to stay. The diversity questions she poses to corporations are, "Do you really want people of color to stay? What are you doing to keep them? Is it working? If it is not, why are you continuing with the same strategies?" She works with organizations to identify diversity principles and practices which will ultimately help the employees, thus enabling the business to move forward successfully.

A native of Alabama, Fenn recalls integration as she entered the ninth grade. She remembers vividly how most of the black teachers, staff and administrators went from top positions in segregated schools to second-in-command in integrated ones - even when many had more advanced degrees in that area of the rural south. Her school was the exception because of the strong leadership and advocacy of the principal of the all-black school that she had attended previously. He ensured that his staff from the all-black school was placed at the appropriate levels in the newly integrated school system.

She attended Tuskegee University, an experience she values highly because the faculty nurtured and encouraged her to do nothing but her best. Her bachelor's and master's degrees in biology took her to Purdue University for a Ph.D. program in the same subject, but the school of business caught her attention. The university's master's of business was a quantitative case-method program, yet she found herself intrigued by the human resources aspect of the business cases, "a focus beyond the numbers."

Her human resources proficiency has led her to Quaker Oats, Sara Lee Corp., and most recently Kraft Foods, where she was senior director of global diversity until January 2006.

The underlying trait that fuels her passion is that of a nurturer. "As individuals come to me for mentoring advice and feedback, I encourage them to be true to themselves and to be truthful to me." This is the only way she's able to help people of color realize their full potential. Fenn mentors them about everything from how to handle complex organizational situations to how to be an active participant in their careers. She balances empathy with candor and practical advice. Whether she's counseling people of color or working with executives to evolve their corporate culture, she follows this philosophy: "Always deliver your best and help others to deliver their best."

Photo by Robert Drea

Celebrating African-American Achievements

Chicago's
INTERESTING PERSONALITIES

Composer, Performer and President

WARRICK L. CARTER, PH.D.

By Markland G. Lloyd

When Daniel Burnham advised, "Make no small plans...," Columbia College President Warrick L. Carter must have been listening.

Dr. Carter arrived at Columbia six years ago from the Disney Corporation, where he was director of entertainment arts for Walt Disney Entertainment, in charge of global education and live arts programs for the entire corporation. Almost as soon as he arrived in Chicago, Dr. Carter committed himself to making Columbia "the best student-centered arts and media college ... *in the world.*"

No small feat, and requiring no small plan. In 2003, under Dr. Carter's leadership, the college's board of trustees approved the institution's first long-range strategic plan.

Today, Dr. Carter presides over one of the hottest colleges anywhere – enrollment has grown since his arrival by nearly 25 percent, to 11,000 students. Applications for next year are up again by 39 percent and student retention levels are higher than ever before in the college's history. Columbia enrolls more students of color in creative arts disciplines than any other private arts and media college in the nation.

Not only has Columbia's growth been remarkable, the college has taken real strides toward realizing Dr. Carter's vision about being student-centered. When compared with other similar colleges in a recent national survey, Columbia exceeded peer averages in virtually every measure of student satisfaction – instructional effectiveness, campus climate, support services, service excellence, and *student centeredness.* In many ways, Columbia now sets the standard, and others are trying to catch up.

Dr. Carter's success at Columbia continues his distinguished academic career, which includes 12 years at the Berklee College of Music in Boston, where he was dean of faculty and then provost/vice president of academic affairs. At Governors State University in Chicago, where he served from 1971 to 1984, he began as chair of the music program and was promoted to chair of the division of fine and performing arts.

He earned a bachelor of science degree at Tennessee State University, and a master of music degree and a Ph.D. in music education from Michigan State University.

Dr. Carter has consulted widely on music education and minority issues in music education. His projects have included work with the Wisconsin Music Educators, the Michigan Council for the Arts, Philadelphia Public Schools, the Los Angeles Board of Education, the National Endowment for the Humanities, and the Ministry of Culture in France.

A composer and performer, Dr. Carter has created commissioned works for the National Endowment for the Arts, the Chicago Symphony Orchestral Association, and the Chicago Chamber Orchestra. His recordings are on Mark and Capital records, and his live performances include work with the Boston Pops Jazz Quartet, Dee Dee Bridgewater, Billy Taylor, Clark Terry, Donald Byrd and many others. He has played at several collegiate and regional jazz festivals, including the International Jazz Festival in Montreux, Switzerland.

Dr. Carter is a two-time recipient of the National Black Music Caucus Achievement Award and is a member of the International Jazz Educators Hall of Fame. He is included in a variety of Who's Who publications, including *Who's Who in Black America.*

Photo by Powell Photography, Inc.

Celebrating African-American Achievements

Chicago's
INTERESTING PERSONALITIES

Using a Different Canvas

DORIS M. LOMAX-JUZANG

By Gregory J. Huskisson

By her own account, Doris M. Lomax might have ended up an "angry victim" of life's circumstance. Mother dies giving birth when Lomax is 2 ½ years old. Father is killed three years later in a tragic car accident. Now black, female and orphaned during the still-segregated 1930s, the St. Louis youngster faces a daunting future.

But a network of black women in her family – including a great-great-grandmother born just after slavery ended – step up to help Lomax beat the odds. They step in to raise the spirited youngster and give her the values she'll need to survive, succeed and serve.

"These women were unassuming but they were giants when it came to instilling morals, values and a commitment to loving and embracing life," Lomax recalled. "They were devoted to giving back and they lived that principle. They taught me compassion and planted the seeds that set me on my social service mission."

That adopted mission would lead Lomax to becoming one of the most influential service providers in Chicago, especially in the area of health care for African Americans.

Lomax said her most significant opportunity to serve came in 1974 when Illinois began deinstitutionalizing mental hospitals, leaving thousands of patients – many of them black men – without a place to turn for mental health services.

Concerned about those men, and about the long-term implications for the black community, Lomax and civic activist Dr. C. Vincent Bakeman joined a group of community advocates to create the Human Resources Development Institute, a Chicago-based agency that today provides health care and human services to more than 15,000 people a year in Illinois and four other states.

Lomax said the longtime support of her late husband, Frank Juzang, and her mentor, Ruth Carey Williams, helped to inspire her to serve. She has performed groundbreaking work at several state and federal agencies – including the U.S. Department of Health and Human Services – and has served on two national task forces to develop public health legislation.

While she has been glad to commit her career to health care for African Americans, Lomax sometimes wishes her life had not veered so far from the creative path.

"I started off in high school as an artist, and because of my talent as a painter, I was one of the first blacks to receive a scholarship to Chicago's Art Institute. In fact, it was my painting talent that brought me to Chicago," she said. "I have not done as much with my artwork as I could have done since I graduated from The Art Institute. Yes, that is a regret."

But using a different canvas, perhaps, Lomax has helped create human services programs in Chicago that she believes will have a long lasting impact on public health.

Weighing all, does Lomax consider herself a success? Well, yes and no.

"I have a lot of successes in my portfolio, but it's hard to use the word 'success' when there is so much work to be done," she said.

"My legacy is not over; I'm still shaping it. I have more to give and more to accomplish," she added. "Combined with my past accomplishments, what I have yet to accomplish will dictate my legacy."

Photo by James Fogerty, Exelon Corporation

Celebrating African-American Achievements

Chicago's INTERESTING PERSONALITIES

Commander on Land and at Sea

PETE TZOMES

By Adam Slahor

For Captain C.A. "Pete" Tzomes, USN (Ret.), mother always knew best.

He fantasized of attending the U.S. Naval Academy, a difficult dream to be fulfilled by an African American in the 1960s. So, Charlotte Tzomes didn't let her son leave the house until he finished his homework. "She preached good grades were more important than girls or sports," Tzomes said.

Tzomes, 61, says his academic prowess opened up doors throughout his life. Good grades helped him get into college, the Naval Academy, and nuclear power.

He grew up in Williamsport, Pennsylvania, a town of 50,000 residents with only two black professionals – a dentist and a social worker. Naysayers like his school counselor said blacks should "focus on something reasonable like teaching." But Tzomes was mesmerized by the Navy from a junior high presentation and the TV show *Men of Annapolis*. "I wanted to be an officer – whatever it took," Tzomes said.

After attending the State University of New York, the Academy accepted him during the height of the civil rights movement. He was one of two black graduates in the class of 1967. Tzomes aspired to be a marine pilot, but "was informed in a flight physical during my senior year that I was too short. If I couldn't fly, I wanted to go subs."

Tzomes was the first black to complete submarine officer nuclear power training and the first to command a submarine (USS HOUSTON in 1983). Eight blacks have commanded submarines in U.S. history.

"I'm most proud of my submarine command tour because of the trip I took to get there," Tzomes said. "There were people who said, 'I'm not going to take orders from a nigger officer.' I made up my mind that I'd make it. I used racial encounters as opportunities. In the end, people looked favorably upon me."

Some credit Tzomes for leading Navy affirmative action into the 21st century, heading its equal opportunity program in the late 80s. He directed unprecedented initiatives aimed at improving minority opportunities and achievements. In 1970, he participated in a special study group that resulted in significant cultural changes throughout the Navy following serious racial incidents aboard ships.

Tzomes and other black military leaders were recently recognized at an inaugural breakfast during the annual Black Engineer of the Year Awards conference in Baltimore. He was one of three recipients of the new Stars and Stripes award for his achievements in paving the way for black officers in the Navy's nuclear submarine force.

Tzomes is now the emergency preparedness manager at Quad Cities Nuclear Generating Station. Quad Cities is part of the Exelon Nuclear fleet, which is the largest operator of nuclear power plants in the U.S. "My military experience has helped me – I know how important it is to work as a team and how vital command and control is," Tzomes said. "There's no difference if you're at sea or working through a crisis situation."

Tzomes came to the Chicago area in the early 1990s when he was assigned as commanding officer of the Navy's boot camp.

"I look favorably upon my military career because I got support from many people – black and white," Tzomes said.

Photo by Rodney Wright, Image Makers Photography

Celebrating African-American Achievements

Chicago's INTERESTING PERSONALITIES

"I don't want to lose this generation."
REV. DR. JEREMIAH A. WRIGHT, JR.

By Maureen Jenkins

Rev. Dr. Jeremiah A. Wright, Jr. is a highly educated pastor with four earned degrees, who, during a sermon, can mix theologian-speak with 50 Cent lyrics. He leads Trinity United Church of Christ, a Chicago congregation of more than 8,000 members, but regularly makes time for "Pizza with the Pastor," an informal chat with Trinity teens.

That's because Wright takes his biggest challenge seriously: "How do you serve this present age? I don't want to lose this generation, and you're up against what they see on TV."

With a 150,000-square foot worship center, this South Side megachurch goes by the motto "Unashamedly Black and Unapologetically Christian." It communicates this message through all 70 Trinity ministries, its generous community and global outreach, and even its pastor's sermons. Coined by Wright's predecessor, Rev. Dr. Reuben Sheares, it reflects Trinity's strong ties to Africa as well as its commitment to a culturally black worship experience that extends into the local community.

In fact, says Wright, outreach to and education of young African Americans about the black church's rich heritage and legacy is the institution's most pressing task. "I see that as foundational for addressing so many other issues like gangs," says Wright, whose own children range from 42 to 16. "Telling that history connects them to the foundation of our faith. Without that, I don't see much hope in terms of reversing the feelings of apathy."

One ministry Wright's most proud of—even though it doesn't attract media attention—is Project Jeremiah, which sends largely retired (but still young) male mentors into nearby public elementary schools. "The demographics show that 60 to 70 percent of African-American children grow up in single-family homes where there is no male presence," says Wright. And unlike decades past, more black kids are growing up without attending church. "They take the church to the brothers," he says.

Since its founding in 1972, Trinity, and Wright, have been committed to support of Africa. The church supports missions in South Africa, Liberia, Ethiopia, Nigeria, and Ghana, among other places—even opening a computer school in Saltpond, Ghana in 2000. A man who grew up in Philadelphia with Liberian friends and attended Howard University along with Africans from many nations, Wright developed a strong African consciousness early in life. Trinity was an early leader in the Free South Africa movement, posting a sign outside its West 95th Street doors for years.

Trinity has taken the admonition in Mark 16:15 to "go ye into all the world and preach the gospel to every creature" to heart. Under Wright, Trinity maintains an interactive Web site, offers live webcasts of its three Sunday worship services, and broadcasts on the radio. And the church now takes the gospel on the road during "F.A.T. Fridays," a 45-minute worship and lunch in the heart of Chicago's Loop with a weekly attendance of about 200.

This is possible because Wright taught his flock the spiritual importance of tithing. "Within a $14 million budget," he says, "$11 million is in tithes and offerings." Trinity gave $100,000 to help Hurricane Katrina and Rita evacuees, and nearly $200,000 to help rebuild UCC-related Dillard University.

Wright is married to the Rev. Ramah Reed Wright, is the father of four daughters and a son, and he has three grandchildren.

Photo by Powell Photography, Inc.

Celebrating African-American Achievements

Chicago's INTERESTING PERSONALITIES

"Inquisitiveness is a wonderful value to have."

MERRI DEE

By Lisa D. Lenoir

Approaching threescore and ten, Merri Dee looks to new horizons. For more than 30 years, she's been a fixture in Chicago media on black radio and as WGN's director of community relations, and she's been an inspirational confidant to people looking for new life perspectives. This agelessness and visibility keep people wondering, *What will she do next?*

"My future is bright," says Dee, who enters a new life decade on October 30, 2006. "I treasure aging. It is such a precious gift we are given each day — to be able to grow through a whole day and into the next. That is fascinating to me."

This positive spirit residing in Dee has evolved from living through the best of times and the worst of them. She survived a less-than ideal childhood by basking in the love of her Southern grandparents. She succeeded in transitioning from corporate America to the image-conscious media world at midlife with more education and tenacity. And she triumphed over being shot and left for dead by the roadside after a man kidnapped her and a television guest, sustaining herself by thinking of her daughter, Toya, and the value of life.

Her inner strength comes from remembering the lessons learned through watching and listening to her grandparents and aunts. Her grandfather was a Southern gentleman who dressed well, always keeping his mended clothes, no matter how worn and tattered, impeccable. "I learned a sense of style from him." An aunt taught her to have fun, yet be action oriented. These elders also taught her that it's important for her to volunteer in her neighborhood, and if she didn't, she wasn't a good neighbor.

Radio and television became the vehicle by which she could share pearls from her family and her own life. She could challenge people one day, have them think about it the next and see them come up with an answer the following day. "I can change people's lives and help them to see themselves better."

She also embarked on countless social initiatives including advocating permanent housing for children, raising money for college education and crafting an Illinois Victims Bill of Rights.

In whatever Dee embraces, she takes the social graces obtained in childhood with her each time. "You must have dignity and grace and be respectful. My grandparents said, 'Always hold your head up high and throw those shoulders back.' That has stayed with me throughout my life."

Dee sees herself moving in new circles, with endless opportunities in sight. "Inquisitiveness is a wonderful value to have. I see myself as a verbal person. I see myself as a writer. I see myself with seniors and children."

Whatever crystallizes in the next chapter, it's sure to be enriched with Dee's brand of joy and wisdom.

Photo by Steve Matteo, Getty Images

Celebrating African-American Achievements

Chicago's
INTERESTING PERSONALITIES

Leader in Workforce Diversity

JAMES H. LOWRY

Contributed by Boston Consulting Group

Jim Lowry joined The Boston Consulting Group (BCG) in November 2000. As senior vice president and director, Lowry leads BCG's workforce diversity, emerging markets and minority business development consulting practice efforts. Previous to his position with BCG, Lowry was president and CEO of his own firm, James H. Lowry & Associates, since 1975. He has directed literally hundreds of engagements in all areas of diversity for corporations, government, nonprofits, and educational institutions. Jim is also part of the Organization and Consumer Goods practices at BCG.

Jim's clients have covered a broad range of industries, including: packaged goods (including soft drinks, beer, and multiple dry grocery); telecommunications/hi-tech; healthcare products and delivery; automotive; steel manufacturing; foundations; and a variety of professional services industries including management consulting.

Although Jim has extensive experience in all phases of diversity, his primary area of expertise is minority business enterprise development (MBED).

- In 1978, he and his colleagues at James H. Lowry and Associates wrote one of the first major studies on MBED for the Department of Commerce, entitled *New Strategy for Minority Business*.

- For the past ten years, he has been the academic advisor for a nationally recognized training course for minority entrepreneurs at the Kellogg School of Management.

- In 2004, he was inducted in the inaugural class of the Minority Business Enterprise Hall of Fame.

Jim is a nationally renowned expert in diversity, who is also an adjunct professor at the J.L. Kellogg Graduate School of Management at Northwestern University, where he also serves on the board of directors. In addition, Jim is chair, Durban, South Africa/Chicago Sisters Cities Committee and a member of The Economic Club of Chicago; Northwestern Memorial Hospital board of directors; Grinnell College board of directors; and the Chicago Public Library Foundation board of directors.

Currently, he is a member of the Howard School of Business board and also serves as chair for the Howard University Entrepreneurship Center. Previously, he was a member of the Chicago Council of Foreign Relations and the Harvard Business School Visiting Committee.

Jim earned his master's degree in public administration from the University of Pittsburgh, and his bachelor of arts degree in political science at Grinnell College. He also attended Harvard Business School's Program for Management Development.

Photo by Powell Photography, Inc.

Celebrating African-American Achievements

Chicago's
INTERESTING PERSONALITIES

Caretaker of a Giant Treasure Chest

ANTOINETTE D. WRIGHT

By Lisa D. Lenoir

Ask Antoinette D. Wright how she views her position as president and chief executive officer of DuSable Museum of African American History and she'll respond: "It's my divine assignment."

As the longest standing leader of the nation's oldest independent African-American history museum, she's taken on the charge to lead an organization whose mission is to educate and preserve artifacts of the African and African-American experience.

Located on Chicago's South Side, the DuSable stands along Cottage Grove Avenue, nestled among the grand trees of Washington Park. It is there where thousands of families make pilgrimages to its galleries to celebrate Martin Luther King, Jr.'s birthday, to admire black arts and crafts, or to explore the history of black hair care giant Annie Malone of Poro Beauty Colleges.

Igniting Wright's spirit to maintain this vessel of knowledge is DuSable's founder Margaret R. Burroughs. The world-renowned artist and educator started the museum in 1961 in the ground floor of her home.

Burroughs' poem, "What Shall I Tell My Children Who Are Black?" provides a meditation for Wright. Words such as "I must find the truth of heritage for myself/And pass it on to them" help to enforce and inspire what needs to be done daily to keep the museum viable and relevant.

With financial acumen and a passion for black culture, she's able to keep focused on the tasks given from above.

She finds her parents' guidance and her immersion in culture on Chicago's South Side helped to lay the groundwork for this assignment. She read the *Chicago Defender*, pored over Langston Hughes' history books, and learned from her elders, who passed on oral traditions. At the same time, a fascination with arithmetic emerged. "I liked the way [math] made my brain feel."

Her math aptitude took her to DePaul University and Mundelein College, where she earned a bachelor of science degree in business. After earning her degree, Wright moved into banking for a few years, worked as comptroller for Operation PUSH, and served as director of finance and administration for the Donor's Forum of Chicago. She joined DuSable from 1990-1993 as deputy director and returned in 1997 to her current position.

Wright's main objective is to keep the not-for-profit museum in the hearts and minds of the community. She has launched the beginnings of a $25 million expansion and capital campaign to move thousands of precious artifacts to a building across the street. But money continues to be the challenge. If only the city's significant African-American population contributed $1 per year, she says, the institution could flourish. "Your culture is good for you and you should support it."

Facilitating this aesthetic experience has become Wright's commission, one she's taken on with fervor. "I am a caretaker of a giant treasure chest. I have been the person assigned to take care of the treasure."

Photo by Powell Photography, Inc.

Celebrating African-American Achievements

Chicago's INTERESTING PERSONALITIES

Energy to Fight for Justice

JAMES MONTGOMERY

By Lisa D. Lenoir

Amidst the hardcover biographies of John Adams and Harold Washington juxtaposed with volumes of legal texts on his office bookshelves, James Montgomery mirrored their depth and heft. Standing well above six feet tall, he overflowed with tome-filling stories of struggle and triumphs as the toughest African-American man in the legal field.

Born in Louise, Mississippi, and raised in Chicago, Montgomery was the middle child, sandwiched by an older and younger brother. "I was one of the guys who had to fight to get attention."

Achieving academically would be the way for him to "grab a place in the sun" with his parents. After meeting his uncle's lawyer and being mesmerized by episodes of *Perry Mason*, he wanted to steer his education into law.

But a counselor at the University of Illinois at Urbana-Champaign had a different idea for him. Montgomery still recalled the woman's name. She told him after evaluating his aptitude test scores that he was below average in some areas, average in others. His abilities, she said, would best be applied in physical education.

"Racism was the next thing that started to drive me. I was trying to prove to her and me that I would do what I was *chosen* to do."

He turned a deaf ear to her criticism and pursued law, but it wasn't easy. "In law school, I was the only African American. The students would ignore me when I wanted to discuss cases. That was the devastating part for me. I never allowed myself, until years later, to deal with [this rejection]."

Being rendered invisible drove Montgomery to perfection after graduating in 1956. The moment he stepped into the courtroom he initiated firebrand tactics. He over prepared his cases, combated with white judges and suppressed evidence. One judge, though, proved to him that not everyone who sat on the bench was racist. "I came to realize my method of operation wasn't the most effective. But that period of my life taught me to thoroughly prepare my cases."

This attention to detail has served him well as he worked on some of the city's most high-profile criminal, civil rights, personal injury and medical malpractice cases through his firm, James D. Montgomery and Associates. Whether he represented the Black Panthers or Black Stone Rangers, Montgomery channeled his bold energy to fight for justice. "I would go out and defend the toughest cases and volunteer for them."

His professionalism and skills landed him the position as corporation counsel under the Harold Washington administration in 1983. In 1999, the Illinois Academy of Lawyers inducted him as a laureate in the academy, describing him "as a lawyer who personifies the greatness of the law profession."

And in 2000, he partnered with the late Johnnie Cochran to start Cochran, Cherry, Givens, Smith and Montgomery, LLC. "What [Johnnie] did by using his great talent ... did more for the image and for the respect of the black lawyer."

Montgomery's challenges reaching the top of his profession, coupled with his legal successes, have shaped him. "That's the milieu that has created the kind of animal I have become."

He is married to Pauline Montgomery and has six adult children. His son, James Jr., works in the law firm.

Photo by Powell Photography, Inc.

Celebrating African-American Achievements

Chicago's
INTERESTING PERSONALITIES

"I keep working it every single day."

S. JERMIKKO JOHNSON

By Maureen Jenkins

S. Jermikko Johnson has come a mighty long way—literally—since breaking into the fashion design business with just "$50, two tree trunks, a home sewing machine, a metal card playing table, three yards of fabric and a six-pound dog."

And to ensure she never forgets her humble Louisiana roots, where she spent her early childhood picking cotton on a former plantation where her family had been slaves, Johnson keeps a small plastic bag containing a cotton boll at her new 6,000-square foot factory in the Pilsen neighborhood.

"You've got to educate people about who you are, what you are, and how you are," says Johnson, who employs 17 employees plus a contractor in Ghana. "I've had to do a lot of that. It works if you work it, and I keep working it every single day."

Known for the colorfully whimsical coats and sportswear she both designs and manufactures here in Chicago, Johnson sells about ten percent of her creations to other companies for their own private labels. The rest bears variations of her "Jermikko" moniker. With women's sizes that range from petite through 3X, Johnson maintains a diverse customer base, one that appreciates both the humor and workmanship that goes into her garments. She has also launched her first retail venture in a small downtown Chicago space.

Johnson first arrived in Chicago from Tallulah, Louisiana, in 1956. Short stints as a hospital candy striper and telephone operator only encouraged the determined young woman to follow her design dreams. She earned a psychology degree from The University of Chicago while also studying fashion design at the School of the Art Institute of Chicago in the early 1970s.

While there, Johnson encountered folks of privilege. A student working three part-time jobs to make ends meet, she realized, "They know something I don't know. They've been somewhere I haven't been. In order to do that, I have to understand them." So she made nice with powerful people like Stanley Korshak, who at the time owned one of Chicago's toniest boutiques, and became his apprentice.

But once she launched her own business, she ran into roadblocks like manufacturers who weren't willing to gamble on a young black woman running a one-person shop. "When I look at what I'm doing today," she says, "I see it as stepping into an industry that barred me."

Today, Johnson's apparel sells in about 640 stores and boutiques, including some in Australia, Japan and Ghana. The first black woman named "Designer of the Year" by Chicago's Apparel Industry Board, Johnson has also created looks for Gladys Knight and Dionne Warwick, and designed Della Reese's coats for the award-winning CBS drama *Touched by an Angel*.

Some folks would rather forget the past, but not Johnson. She's probably still got every pattern she's ever designed hanging on rolling racks and several vintage mannequins—not to mention every article written about her. Because she's seen so much, Johnson wants to provide a training ground for design students.

"It finally occurred that God put me through all this to do something about it," she says. "I'm interested in building an empire through young people's energy. I want to bring 'em in here and teach them how to do this. I want to help rebuild manufacturing here."

Photo by Powell Photography, Inc.

Celebrating African-American Achievements

Chicago's
INTERESTING PERSONALITIES

"It's one of the best jobs in the world."

ALDON D. MORRIS, PH.D.

By Maureen Jenkins

African Americans who survive and thrive in the competitive world of academia don't have the luxury of hiding out inside ivy-covered walls. Rather, thoughtful ones consider it their duty to help black scholars navigate the university system and emerge as successful professionals.

That's a role that Aldon D. Morris, Ph.D., gladly has accepted at Northwestern University in Evanston, Illinois. As professor of sociology in the Weinberg College of Arts and Sciences and associate dean for faculty, he'll be helping mold future scholars and shape this prestigious university for decades to come. For the past three years, he's handled issues dealing with recruitment, promotion, tenure, and staff diversity.

"I've been in the academy long enough to be able to effect some change," says Morris, a Chicago native appointed by Northwestern's provost to serve on the standing faculty diversity committee. "Diversifying the faculty at a university like Northwestern is incredibly challenging. Once you get a very strong African-American studies department, you can use that as leverage to diversify the faculty generally. We're working very diligently to make that happen."

Morris, who has played a major role in this task, is especially excited that come fall, this department will matriculate its first graduate students. He says that Northwestern is just one of seven schools in the nation that will offer such a degree at the doctorate level. "Now," he says, "it's one of the largest in the country," with about a dozen tenured and tenure-track professors. "I feel a strong desire to help young people get involved in this, to know they can do it." And he's supervised doctoral work for many who have themselves become professors at major universities.

Not only has Morris made his mark on African-American studies, but this academician also directed the school's Asian-American studies program from 2002 to 2005. While it might sound strange for a black professor to head this discipline, Morris "accepted the position because I really wanted to understand the Asian-American situation in a different way."

As a scholar, Morris' teaching and research interests include social movements and change, the study of social inequality, and the roles race, class and gender play in this imbalance. In 1984, Morris published *The Origins of the Civil Rights Movement: Black Communities Organizing for Change,* one of academia's definitive books on the subject and the recipient of numerous awards. He also consulted on the groundbreaking 1987 documentary, *Eyes on the Prize.*

Morris is currently writing on the sociology of activist and scholar W.E.B. DuBois, as well as researching the National Baptist Convention, the largest black religious denomination in the world. A versatile scholar who can write as easily and knowledgeably about the film *Barbershop* as politics in Israel, Morris believes it's critical that black academicians develop a global perspective.

"There's always been an interest of African-American scholars on the global picture dealing with race and inequality," says Morris, referring to legends such as DuBois. "One can't understand race in America without understanding it in a global sense." And it's this ongoing learning that keeps him excited about scholarship.

After all these years, Morris is still amazed his work allows him "to actually get paid to read, write and study. It's one of the best jobs in the world."

Photo by Powell Photography, Inc.

Celebrating African-American Achievements

Chicago's
INTERESTING PERSONALITIES

The Right Combination to Win

CAROLYN ADAMS

By Lisa D. Lenoir

A menagerie of all things lucky surrounded Carolyn Adams' office. Lucky bamboo stalks stood in a vase. Lottery signs screamed out the winning pot amounts. And the framed picture of a handsome, young nine-year-old boy's face posed with his mother said enough.

Adams, Illinois lottery superintendent, has appeared to be a commanding woman who knows how to "move the needle" and facilitate change in the public sector. Since she started heading the lottery in 2003, she has launched new tickets such as Ticket for the Cure, which is the nation's first lottery ticket formed to help fund breast cancer education, research and patient services, and Veterans Cash, the first instant ticket to support 100 percent the Department of Veterans Affairs in Illinois. And she's been able to increase total contributions to the State Common School fund by more than $74 million during her term.

These have been initiatives and accomplishments Adams was proud of — they made the lottery even more advocacy-oriented. "Along with great power comes great responsibility."

This take-charge personality has always existed in her life. After attending Illinois State University for two years and then receiving her degree from Columbia College Chicago in communications, Adams found herself not ready after graduation to embrace corporate America and get serious about her career. So, she became a flight attendant for a major airline.

Bangkok, Japan, Hong Kong were destinations she visited. While seeing the world was her goal, she found herself elevated to leadership roles on flights. "Flying international meant I was the only American and I would become the lead attendant." This meant she dealt with customer service and personnel issues.

These were just the building blocks that would take her to new heights. "I set goals, and I like accomplishing those goals. I have a strong faith base and without that you can't do what you are set in life to do."

After flying for five years, she worked in sales and marketing. While at places such as Clear Channel Communications, WVON and WGN radio, she mastered skills in cross media marketing, special events and ad sales.

From these experiences, she learned how to meet consumers where they were. And this was why she moved at a fast-clip to effect change at the lottery. She fostered better communications with lottery partners; she improved machine technology and visibility; she hired a top-flight staff; she spiced up the games; and she retained Danielle Ashley Communications, a black advertising and public relations firm, to handle the lottery account.

"I wanted to make a difference, help people and institute change. When you are an African American, you have a responsibility to institute change, level the playing field and raise the bar. The field was not level. When you are put here, you have to make a difference."

Adams has discovered the right combination to win.

Photo by Powell Photography, Inc.

Celebrating African-American Achievements

Chicago's INTERESTING PERSONALITIES

In Pursuit of Others' Creative Greatness

HARRY PORTERFIELD

By Maureen Jenkins

For nearly 30 years, broadcaster Harry Porterfield's legendary "Someone You Should Know" reports have shone a spotlight on thousands of Chicagoland residents that dedicate their lives to the pursuit of creative greatness without much fanfare.

The same can be said for Porterfield, a real-life Renaissance man who doesn't seek personal accolades but earns them anyway for his humble dedication to his craft—and to the viewers who watch him.

A chemistry major at Eastern Michigan University, this former U.S. Army sergeant joined radio station WKNX in Saginaw, Michigan, as a gospel and jazz disc jockey. He soon found himself writing copy for commercials.

"What I liked about it was the opportunity to be creative," remembers Porterfield, "which you don't get much opportunity for in a chemistry lab."

He started working part-time at night as a stagehand and cameraman for a Saginaw television station owned by the same company as WKNX. "I could see all sorts of challenges to do creative things, create different kinds of programming," he says.

Little did Porterfield know that his big broadcasting break would come *in front* of the camera. He had a choice: use his chemistry education in a metallurgical lab, or take a writing job at Chicago's CBS affiliate, WBBM-Channel 2. He chose the latter, and still believes it's one of the smartest career moves he made. That was in 1964, when African-American journalists in mainstream newsrooms were scarce.

"The challenge was to come into a job I didn't know and *learn* to be a journalist," Porterfield says. Always mindful of some advice he'd gotten years before from a radio salesman—"Be a good listener"—he eventually found himself anchoring the station's 6 p.m. weekday newscast and launching the "Someone You Should Know" series.

"I really wasn't enamored with the name," Porterfield admits. The executive producer's original idea "was to look for goofy people, zany people, oddballs. I tried it a couple of times but they were so profane we couldn't use them on the air." But Porterfield heard about a handicapped hospital worker who used "puff and sip" adaptive technology in her administrative work. "That one elicited a lot of response and we figured we were on to something," he says. "We look for people who are doing exceptional things, doing incredible things in the lives of other people."

Porterfield, who also holds a law degree from DePaul University, moved from Channel 2 to ABC affiliate WLS-Channel 7 in 1985, bringing the "Someone You Should Know" concept with him. He still has one minute and 50 seconds to tell compelling stories, which he does during the 5 p.m. newscasts every Tuesday and Thursday.

"It seems to work because there's really nothing like it on TV," he says. And in his office sit countless honors from civic groups, community organizations, and even schoolchildren he's met over the years.

An 11-time Emmy Award winner for news and features reporting, Porterfield is also an accomplished jazz violinist, skilled narrator and acoustic guitarist.

"One of the goals of every musician I've ever met is to get better," he says. And he feels the same way about his journalistic work. "I want to do a better story the next time than I did today, because every story is a learning experience."

Photo by Powell Photography, Inc.

Celebrating African-American Achievements

Chicago's INTERESTING PERSONALITIES

For the Love of It: Conversations with Canvas

ANDRE GUICHARD

By Lisa D. Lenoir

A three-story building in Chicago's historic Bronzeville often illuminates the block of 35th and Martin Luther King, Jr. Drive. The sand-colored exterior, with large oblong windows providing glimpses of artwork inside, serves as a creative beacon in the city's revitalized Black Metropolis.

Artist Andre Guichard helps to fuel this structure's aura. Started in 2004, Gallery Guichard not only features his own works but those of African and African-American artists throughout the country and the world. This well-designed building's high ceilings, track lighting and peek-a-boo columns complement the sculptures, oil pastels, collages, acrylics, sculptures and lighting fixtures.

This is Guichard's vision realized; he always wanted a place to feature the black experience through fine art. The son of a self-taught artist, the Chicago native found himself receiving the gift through osmosis. He remembers going to Lake Michigan with his father to watch him create beautiful landscapes. "My father was an artist for the love of it."

Doodling for fun between high school classes was the extent of Guichard's artistic expression. He went on to Illinois State University in Bloomington, graduated with a degree in economics and went into the insurance industry. But there was restlessness — until he went on a trip to Jamaica and received clarity.

"Everyone who had a talent was creating art. Everyone was doing what he was blessed to do … not allowing financial constraints to keep them from doing what they were supposed to do. In Jamaica, it was about being who you are and tapping into it."

Upon returning to the States, he bought art supplies and started making art. "All of the blood, sweat and tears inside me came out onto the canvas. It was the end of a creative constipation."

With each stroke, his confidence and proficiency as an artist grew. His jazz series paintings, inspired by his grandfather, a jazz musician, fueled what appeared on his early canvases. He started to enter works in juried shows and display them at smaller galleries — all while he worked his day job as an insurance adjuster. The more exposure he received, the faster he moved into making art a full-time commitment. "The confidence came through when people began purchasing the work. This led me to want to create my own venue."

Layers of oil or acrylic paint produce large-scale sculpture-like works. This technique is part of his visual vocabulary, helping him to emphasize his thoughts about love and relationships, jazz and spirituality. "It starts with giving something of yourself. By having conversations with the canvas, you are able to create something that speaks to the collector in a way that's deeper than the aesthetic. The artwork helps them to look at the world differently."

Establishing an environment for this exchange to take place is vital for the black community, he says. Seeing like images helps to build self-esteem and pride. "I want to continue to reach back and work with young, emerging artists. They can see the example of an artist and businessman."

And this, he says, can help to grow the Bronzeville community and beyond.

Guichard is married to Frances, who is also his gallery business partner, and is the father of Miles, from a previous marriage.

Photo by Billy Smith

Celebrating African-American Achievements

Chicago's
INTERESTING PERSONALITIES

Transforming the Urban University

DR. ELNORA D. DANIEL

By Robyn E. Wheeler

The remarkable transformation that Chicago State University (CSU) is experiencing today is, in no small measure, the result of the visionary leadership of President Elnora D. Daniel. In her eight years as president, the university has enjoyed myriad enhancements and first-time achievements. They include securing funding for five new buildings, (the first state-supported capital projects at the university since 1972), and operating with four consecutive years of balanced budgets following four prior years of deficits.

Since her appointment in 1998, the university's academic standing has been profoundly enhanced by achieving a major higher education milestone, namely the approval of two new doctoral programs: the Ed.D. in educational leadership through the College of Education and the Pharm.D. degree through the College of Health Sciences. The university's expansion to a doctoral degree-granting university in tandem with increased accreditations and the aforementioned capital projects (including a $35 million state-of-the-art library and a $32 million, 7,000-seat convocation center), equal a phenomenal eight-year presidential track record.

The discipline, talent and leadership that Daniel exhibits as CSU's president can be seen early in her career. After receiving her master's degree in nursing education, she launched a career as an educator at Hampton University and a military career in the Air Force Reserve and then the Army Reserve Nurses Corp. Along the way, Daniel's dedicated work and service to her country was punctuated with continued ascension. She ultimately reached the position of colonel in the Army Reserve before retiring, and executive vice president and provost at Hampton before her appointment to CSU. "I rely on my three decades of higher education experience and my military training in my role as president. Every experience has prepared me for this," explained Daniel.

The university's relationships with business and civic organizations have substantially increased under the president's direction. "Higher education institutions cannot solely depend on federal and state funds if they want to thrive. University leadership must cultivate relationships and collaborate with corporate and community constituents in order to realize their educational objectives," says Daniel. Her fundraising efforts have more than doubled the size of CSU's endowment and contributions to the foundation have also increased significantly.

The illustrious career of Daniel, and the transformation that she continues to lead at Chicago State University, has earned her an international reputation as is reflected in her appointment by the W.K. Kellogg Foundation. In that role, she served as a consultant in the area of regulatory health care reform to Lesotho, Botswana, Zimbabwe and Swaziland. Additionally, she served as a consultant for Operation Smile International in Liberia, Kenya and Ghana, and was invited by former Governor George Ryan of Illinois to represent the higher education community in a trade mission to South Africa.

Many national and local organizations have recognized Daniel's extraordinary leadership by appointing her to their boards. She has also published extensively and holds numerous academic and civic awards.

Daniel says, "The changes underway at Chicago State are exciting, surpassed only by the endless possibilities realized in the lives of students that attend the institution." With Dr. Daniel at the university's helm, Chicago State will continue to have a positive impact on its students.

BeInspired

BeRewarded

BeYourself

Be **KRAFT**

Where Do You Want Your Career to Be? If you are seeking a rich environment that provides challenging opportunities, rewards you for your contributions, and values your individuality, then choose KRAFT. Join a global organization where you become part of a high quality, dedicated team while bringing your unique and innovative ideas to the table to help grow the business. It is what makes you – and KRAFT – special. A company that simply allows you to Be.

The choice is yours. The answer is KRAFT.

Explore exciting career opportunities at
www.kraft.com/careers

Kraft is an Affirmative Action/Equal Opportunity Employer M/F/V/D.

©2005 KF Holdings

CHICAGO'S PREMIER HOTEL

EXPERIENCE THE ESSENCE OF THE CITY AT HYATT REGENCY CHICAGO

A vibrant hotel standing at the top of Chicago's Magnificent Mile, near world-class shopping, international cultural attractions, Navy Pier, Millennium Park, and so much more. The hotel features 2,019 guestrooms & suites and six restaurants & lounges. Wireless and high-speed Internet access is available in all guestrooms and suites. This is not your typical hotel story, this is the Hyatt Touch.™ To find out more or to book your next meeting, call our sales representative at 312 239 4540 or visit **chicagohyatt.com**.

HYATT REGENCY CHICAGO
ON THE RIVERWALK®

Celebrating African-American Achievements

ACROSS THE NATION

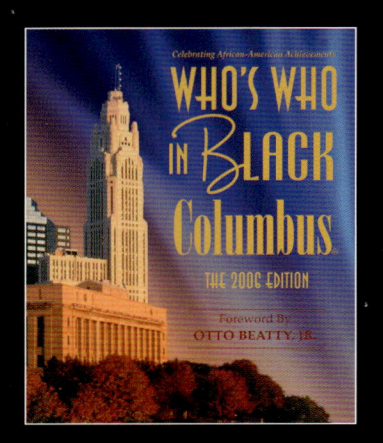

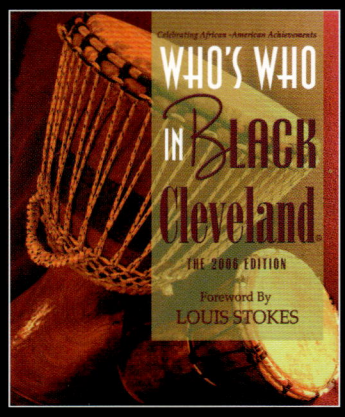

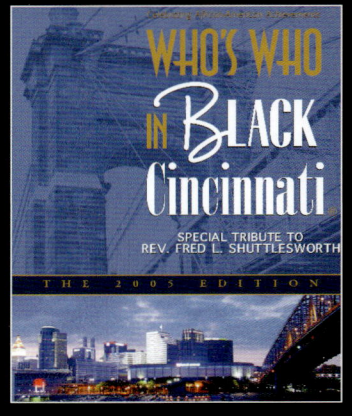

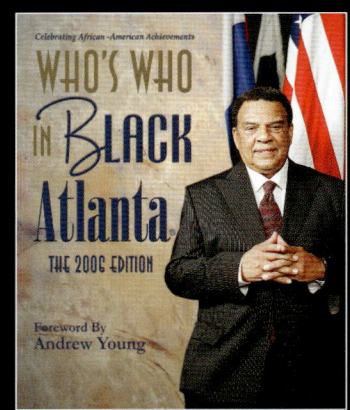

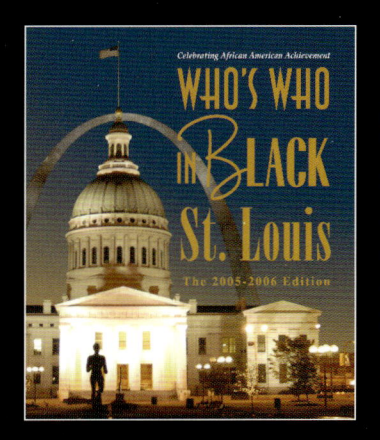

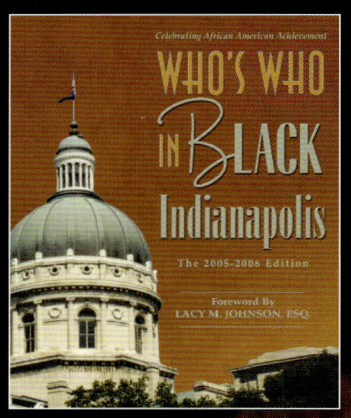

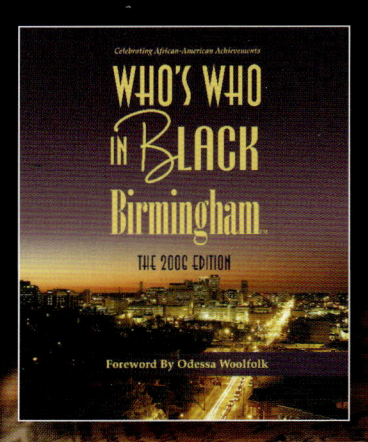

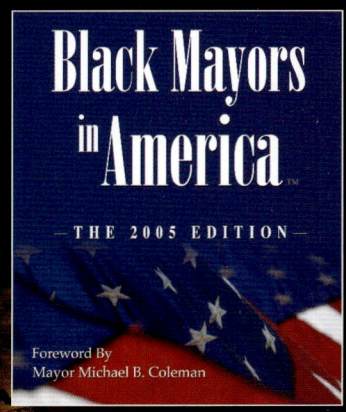

WHO'S Who
PUBLISHING CO., LLC

Visit Us Online@ *www.whoswhopublishing.com*
Or Call (614) 481-7300

Real People, Real Solutions

We value our diversity.

Diverse products that address a spectrum of health care needs. Diverse technologies that enable us to develop better health care solutions. Diverse markets that challenge our thinking and help strengthen our capabilities through collaboration.

And diverse people with diverse perspectives that inspire new and better ways to improve health.

For more than a century, Abbott has been working to advance health care. Headquartered in Chicago with more than 60,000 employees around the world, we don't just see a better world—we're positioned to make it happen.

Learn more at **www.abbott.com**.

Abbott
A Promise for Life

Work with the best.

At CDW, we take great pride in the work we do — and it shows. For the eighth consecutive year, CDW has been named one of Fortune's 100 Best Companies to Work For.

Visit us at CDW.com

FORTUNE® 100 BEST COMPANIES TO WORK FOR

CDW®

The Right Technology. Right Away.™
CDW.com • 800.800.4CDW

Supplier Diversity
A Natural Resource

In today's naturally evolving business climate, developing opportunities for diverse suppliers is not just our corporate responsibility, it's good for business and ultimately makes us a stronger, more productive, and increasingly successful company.

To learn more about Nicor's Supplier Diversity Program, please contact Rona Fourté at 630 388-2870.

nicor
GAS

Order Additional Copies Online
www.whoswhopublishing.com
614-481-7300

Pioneers in a new thought process called ethnic fusion.

FCG

FLOWERS COMMUNICATIONS GROUP

Find out how we can build your brand with multicultural marketing communications.
Contact D. Michelle Flowers, CEO, at 312-986-1250.

www.flowerscomm.com

play style

What's your style? Pick 3, Pick 4, Little Lotto, Instants, Lotto or Mega Millions...

No matter how you play, play.

Illinois Lottery

HAVE A BALL!
illinoislottery.com

Have fun! Play responsibly. Must be 18 or older. If you believe you or someone you know has a gambling problem, call 1-800-GAMBLER for assistance.

BOEING

CORPORATE SPOTLIGHT

BOEING — Corporate Spotlight

Joyce E. Tucker
Vice President
Global Diversity and Employee Rights
The Boeing Company

Joyce E. Tucker is the vice president of global diversity and employee rights for The Boeing Company. She is responsible for developing and implementing cultural diversity initiatives, affirmative action plans, and resolving internal and external equal employment opportunity (EEO) complaints. She also ensures compliance with federal, state, and local EEO mandates, and manages Boeing's alternative dispute resolution and corrective action processes.

Before joining Boeing, Tucker was president of Tucker Spearman & Associates, a consulting company specializing in EEO and diversity management. She served as a court-approved monitor on the consent decree between the Equal Employment Opportunity Commission (EEOC) and Mitsubishi Motor Manufacturing of America.

Former President George H. W. Bush appointed Tucker as commissioner of the U.S. EEOC, where she served from 1990 to 1996. From 1980-1990, Tucker was the first director of the Illinois Department of Human Rights. Additionally, President George H. W. Bush appointed Tucker to serve on the White House Advisory Board for HBCUs.

A native of Chicago, Tucker received a juris doctorate from The John Marshall Law School. She is a member of the Illinois Bar.

Mike Carnette
Director, Finance
The Boeing Company

Mike Carnette is a director of finance in The Boeing Company. He has been in this position since October of 2003.

Carnette reports to James Bell, executive vice president and chief financial officer (CFO) of the Boeing Company. He ensures the responsibilities of the CFO's office are met through integration of the functional finance organizations and the business unit financial organizations.

Carnette has been with Boeing for ten years. He has held leadership positions in both Boeing's commercial and government businesses. Prior to his current assignment, Carnette was responsible for implementation of strategic initiatives such as e-commerce and lean manufacturing for Boeing rotorcraft products. Before that, he was responsible for all aspects of production quality for the 757 commercial jetliner factory.

Prior to joining Boeing, Carnette was an engineer in General Electric's aircraft engine division.

Attending the Massachusetts Institute of Technology, Carnette earned a bachelor's and a master's degree in mechanical engineering. He also holds a master's degree in management from the MIT Sloan School.

Corporate Spotlight — **BOEING**

Karen F. Johnson
Director, Employee Rights
The Boeing Company

Karen Johnson is director of employee rights within human resources at The Boeing Company. There, she is responsible for providing strategic development and alignment of enterprise-wide policies and procedures related to employee corrective action and alternative dispute resolution.

Karen's 25-year professional career at the company includes increasing levels of responsibility in several positions. A few of which include, staffing representative, senior equal opportunity representative, compensation specialist, manager/director of human resources/communications, ethics advisor, and director of regulatory compliance, and most recently, employee rights. Her corporate social responsibilities include participation in various community events throughout Chicago and other U.S. cities.

A native of Alabama, Karen earned a bachelor of science degree in business administration at the University of Alabama, Huntsville. She previously lived in Houston and Seattle, prior to moving to Chicago.

A member of the Society of Human Resources Management, Karen is also a member of Delta Sigma Theta Sorority, Inc. She enjoys shopping, watching The Learning Channel, social time with family and friends, and sharing her cooking skills while testing new recipes.

Linda D. Martin
Director, Global Corporate Citizenship
The Boeing Company

Linda Martin is director of global corporate citizenship for The Boeing Company. In 2003, she spearheaded the creation of the company's first-ever global contributions strategy, and is now managing its multi-phase implementation. In her role, Martin is responsible for ensuring that these charitable contributions and grant-making activities comply with all applicable rules, regulations, and legal requirements. Some of which include, the Executive Order, 13224/USA Patriot Act and Foreign Corrupt Practices Act, as well as Boeing's internal code of conduct.

A Boeing employee since 1974, in a prior position Martin served in Washington, D.C., as director of government relations for human resources, labor relations, education relations, and employee benefits policy.

Martin currently serves as a trustee of United Way International and board member of National Merit Scholarship, Inc.

Receiving a bachelor of arts degree from Seattle University, Martin obtained a master of science degree in management from Stanford University where she was a Sloan fellow. She also attended the executive management program at Dartmouth College, Tuck School of Business in Hanover, New Hampshire.

BOEING — Corporate Spotlight

Denise B. McKinney
Director
Corporate & Strategic Development
The Boeing Company

Denise McKinney is a director of corporate and strategic development at Boeing's corporate headquarters in Chicago, Illinois. In this position, she provides leadership and support to Boeing's business units in the initiation and execution of merger and acquisition, joint venture, and divestiture activities.

In addition to her seven years of transaction experience, Denise has also spent 11 years in business operations with multi-year assignments in product management, including P&L, strategic planning responsibilities, and sales.

Denise received a bachelor's degree in chemical engineering from Georgia Tech, and a master's degree in business administration from the University of Michigan.

An active member of Jack & Jill of America and the Chicago Chapter, she is a member of Delta Sigma Theta Sorority, Inc. A native of Columbia, Maryland, Denise and her husband Antonio have two children, Uriah and Trinity.

Verett Mims
Assistant Treasurer
The Boeing Company

As assistant treasurer of Boeing, Verett Mims has many responsibilities including forecasting and reporting on short-term cash balances, maintaining sufficient liquidity, enhancing return on assets, and standardizing cash and banking processes. She provides guidance to address risks related to foreign currency transactions and letters of credit. Previously, she served as Boeing's director of international finance and was responsible for currency hedging strategy as well as related compliance with applicable accounting standards.

Before joining Boeing, Verett oversaw foreign exchange, interest rate, and equity risk management as a senior treasury manager at Sun Microsystems in Palo Alto, California.

A native of Shreveport, Louisiana, she received a bachelor's degree in physics from Southern University and a master's degree from MIT. After completing her master's thesis, she joined Hughes Aircraft. Completing an MBA from Stanford University in 1993, Verett spent seven years as a sales trader with Citibank's foreign exchange sales desk in New York. Additionally, she served NationsBank in the Chicago sales desk where she developed new business and advised corporate treasurers and treasury managers on risk management.

Corporate Spotlight

BOEING

Lawrence Oliver
Chief Counsel, Investigations
The Boeing Company

Ozzie Pierce
Director, EEO Compliance
The Boeing Company

In September of 2004, Oliver joined The Boeing Company as its chief counsel of investigations, where he manages the company's internal legal investigations. The following month, he received a gubernatorial appointment to the state's first-ever Executive Ethics Commission.

Prior to joining Boeing, Oliver was a partner at the law firm of Perkins Coie in Chicago. During his tenure at Perkins Coie, he was appointed by the mayor of Chicago to investigate the E2 Nightclub tragedy of February 2003 that left 21 people dead. Oliver also investigated the alleged cover up of beatings of inmates by jail guards at the Cook County Jail. He is a former federal prosecutor and federal judicial law clerk.

In 1991, Oliver received his law degree from the Detroit College of Law and was the Charles H. King award recipient for graduating first in his class. In 1984, he received a bachelor of science degree in industrial engineering from Purdue University.

Oliver is an ordained minister and serves on several nonprofit boards.

Ozzie Pierce is director of equal employment opportunity (EEO) compliance at The Boeing Company. He is responsible for providing direction, leadership, and guidance for enterprise-wide EEO strategies and initiatives. His corporate social responsibilities include participation in diversity events throughout Chicago and other cities where Boeing has employees.

Ozzie's professional career includes private and public sector experience. Previously, he was senior EEO and diversity management consultant with Tucker Spearman and Associates, Inc. Additionally, Ozzie served as branch manager of the opportunity programs department at Mitsubishi Motor Manufacturing of America, Inc., and was charge processing assistant manager at the Illinois Department of Human Rights.

Earning a bachelor of arts in political science at Valdosta State College, Valdosta, Georgia, Ozzie also holds a master of arts in legal studies at the University of Illinois, Springfield.

Enjoying sports and music, Ozzie appreciates spending time with family and friends.

BOEING — Corporate Spotlight

Phillip "Phil" B. J. Reid
Director of Security
Boeing Corporate Center

Phillip B. J. Reid is the director of security for Boeing's Corporate Center in Chicago, Illinois, and of their Executive Flight Operations in Gary, Indiana.

Phil retired from the FBI in May of 2005, as the special agent in charge of the Denver FBI Division, which is responsible for all of the FBI's federal investigations for the states of Colorado and Wyoming. During his 28-year career with the FBI, Phil was assigned to several FBI offices. His investigations involved FBI employee misconduct and international terrorism, where Americans were victims of murder and kidnappings in Europe, Asia, and the Pacific Rim countries. Most notablably was the Pan Am 103 Lockerbie bombing investigation.

Phil received an associate degree in law enforcement from the Baltimore Community College and a bachelor of arts degree in sociology from Morgan State University.

A native of Baltimore, Maryland, Phil now resides in the western suburbs of Chicago with his wife, Bernadette. He is the proud father of his daughter, who graduated from Howard University's Business School, and two granddaughters.

Darcel M. Stewart
Director, International Finance
The Boeing Company

Darcel Stewart is director of international finance for The Boeing Company where she is responsible for the leadership of all international financial reporting, processes, and systems for non-U.S. entities of the company. She also chairs the international finance process action team of The Boeing Company.

Previously, Darcel was director of financial planning and analysis, responsible for competitive analysis and benchmarking, financial planning, reporting, and analysis for the corporation.

Prior to Boeing, Darcel spent 13 years in numerous financial management positions at Motorola Inc. She also worked for United Airlines and Deloitte, Haskins & Sells (currently Deloitte & Touche).

Darcel is active in many professional associations in the Chicagoland area including the National Association of Black Accountants and the National Black MBA Association. She is an officer of Jack and Jill of America, Inc., and a member of Delta Sigma Theta Sorority, Inc.

Holding an MBA in finance from The University of Chicago, Darcel earned a bachelor of science degree in accounting from the Wharton School, University of Pennsylvania, and is a certified public accountant.

Corporate Spotlight — **BOEING**

Deb Telman is assistant corporate secretary and counsel for The Boeing Company. In this position, she is the lead lawyer managing Boeing's mergers, acquisitions, divestitures, and joint ventures. Deb also provides legal oversight for Boeing's pension plan, treasury department, and community relations programs.

Prior to joining Boeing, Deb was a partner at Winston & Strawn, and previously worked at Morgan Stanley and Merrill Lynch.

Active in many community and civic affiliations, Deb was named to *Crain's Chicago Business* "40 under 40" rising stars in business, government, and arts. She is a 1999 fellow of Leadership Greater Chicago, and serves on the board of directors of Jamal Place and Chicago Bar Association Foundation.

Receiving a bachelor of arts degree from the University of Pennsylvania, Deb holds a juris doctorate from Boston University School of Law. A native of New York, she has lived and worked in Chicago for the last 13 years.

Deb is the wife of Nigel F. Telman and the proud mother of two sons, Nigel, II and Nicholas.

Deborah H. Telman
Assistant Corporate
Secretary & Counsel
The Boeing Company

Dream BIG!

Order Additional Copies
(614) 481-7300

THE INAUGURAL EDITION *Who's Who In Black Chicago*®

SPEAKING TRUTH TO POWER

We live in a world where our views are shaped by the voices that present them. For 100 years, the Chicago Defender has been an independent news source that covers today's issues through OUR eyes. Whether it's OUR news, OUR faith, OUR lifestyle, OUR business, OUR books or OUR opinions, we report the news from OUR perspective.

CHICAGO DEFENDER
Honest. Balanced. Truthful. Unapologetically Black.

Join with us as we head into our second century by subscribing today.

Subscribe Online
ChicagoDefender.com
or call 312.225.2400

Chicago Defender, 200 S. Michigan Ave.
Suite 1700, Chicago, IL 60604

Exelon

CORPORATE SPOTLIGHT

Exelon

Corporate Spotlight

Richard H. Glanton
Senior Vice President
Corporate Development

Joyce L. Carson
Vice President, Investor Relations

Richard H. Glanton is senior vice president of corporate development for Exelon and is responsible for mergers, acquisitions, and divestitures. He served on PECO Energy's board of directors before PECO merged with Unicom to form Exelon. He was also a director of Exelon until 2003.

Before joining Exelon, Glanton was a partner in the law firm of Reed Smith LLP and was deputy counsel to Richard L. Thornburgh, former governor of Pennsylvania.

A member of the board of directors of Aqua America and The GEO Group, Inc., Glanton is a trustee of Lincoln University and serves on the national board of advisors for the Whitney M. Young, Jr. School of Social Work at Clark College. He was president of the Barnes Foundation and was awarded the title of Commander of the Order of Arts and Letters by Francois Mitterrand.

Glanton received an honorary degree from his alma mater, the University of West Georgia, in 2005. He received his bachelor's degree in English from West Georgia College in 1968 and his juris doctor degree from the University of Virginia School of Law in 1972.

Joyce L. Carson is vice president of investor relations for Exelon and manages the primary interface with major shareholders, equity and fixed-income analysts, and other stakeholders regarding Exelon's financial projections, operational performance, and company strategy.

Carson joined the company in 1997. She served as director of finance from 2002 to 2005, much of which was spent in the treasury group where she was responsible for planning and implementing long-term external financings, managing the credit rating agency, banking relationships, and credit ratings. In 2005, she was promoted to vice president, Exelon Business Services Company support services, where she managed a variety of shared services.

Prior to joining Exelon, Carson held finance positions at Jane Addams Hull House Association. She has six years of internal and external audit experience with American Stores Company and Deloitte and Touche.

Carson is a member of the board of Chicago House, where she has served as trustee and/or treasurer for more than ten years.

She is a 1989 graduate of DePaul University and has bachelor's and master's degrees in accountancy.

Corporate Spotlight

Jerrold Martin is vice president of IT (information technology) energy delivery for Exelon Business Services Company. Martin leads the energy delivery-specific areas of IT: customer/marketing, operations, asset management, support services, and real time operations. He is also accountable for the overall delivery of all IT services for the regulated delivery companies.

Prior to joining Exelon subsidiary ComEd in 1998, Martin held multiple IT senior management positions at both Ameritech (SBC) and Accenture (Andersen Consulting), including senior marketing manager of database and applications, IT customer relations general manager, and manager of field support.

He is a member of the board of directors of the American Red Cross of Greater Chicago.

Martin holds a master's degree in business administration from Roosevelt University and a bachelor's degree in economics and business from Eureka College. He has also been an adjunct professor of MBA programs at Roosevelt University.

Martin and his wife have two children.

Jerrold Martin
Vice President, IT

WHO'S Who
"Reaching America's Most Influential and Affluent African Americans"

ACROSS THE NATION

VISIT US ONLINE @ www.whoswhopublishing.com
or Call (614) 481-7300

ComEd
An Exelon Company

Corporate Spotlight

Frank M. Clark
Chairman and Chief Executive Officer

John T. Hooker
Senior Vice President
Legislative and Governmental Affairs

Frank M. Clark, chairman and CEO of ComEd, is responsible for the overall operations and strategic, regulatory and legislative efforts of the Chicago-based utility, which provides electric service to approximately 3.7 million customers in northern Illinois. Since joining ComEd, Frank has served in several key leadership positions before being named the company's first African-American president in 2002.

An active community servant, Frank provides leadership to numerous community efforts, such as the $6 million African American Legacy Fund and the capital campaign to expand DuSable Museum – one of the nation's oldest African-American museums. Frank also serves as the chairman of the board of the Adler Planetarium and Astronomy Museum, and Metropolitan Family Services of Chicago.

Named one of *Fortune* magazine's 50 Most Powerful Black Executives in 2002, he has received numerous business and humanitarian awards including honorary doctor of humane letters from Governors State University and honorary doctorate of law from DePaul University's College of Law.

Frank earned a bachelor's degree in commerce and a law degree from DePaul University in Chicago.

Frank and his wife, Vera, have two sons, Frank III and Steve.

John Hooker, senior vice president, legislative and governmental affairs, is responsible for managing ComEd's relationship with the Illinois General Assembly, Chicago's City Council and other state agencies. ComEd provides the delivery of electric service for approximately 3.7 million customers throughout northern Illinois.

With nearly four decades of service, John has held management positions in industrial relations, marketing, governmental affairs and regulatory affairs. John is also a founding member of the Exelon African-American Members Association, an employee network group established to develop and promote programs that enable members to recognize and utilize resources to enhance their capabilities in networking and in securing career-rewarding opportunities within the company.

Active in many organizations, John serves on the boards of directors of the Peoples Consumer Cooperative, which provides affordable housing for the elderly, and the Safer Foundation, which helps former offenders find a road to lawful and productive living by offering a variety of programs and services.

John earned a bachelor's degree in marketing from Chicago State University.

John and his wife, Kim, reside in Chicago and have three children, Felicia, LaToya and Sandor.

Corporate Spotlight

ComEd
An Exelon Company

Phyllis Batson
Vice President, Customer Contact

Kevin B. Brookins
Vice President, Customer Field Operations

Phyllis Batson, vice president of customer contact, is responsible for managing all call center operations. Her primary focus is improving the quality of customer interactions with residential, small business and industrial customers. ComEd, a subsidiary of Exelon Corporation, provides electric delivery service for approximately 3.7 million customers in northern Illinois.

Prior to her current position, Phyllis served more than three years as director, Customer Contact Center for ComEd, where she strengthened the organization's focus on performance management, process improvement, systems enhancement and staff development. The organization's achievements included increased use of customer self-service technology from 15 percent to 42 percent, improved call-handling performance and reduced overall costs by more than $10 million.

Prior to joining Exelon in 2001, Phyllis directed customer services at the TeleServices Division of Sears, Roebuck and Company, managing a staff of 3,500 in seven call centers. She also directed customer services at Damark International, based in Minnesota, and spent 16 years in various front-line and management positions in customer service at Northwest Airlines, Inc.

Kevin Brookins, vice president of customer field operations, is responsible for field services, meter services and meter reading. ComEd, a subsidiary of Exelon Corporation, provides electric delivery service for approximately 3.7 million customers in northern Illinois.

A versatile electric utility manager with more than 22 years experience, Kevin's recent accomplishments include increasing the number of meters read at ComEd, which ensures accurate bills for customers. In a previous role in Operations, he led efforts that reduced the number of service interruptions in Chicago as well as the city's south suburbs.

Kevin also serves on the boards of First Northern Credit Union and Chicago United. He completed the Fellows Program of Leadership Greater Chicago in 2003.

Kevin earned a bachelor of science degree in electrical engineering from Howard University in Washington D.C. and a master of business administration degree from Governors State University in University Park, Ill.

Kevin resides in Olympia Fields, Ill., with his wife, Melonese, and his two children, Courtney and Kyle.

ComEd
An Exelon Company

Corporate Spotlight

Stephanie J. Hickman
Vice President, Legislative Affairs

George W. Lofton
Vice President
External Affairs and Claims

Stephanie Hickman, vice president – legislative affairs for ComEd, is responsible for managing legislative issues, initiatives and relationships for the Chicago-based utility company. ComEd, a subsidiary of Exelon Corporation, provides electric delivery service for approximately 3.7 million customers in northern Illinois.

With more than 20 years of human resources and labor relations experience, Stephanie was an attorney with the National Labor Relations Board in Chicago before joining Exelon in 1999.

Stephanie is a board member of the Hubbard Street Dance Chicago and the American Association of Blacks in Energy. She is a former board member of the National Coalition of 100 Black Women (Chicago). She is also a 2006 Fellow of Leadership Greater Chicago and a member of the Alpha Kappa Alpha Sorority, Inc.

Stephanie earned a bachelor's degree in business administration from Eastern New Mexico University. She earned her law degree from the University of Mississippi and completed the Management Program for Executives at the Joseph M. Katz Graduate School of Business, University of Pittsburgh.

Stephanie has one son and resides in Chicago.

George Lofton, vice president of external affairs and claims for ComEd, oversees the company's external affairs, community relations, economic development, community development and corporate relations activities. ComEd provides the delivery of electric service for approximately 3.7 million customers throughout northern Illinois.

During his 31-year career, George has served ComEd in several management positions including engineering, sales, marketing, public affairs, economic development and commercial operations. George's accomplishments include the creation of STRATEGIC ILLINOIS – an innovative economic development strategic plan, the establishment of a database of every marketable industrial building and site in the six-county Chicagoland region and negotiating the creation of the Chicago Southland Alliance.

George serves on several corporate and economic development agency boards, including the Chicagoland Entrepreneurial Center, the Illinois Development Council, Illinois State Chamber of Commerce, The First National Bank of Chicago Heights, the National Utility Economic Development Association, Roosevelt University and the National Brownfield Association.

George holds a bachelor's degree in architectural engineering from Chicago Technical College.

George and his wife, Felecia, have three daughters, Hillary, Heather and Hailey. They reside in Homewood, Ill.

Corporate Spotlight

PECO
An Exelon Company

Doyle N. Beneby
Vice President, Electric Operations-East

Lisa Crutchfield
Vice President
Regulatory & External Affairs

Doyle Beneby, vice president of electric operations, is responsible for the construction and maintenance, operations, and emergency response for the electrical distribution infrastructure that provides service to 1.6 million electric customers in southeastern Pennsylvania. He manages about 1,000 employees. PECO, a subsidiary of Exelon Corporation, is a regulated delivery service utility company with 1.6 million electric and 470,000 natural gas customers in southeast Pennsylvania.

An industry veteran of more than 20 years, Doyle joined PECO from Exelon Power, where he served as a general manager for the Exelon Power fleet of peak demand power plants, based in Philadelphia. Prior to joining Exelon Power, Doyle worked at Consumers Energy in Michigan, serving as site general manager for the Dan E. Karn/Weadock Electric Generating Complex. He also serves as a board member for the Delaware County (Pennsylvania) Chamber of Commerce.

Doyle earned a bachelor of science degree in mining engineering from Montana Technical College and a master of business administration degree from the University of Miami.

Doyle and his wife, Christine, reside in Glenn Mills, Pennsylvania.

Lisa Crutchfield, vice president of regulatory and external affairs for PECO, is responsible for managing the company's regulatory, governmental affairs, economic development, and external affairs divisions. PECO, a subsidiary of Exelon Corporation, is a regulated delivery service utility company with 1.6 million electric and 470,000 natural gas customers in southeast Pennsylvania.

In her more than 15 years of utility industry experience, Lisa has also served as an executive for Duke Energy Corporation and as vice chair of the Pennsylvania Public Utility Commission. As vice chair of the Pennsylvania Public Utility Commission, Lisa influenced national public policy regarding restructuring the electric utility industry. She crafted provisions in the 1996 Electric Competition Generation Choice Act for customers, which deregulated the electric generation market in Pennsylvania.

Lisa currently serves on the boards of the United Way of Southeastern Pennsylvania, the Urban League of Philadelphia, and the African-American Museum of Philadelphia.

Lisa earned a bachelor of arts degree in economics and political science from Yale University, and a master of business administration degree from Harvard Business School, with a concentration in finance.

You've seen our work...

...now join our list of satisfied clients.

POWELL
PHOTOGRAPHY & DIGITAL IMAGING
531 S Plymouth Ct
Chicago, IL 60605
312/922-6366
www.powellphotography.com

more than just photography...

116 *Who's Who In Black Chicago*® THE INAUGURAL EDITION

LaSalle Bank
ABN AMRO

CORPORATE SPOTLIGHT

LaSalle Bank
ABN AMRO

Corporate Spotlight

Willie J. Miller, Jr.
Executive Vice President &
Chief Legal Officer
LaSalle Bank Corporation

Willie J. Miller, Jr. is an executive vice president and chief legal officer for LaSalle Bank Corporation. He has been with the corporation since 1981. He is a key member of the senior management team, providing legal perspective and business advice on the ramifications of strategic decisions made throughout the organization. This includes its major subsidiaries, LaSalle Bank N.A. in Chicago and Standard Federal Bank in Troy, Michigan.

Miller is a member of the Chicago and Illinois Bar Associations and is a 20-plus-year member of the Fellowship of African-American Men (F.A.A.M.). He is a member of the F.A.A.M. Hall of Fame. Miller is an active leader in civic endeavors, including serving on the Board of Education for Evanston Township High School for ten years, where he served three terms as president. He is one of the inaugural recipients of the Chicago United Business Leaders of Color Award, which he received in October of 2003.

Miller earned his bachelor's degree from the University of Illinois at Urbana-Champaign in 1975, and he received his law degree from Loyola University Chicago in 1979.

Donna N. Smith
Group Senior Vice President
Commercial Bank
LaSalle Bank Corporation

Donna N. Smith is a group senior vice president in LaSalle Bank's commercial bank. She manages six lending divisions with the overall responsibility of relationship management and business development for commercial and private equity clients.

Smith joined LaSalle Bank in 1997 as a senior vice president and division head with responsibility for a middle-market lending division, providing services for an array of companies throughout the Midwest. Prior to joining LaSalle, she managed a group of relationship managers at the Harris Trust and Savings Bank.

Smith received her MBA in finance from Northwestern University's Kellogg Graduate School of Management and her bachelor's degree from the University of Illinois at Chicago.

Smith serves on the board of directors of the Adler Planetarium, the Barrington Area Community Foundation, and the executive committee of the board of directors of the Gateway Foundation. Additionally, she is a member of the Kellogg Alumni Association, the Association for Corporate Growth, and the Executives' Club of Chicago.

Corporate Spotlight

LaSalle Bank
ABN AMRO

Ellamae Brown
Senior Vice President
Capital Markets Group
LaSalle Bank Corporation

Ellamae Brown is a senior vice president and money desk manager in LaSalle Bank's capital markets group. She is responsible for the management of the daily funding, reserve, and payments system risk positions at the Federal Reserve Bank in Chicago for both LaSalle Bank and LaSalle Bank Midwest, based in Troy, Michigan. In addition, Brown is responsible for direct trading for federal funds, repurchase agreements, and Eurodollars in the financial markets for LaSalle Bank and LaSalle Bank Midwest.

Brown is a member of LaSalle Bank Corporation's wholesale funding committee. She received a bachelor's degree from Mundelein College and an MBA from DePaul University's Charles H. Kellstadt Graduate School of Business.

Karen Caldwell
Senior Vice President
Capital Markets Group
LaSalle Bank Corporation

Karen Caldwell is a senior vice president in LaSalle Bank's capital markets group and manages a $6.7 billion portfolio of securitized credit products. She is responsible for developing both credit underwriting procedures and a relative value matrix for the securitized book. Karen also creates hedging strategy for the portfolio; contributes to decisions of macro duration and curve risk taken in the Domestic Treasury Mortgage portfolio; and manages the Bank Owned Life Insurance (BOLI) program.

Before joining LaSalle Bank in 1994, she was a vice president with JPMorgan Chase and a financial analyst with US Steel.

Karen is a member of LaSalle Bank's investment portfolio and BOLI committees. She is active in her community as board vice chair of finance for the Southside YMCA, a board executive committee member and board secretary for South Central Community Services, and board chair of the audit and investment committee of the Chicago Alumnae Chapter of Delta Sigma Theta Sorority, Inc.

Karen received a bachelor's degree from Florida A&M University and a master's degree from Northwestern University. She is also a CPA and a CFA Society member.

LaSalle Bank
ABN AMRO

Corporate Spotlight

Lamont Change
Senior Vice President
Wealth Management Group
LaSalle Bank Corporation

Lamont Change serves as a senior vice president in LaSalle Bank's wealth management group and global securities and trust services. In this role, his responsibilities include new business development and marketing the entire suite of wealth management and global securities and trust products and services.

Change joined LaSalle Bank in 1986. Prior to his current position, he managed a division of LaSalle's Midwest commercial lending group, targeting companies with annual sales of $25 million to $500 million. He also served as president of LaSalle's community development corporation (CDC) and as senior vice president of its community reinvestment division (CRD). As president of the CDC, Change was responsible for equity investments in both small businesses and real estate developments. As senior vice president of the CRD, he developed and implemented strategic objectives and reporting requirements for compliance with the Community Reinvestment Act. Before heading to the community reinvestment division, Change developed and managed LaSalle's small business lending division.

Tim Ervin
Senior Vice President
Real Estate Capital Markets Group
LaSalle Bank Corporation

Tim Ervin is a senior vice president and managing director in LaSalle Bank's real estate capital markets group. He is responsible for managing the production process of commercial real estate loans from $1 million to $5 million, which are eventually securitized as commercial mortgage-backed securities (CMBS). Ervin also oversees a team of analysts, underwriters, and closers who, as a team, finalize all the loans for securitization to ensure each loan can be sold on the CMBS market.

Prior to joining LaSalle Bank in 1998, Ervin worked as an associate at both Nomura/Capital Company of America and Heller Financial in Chicago.

He is active in his community where he is the chief financial officer for New Mount Pilgrim Baptist Church, and a founder and president of the Chicago Knights Foundation. Ervin earned his bachelor's degree from Purdue University.

Corporate Spotlight

LaSalle Bank
ABN AMRO

Pamela Daniels-Halisi
Senior Vice President
Community Development Lending
LaSalle Bank Corporation

Pamela Daniels-Halisi is a senior vice president and the head of LaSalle Bank's community development lending department, which is committed to revitalizing Chicago's low-to-moderate-income neighborhoods by offering real estate loan products and services to entrepreneurial clients. These clients include both private investors and community groups who have a can-do attitude and an interest in Chicago area real estate.

Before she joined the Bank in March of 1994, Daniels-Halisi was a real estate officer at Continental Bank of Chicago and a liquidation specialist with the Federal Deposit Insurance Corporation.

Daniels-Halisi serves on the board of the Woodstock Institute, is a member of the housing committee of the Metropolitan Planning Council, and serves on the ULI Chicago board of advisors and Leap Learning.

She received her bachelor's degree in finance and business administration from The University of Tennessee and her MBA from Indiana University.

She and her husband, Anthony, currently reside in Chicago's south loop area with their two children.

Selina Horton
Senior Vice President
Check & Wire Processing Group
LaSalle Bank Corporation

Selina Horton is a senior vice president in LaSalle Bank's check and wire processing group, which is a division of transaction banking. She is responsible for 28 operations team members who perform domestic and international wire functions, the Office of Foreign Asset Control (OFAC), compliance validation, and wire investigations. Horton is also responsible for an annual operating budget of $3 million and oversees more than 15,000 wire transactions per day, totaling $17 billion. In addition, she is the Global Wire Project representative and is responsible for providing detailed requirements, working through current processes and procedures, defining direction for configuration, and setup.

Horton is a member of LaSalle Bank's payments committee, which oversees and reviews LaSalle Bank payments processing related to global and domestic payments and compliance. She is also a member of the Federal Reserve Bank's wholesale customer advisory group.

She is active in her community as an outreach and hospitality committee member for Broadview Baptist Church and a volunteer tutor at Tilton Elementary School. She earned an associate degree from Loop Junior College and is currently attending DePaul University.

LaSalle Bank
ABN AMRO

Corporate Spotlight

Oscar Johnson, Jr.
Senior Vice President
Commercial Banking Group
LaSalle Bank Corporation

Oscar Johnson, Jr. is a senior vice president in LaSalle Bank's commercial banking group. He manages a $200 million loan portfolio consisting of 20 clients, and he is responsible for underwriting new and existing commercial relationships in addition to cross-selling other LaSalle Bank products and services.

Prior to joining LaSalle Bank in 1998 as an assistant vice president in the commercial banking group, Oscar was an assistant vice president with M&I (Marshall & Ilsley) Bank and a director of marketing at Fiserv Corporation, both in Milwaukee.

Oscar is a member of the Black Leadership Council and the lead on-campus LaSalle Bank recruiter at Howard University. He is active in his community and is involved with Big Brothers Big Sisters as a board member and a volunteer; board member of the West Suburban Hospital in Oak Park, Illinois; and a junior board member of the Scene Makers Council for Goodman Theatre.

Oscar received a bachelor's degree from Howard University and an MBA from Marquette University.

Regina Ward
Senior Vice President, Business &
Association Banking Department
LaSalle Bank Corporation

Regina Ward is a senior vice president of LaSalle Bank's business and association banking department.

Ward manages the nonprofit banking marketing and service team that services more than 250 association account relationships. Nonprofits typically have special servicing and product needs that are not always recognized by traditional commercial banking areas of financial institutions.

Ward joined LaSalle National Bank in 1987 and is a member of the Association Forum, Union League Club, and the ABN AMRO Black Leadership Council. She received a bachelor's degree in economics from Loyola University Chicago and has served on the board of several cultural and community organizations. Presently, she serves on the board of trustees of the DuSable Museum of African American History.

Corporate Spotlight

LaSalle Bank
ABN AMRO

Gary S. Washington
Senior Vice President
Chief Fair Lending Officer
LaSalle Bank Corporation

Gary S. Washington is senior vice president and chief fair lending officer of LaSalle Bank Corporation. He is responsible for fair lending compliance strategy and policy as well as advising on Community Reinvestment Act strategy.

Washington was a senior vice president and CRA officer for LaSalle Bank from June of 1992 to 1997. He was responsible for the bank's community development lending strategy, charitable donations to community-based organizations, and assisting the bank in meeting credit needs of income-challenged communities, resulting in the formation of the LaSalle Community Development Corporation.

Washington received a bachelor's degree from Oberlin College and a master's degree in city and regional planning from the John F. Kennedy School of Government at Harvard University.

He serves on the boards of directors for the Community Investment Corporation and the National Association of Affordable Housing Lenders. Washington also serves on the Consumer Bankers Association's fair lending committee; he completed terms on the Federal Reserve Board, on the consumer advisory council and as chair of the deposit and delivery systems committee; and he served on the Illinois Facilities Fund loan committee.

Sarah Webb
Senior Vice President
Trust Group
LaSalle Bank Corporation

Sarah Webb is a senior vice president in LaSalle Bank's trust group and is the manager of the corporate trust services division. She is responsible for daily management; budget and operations of a business unit with $6.8 billion in assets consisting of debt offerings in the secondary market, insurance specialty products, municipal escrows, default administration; and she supervises numerous legal and professional technical personnel.

Webb is on LaSalle Bank's corporate trust review committee, fiduciary administrative committee, Black Leadership Council, Global Securitization and Trust Services (GSTS) strategic roundtable committee, and GSTS InterAction's Task Force. She is on three industry committees including the advisory board of the Institute of Certified Bankers, the American Banking Association's corporate trust committee, and the Illinois Corporate Fiduciary Association.

She is a ministerial board member, board of trustees member and financial director for the Christian Family Faith Center. She is also on the strategic planning committee for Roseland Christian Elementary School.

Webb earned a bachelor's degree from the University of Illinois at Chicago, an MBA from Roosevelt University in Chicago, and she is a certified corporate trust specialist (CCTS).

Powered and Driven by Diversity

More than meets the eye.
It's about looking up the road, anticipating the demands of the future and exceeding your expectations. It's about people who are driven to set new standards for performance, reliability and service.

International Truck and Engine Corporation
Supplier Diversity Department
10400 West North Avenue
Melrose Park, Illinois 60160

We all smile in the same language

Blue Cross Blue Shield

To Us, it's all Blue.

It's easy to see the difference diversity can make.

Our employees will always be the heart of our company; united through different ideas, opinions and approaches, which are encouraged and valued. The best outcome is that the company, employees, suppliers, members and the communities we serve, benefit as a whole.

We're **Health Care Service Corporation (HCSC)**, the company behind the Blue Cross and Blue Shield divisions of Illinois, New Mexico, Oklahoma and Texas. Our workforce is as diverse as the communities we serve, because to HCSC, diversity is a company-wide commitment. We are committed to partnering with minority, women-owned and other diverse businesses for products and services because it adds value to what we do for our customers, as well as promotes prosperity in the communities where we live and work.

We're proud to recognize the many differences that make us Blue. We hope you'll join us as we continue on our journey of promoting diversity and a healthier world for all.

Blue Cross Blue Shield of Illinois
Blue Cross Blue Shield of New Mexico
Blue Cross Blue Shield of Oklahoma
Blue Cross Blue Shield of Texas

www.bcbsil.com
www.bcbsnm.com
www.bcbsok.com
www.bcbstx.com

To learn more about our company, our services, our careers and procurement opportunities, log on to our company web sites.

Divisions of Health Care Service Corporation, a Mutual Legal Reserve Company, an Independent Licensee of the Blue Cross and Blue Shield Association.
This drawing was created by an employee's child for our annual Diversity Calendars, which span several years.

Northern Trust
CORPORATE SPOTLIGHT

Northern Trust — Corporate Spotlight

Richard L. Bordelon
Equal Employment Opportunity Officer
Northern Trust Company

Richard L. Bordelon is the corporate equal employment opportunity (EEO) officer at the Northern Trust Company. He serves in the corporate policy division of the human resources department.

As EEO officer, Bordelon is responsible for overseeing EEO administration for the corporation. He monitors EEO activity at all levels of the organization, and ensures that the corporation is in compliance with federal, state, and local rules and regulations. Bordelon is responsible for investigating complaints alleging discrimination, harassment, unfair treatment and other employee relations issues. He is a member of the human resources senior management team and several compliance committees.

Prior to joining Northern Trust in April of 1985, Bordelon served as an attorney for the Illinois Environmental Protection Agency, the Illinois Fair Employment Practices Commission and the Illinois Department of Human Rights.

Bordelon received a bachelor's degree from Washington University in St. Louis, Missouri, and a juris doctorate degree from Northwestern University School of Law. He is an active member of the Illinois Bar.

Clark Delanois
Managing Director
Schaumburg Financial Center
Northern Trust Company

Clark Delanois is the managing director of Northern Trust's Schaumburg Financial Center in Illinois-West Region. As part of the Illinois-West Region senior leadership team, he manages trust, investment services and private banking at the Schaumburg center.

Delanois joined Northern Trust in 1994. His responsibilities, including management duties, began with the commercial banking group in Oakbrook Terrace. As the manager, he monitored the group's credit quality, developed tactics for expanding new business and implemented new client servicing procedures. The group serves family enterprises with sales ranging from $10-200 million.

Delanois also worked in the middle market client group, working with senior management to formulate the strategic plan to enhance Northern Trust's DreamMakers' Forum. This initiative attracted some of the most affluent individuals from African-American communities across the country.

Before joining Northern Trust, Delanois worked at Bank One (now Chase) in a variety of commercial banking assignments, and he managed a number of corporate relationships.

Corporate Spotlight — **Northern Trust**

Kevin Hardy
Senior Vice President
Global Director of Transition Management
Northern Trust Global Investments

Kevin Hardy is a senior vice president in Northern Trust Global Investments (NTGI). He has responsibility for the global transition management business sites based in Chicago and London. He joined NTGI in 2003 and now leads the firm's global transition management business. Since joining NTGI, Hardy has been instrumental in enhancing the transitions product by revising the internal transitions process, improving both internal and external marketing and communications. Among his achievements, Hardy has been responsible for the growth in global equity and fixed-income transitions within the group.

Hardy has more than ten years of industry experience. He is a member of two FTSE index advisory committees, and holds a bachelor of science degree in business studies with honors from the City University Business School.

Originally from London, England, Hardy temporarily relocated to Chicago in 2004. He and his wife, Lynndi, are the proud parents of Grace, born in November of 2005.

Darrell B. Jackson
President & Chief Executive Officer
Illinois West Region
Northern Trust Company

Darrell B. Jackson is president and chief executive officer of Northern Trust Company's Illinois West Region. He is responsible for the Oak Brook, Hinsdale, Naperville, Schaumburg, Barrington and Wheaton financial centers. He is also responsible for personal and private banking, investment management and fiduciary and commercial banking services in DuPage and Northwest Cook/Lake counties.

Previously, Jackson was a senior vice president and division manager in private banking at Northern Trust. He managed a team of bankers that provided credit, financial planning, trust, and investment services to corporate executives in Illinois and the northeastern states. He began his career at South Shore Bank and then moved to Harris Bank, where he spent 14 years in commercial and private banking.

Jackson received a bachelor's degree from Saint Xavier University and an MBA from Northwestern University's Kellogg School of Management.

Jackson serves on the boards of the Conservation Foundation, the Executives Breakfast Club of Oakbrook, the Chicago Shakespeare Theater and Saint Xavier University. He is a member of the Union League Club, the DuPage Club and Saint Xavier University's Graham School of Management advisory council.

Northern Trust — Corporate Spotlight

Connie L. Lindsey
Segment Head
Public Entities & Institutions
Northern Trust Company

Connie L. Lindsey is a senior vice president at the Northern Trust Company. She is segment head of the public entities and institutions segment in the Corporate and Institutional Services business unit.

Lindsey received a bachelor of arts degree in finance from the University of Wisconsin-Milwaukee and is a certified cash manager.

She is a member of the INROADS, Inc. policy setting board; board president of the Leadership Council for Metropolitan Open Communities; national board director of the Girl Scouts of the USA; immediate past president of Bottomless Closet; a 2001 Leadership Greater Chicago fellow; and a member of the board of governors of the Metropolitan Club of Chicago. She is also a board member of the Joffrey Ballet, Women Employed, the Neighborhood Housing Services, the Chicago Finance Exchange and a member of the Economic Club of Chicago.

Lyle Logan
Investment Services Manager
Northern Trust Global Investments

Lyle Logan is managing director of institutional sales and client servicing for Northern Trust Global Investments. Previously, he was senior vice president and head of Chicago private banking in Personal Financial Services (PFS). Logan joined Northern Trust in April of 2000 as a senior vice president in PFS-Midwest. He oversaw the business unit's growth strategies and focused on the development and marketing of Northern Trust's services to current and prospective clients. He has been involved in a wide range of marketing and product development activities throughout PFS, and most recently oversaw the marketing area of the PFS business unit.

Prior to Northern Trust, Logan worked at Bank of America (formerly Continental Bank) in Chicago. Beginning there in 1981, he held several leadership positions as a senior vice president in the private bank and domestic portfolio management group.

Logan has an MBA degree in finance from the University of Chicago and a bachelor of arts degree in accounting and economics from Florida A&M University. He is on several boards of directors, including Children's Memorial Hospital, Roosevelt University and the Field Foundation.

Corporate Spotlight — Northern Trust

Kerry Nelson
Senior Vice President
Public Funds & Taft-Hartley Division
Northern Trust Company

Kerry Nelson is a senior vice president in the public funds and Taft-Hartley division for the Northern Trust Company. In this position, he manages a staff that is responsible for serving the custody needs of public funds and Taft-Hartley clients.

Nelson is a member of Beta Gamma Sigma, Inc., an international business honors society, and is a graduate of the Pacific Coast Banking School. He is a 2003 Leadership Greater Chicago fellow and a member of the board of directors for the Advocate Healthcare Charitable Foundation. Nelson is a member of the Northern Trust strategic philanthropy committee and is past chairperson for the Northern Trust Corporate and Institutional Services diversity council. In 2005, he was inducted into the Hall of Fame of Lima Senior High School (Lima, Ohio).

Nelson received a bachelor of business administration degree, magna cum laude, from Howard University. He also received a master of business administration degree from Howard University.

A native of Lima, Ohio, Nelson is the husband of Patience Nelson and is the proud father of two sons, Joshua and Noah.

Wesley L. Ringo
Institutional Trust
Compliance/Risk Counsel
Northern Trust Securities, Inc.

Wesley L. Ringo is institutional trust compliance/risk counsel for Northern Trust Securities, Inc., an affiliate of the Northern Trust Corporation of Chicago. He is primarily responsible for broker/dealer compliance.

Prior to joining Northern Trust in April of 2001, Ringo was a managing director, assistant general counsel, and director of regulatory affairs at U.S. Bancorp Piper Jaffray in Minneapolis where he also served as director of compliance. Likewise, he served as commissioner of securities for the state of Wisconsin following his appointment by former Wisconsin Governor Tommy Thompson.

Ringo has served on the board of directors of the National Society of Compliance Professionals and the executive committee of the Minnesota Securities Industry Association. He is currently a member of the Securities Industry Association's compliance and legal division. Ringo also serves on the Industry/Regulatory Continuing Education Council. He is an active member, in good standing, of the Wisconsin, Missouri and American Bar Associations.

Northern Trust — Corporate Spotlight

Barbara W. Smith
Manager
Banking Support Services
Northern Trust Company

Barbara W. Smith joined the Northern Trust Company in February of 1999. She has held several roles since joining Northern Trust, but currently leads the banking support services group, providing banking servicing/support for both institutional and personal clients.

Prior to joining Northern Trust, Smith spent eight years as vice president of corporate planning for Johnson Publishing Company, and six years as manager of financial planning at Federal Express Corp. Additionally, she served 13 years at Union Planters National Bank (Memphis, Tennessee) as manager of credit analysis and vice president/senior credit officer.

She has an undergraduate degree in marketing and an MBA degree in finance from the University of Memphis.

Smith is a member of the governing councils for the Advocate Christ Hospital and Medical Center. She has a consulting role with the United Church of Christ's national office, and is active in various organizations of the Covenant United Church of Christ (South Holland, Illinois) where her husband is senior pastor.

Smith and her husband, Rev. Dr. Ozzie E. Smith, Jr., have three children and reside in Flossmoor, Illinois.

Eric Strickland
Senior Institutional Trust
Relationship Manager
Northern Trust Company

Eric Strickland is a senior institutional trust relationship manager at Northern Trust Company. In this position, he manages some of the company's largest client relationships in the Northeast, Midlantic and Midwest areas. In addition to his relationship management responsibilities, Strickland conducts new business developments with a select group of large corporate institutions.

During his 20-year career at the Northern Trust Company, Strickland has held a number of positions within the bank, all of which have centered on new business development, relationship management and banking and credit analysis.

Prior to joining the Northern Trust Company, he was a policy assistant to the governor of the State of Illinois. He also served as a senior staff member of the House of Representatives of the State of Illinois.

Strickland holds a bachelor's degree from Loyola University Chicago where he studied political science and public policy administration.

A native of Chicago, he is a former Michael Curry fellow, a Leadership Greater Chicago fellow (Class of 1984-'85) and a Mellon scholar. Strickland is a member of the Leadership Council of Chicago United.

Corporate Spotlight — Northern Trust

Anthony E. Wilkins
Institutional Investment, Sales Representative
Northern Trust Global Investments

Tony Wilkins is an institutional investment sales representative for Northern Trust Global Investments. He leads a team that is responsible for managing Northern Trust's relationships with global and domestic institutional asset-management consulting firms. A 20-year investment veteran, Wilkins began his career as an electrical engineer. After seven years in that industry and completing an MBA through night courses at the University of Chicago, he switched to asset management.

He began his investment career as a portfolio manager at Stein Roe & Farnham in 1986, then was affiliated with Weiss, Peck and Greer as director of new business, and has been with Northern Trust since 1997.

Wilkins is married to Dorothy Tucker and has three children. He serves on a variety of educational, charitable, and professional boards, including the Canter Middle School Local School Council, the Chicago Abused Women Coalition, AIMSE and the CFA Institute disciplinary review committee. In whatever spare time he has left, he coaches boys' soccer.

Arlynn Woodley
Senior Audit Manager
Northern Trust Company

Arlynn Woodley is a senior audit manager at the Northern Trust Company. In this position, she manages the risk management, compliance and professional practice functions for the department.

Woodley has more than 20 years of audit and risk assessment related experience in the financial services and manufacturing industries. She has worked for three Fortune 100 companies and, at each, held progressive audit and leadership positions. She has managed a staff of up to 16 professionals and served in key project management roles, including re-engineering and Six Sigma quality efforts.

Woodley graduated with highest honors as an accounting major with a minor in English from Hampton University in Hampton, Virginia. A native of Southampton County, Virginia, she is a very active church member, is single and enjoys traveling, reading and all types of music. One of her favorite quotes is "In everything, give thanks!"

The positive effect of being yourself is too great to measure.

At Ernst & Young, we want you to grow and succeed. That's why we've created an environment that values all aspects of diversity, including ethnicity, gender identity and expression. This fact has not escaped *Fortune* magazine, *Working Mother* magazine, nor the National Association of Business Resources who named us Chicago's best place to work in 2005. Visit us at ey.com/us/careers and see how we measure up.

Audit • Tax • Transaction Advisory Services

ERNST & YOUNG
Quality In Everything We Do

Sara Lee SALUTES

CORPORATE SPOTLIGHT

Sara Lee SALUTES

Corporate Spotlight

Roderick A. Palmore
Executive Vice President
General Counsel & Secretary
Sara Lee Corporation

Roderick A. Palmore is executive vice president, general counsel, and secretary of Sara Lee Corporation. In addition, he chairs Sara Lee's global business practices committee, and is responsible for the company's internal audit, special investigations, risk management, safety, and environmental affairs functions.

Formerly, Palmore was a partner with Sonnenschein Nath & Rosenthal in Chicago, a partner with Wildman, Harrold, Allen & Dixon, and an assistant U.S. attorney in the Northern District of Illinois.

He is a director of Nuveen Investments, Inc., the Chicago Board Options Exchange, the United Way of Metropolitan Chicago, and the Association of Corporate Counsel.

Palmore received a bachelor of arts degree in economics from Yale University and a juris doctorate degree from The University of Chicago Law School.

Sara Lee Corporation is a Chicago-based global manufacturer of high quality, brand name products in the food, beverage, and household and body care categories. The company markets its products under such well-known brands as Ball Park, Douwe Egberts, Hillshire Farm, Jimmy Dean, Kiwi, Senseo, and its namesake, Sara Lee.

Diana S. Ferguson
Senior Vice President
Strategy & Corporate Development
Sara Lee Corporation

Diana S. Ferguson is senior vice president of strategy and corporate development of Sara Lee Corporation. She is responsible for corporate strategy and leading the company in transforming its portfolio of businesses.

Ferguson joined Sara Lee in 2001 as vice president and treasurer. Prior to Sara Lee, she was vice president and treasurer of Fort James Corporation. Before joining Fort James, she held a variety of treasury management positions at Eaton Corporation. Earlier, she held financial positions at Fannie Mae, the First National Bank of Chicago, and IBM.

Ferguson is a director of Franklin Electric and Peoples Energy. She also serves on the nonprofit board of Metropolitan Family Services.

Ferguson holds a bachelor of arts degree from Yale University and a master of management degree from Northwestern University's J.L. Kellogg School of Management.

Sara Lee Corporation is a Chicago-based global manufacturer of high quality, brand name products in the food, beverage, and household and body care categories. The company markets its products under such well-known brands as Ball Park, Douwe Egberts, Hillshire Farm, Jimmy Dean, Kiwi, Senseo, and its namesake, Sara Lee.

Corporate Spotlight

Sara Lee SALUTES

Richard L. Armstrong
Chief Supply Chain Officer
Food & Beverage
Sara Lee Corporation

Richard L. Armstrong is a vice president of Sara Lee Corporation and serves as chief supply chain officer of Sara Lee Food & Beverage, the North American retail food organization of Sara Lee Corporation.

Armstrong began his career as an hourly employee at Hygrade Food Products Corporation where he held a variety of positions, rising to general manager. Since Sara Lee's acquisition of Hygrade in 1989, Armstrong has served in several positions of increasing responsibility throughout the company's North American food business, including general manager of Hillshire Farm & Kahn's, president of King Cotton Foods, and president of Galileo Foods. He was appointed to his current position in March of 2001.

Sara Lee Corporation is a Chicago-based global manufacturer of high quality, brand name products in the food, beverage, and household and body care categories. The company markets its products under such well-known brands as Ball Park, Douwe Egberts, Hillshire Farm, Jimmy Dean, Kiwi, Senseo, and its namesake, Sara Lee.

Brett J. Hart
Senior Vice President
Deputy General Counsel
Sara Lee Corporation

Brett J. Hart is a vice president of Sara Lee Corporation and serves as senior vice president, deputy general counsel, as well as global business practices officer.

Hart joined Sara Lee in 2003 as assistant general counsel. Prior to Sara Lee, he was a partner with Sonnenschein Nath & Rosenthal in Chicago. Before that, he served as special assistant to the general counsel at the U.S. Department of the Treasury in Washington, D.C.

Hart received his bachelor's degree in philosophy and English from the University of Michigan and a juris doctorate degree from The University of Chicago Law School.

Sara Lee Corporation is a Chicago-based global manufacturer of high quality, brand name products in the food, beverage, and household and body care categories. The company markets its products under such well-known brands as Ball Park, Douwe Egberts, Hillshire Farm, Jimmy Dean, Kiwi, Senseo, and its namesake, Sara Lee.

LEADING THROUGH INSPIRATION

By leading through inspiration, we can affect education, economic development and community empowerment. From one dynamic organization to another, we congratulate your accomplishments and support your future.

www.uscellular.com

U.S. Cellular
We connect with you.

We are a drug-free workplace and an equal opportunity employer dedicated to DIVERSITY AND INCLUSION.

U.S. Cellular
CORPORATE SPOTLIGHT

U.S. Cellular — Corporate Spotlight

Ronald E. Daly
Board Member
U.S. Cellular®

Ronald Daly is a private investor and serves on the board of directors at U.S. Cellular®. He was the president and chief executive officer of Océ-USA Holding, Inc. between November of 2002 and September of 2004. Océ-USA Holding is the North American operations of Netherlands-based Océ-N.V., a publicly held company. Océ-N.V. is a global supplier of high-technology digital document management and delivery solutions.

Prior to joining Océ-USA Holding, Daly worked 38 years for RR Donnelley, most recently as president of RR Donnelley Printing Solutions. He also serves as a director of SuperValu, a major distributor, wholesaler, and retailer in the food service industry.

Daly holds a master of business administration degree from Loyola University and a bachelor of arts from Governors State University.

His numerous civic activities include several leadership positions: Metropolis 2020 board member, Leadership Greater Chicago fellow, member of the board of trustees for the Chicago Symphony Orchestra, business school advisory board member for Loyola University Chicago, and the Conference Board Council of Operating Executives.

Elliot Rawls
Senior Director, Strategic Analysis
U.S. Cellular®

Elliot Rawls is senior director of strategic analysis at U.S. Cellular®. He has overseen the strategic and financial evaluation of more than $1 billion in proposed and/or executed acquisitions and divestitures. His responsibilities also include corporate level strategic analysis and telecom industry analysis.

Before his current role, Rawls held director level positions at U.S. Cellular® in pricing strategy, intercarrier business, intercarrier revenue and networking, and corporate research and communications, where his responsibilities included business development, decision and risk analysis, pricing strategy, negotiation strategy, and market research.

Before joining U.S. Cellular®, Rawls was president of The Cambaire Corporation, a consultancy that provided market research, financial, and general management services to a variety of clients.

Rawls received a bachelor of arts degree in architecture in 1982 and a bachelor of architecture degree in 1984, both from Rice University. He also received an MBA from Stanford Business School in 1986.

He serves on the board of Marwen, a Chicago-based organization for arts education and youth development.

Rawls and his wife live in Chicago with their daughter. Rawls, a pianist, counts jazz and architectural drawings among his many interests.

Corporate Spotlight

U.S. Cellular

Dana D. Dorcas
Director of Business Sales-Midwest
U.S. Cellular®

Dana Dorcas is director of business sales for the Midwest region of U.S. Cellular®, located in Itasca, Illinois. With more than 20 years of telecommunication experience, he is responsible for regional operation of U.S. Cellular's business-to-business unit. This unit employs more than 40 associates dedicated to providing solution-based offerings that are focused on convenience, value, and individual attention.

Dorcas joined U.S. Cellular® in 1990 and has held positions as market general manager (Pennsylvania area), general manager (West Virginia, Maryland, Ohio), and director of sales (Virginia, Florida).

Prior to joining U.S.Cellular®, Dorcas held leadership roles at Metrocast of New York, Mobile Communications Corporation, Ryder Truck Systems, and Photo Corporation of America.

He is active in the community and is dedicated to supporting youth and seniors. In addition, he is a board member of the Cosmopolitan Chamber of Commerce and a supporter of the Mercy Home for Boys and Girls.

Dorcas lives in Geneva, Illinois and has two children. In his free time, he enjoys boating and golfing.

Yuri Brown
Director of Diversity & EEO Compliance
U.S. Cellular®

Yuri Brown is the director of strategic diversity and EEO compliance at U.S. Cellular®. She is responsible for ensuring the successful design and development of the strategic inclusion plan within the dynamic organization business model and customer-focused strategy of U.S. Cellular®.

Brown has 17 years of experience, including the design and implementation of recruiting and training programs for Fortune 500 companies and the management of multi-million dollar procurement and financial projects.

Brown belongs to the board of Lawrence Hall Youth Services, The Conference Board, the World Diversity Leadership Summit, the League of Black Women, the RainbowPUSH Coalition, and the National Urban League.

She earned a bachelor of science degree in economics from the University California, Berkeley with abroad study at Oxford University in Oxford, England.

Brown lives in Olympia Fields with her family. When not working, she enjoys spending time with her family, traveling, exercise activity, and reading.

THE INAUGURAL EDITION *Who's Who In Black Chicago*®

U.S. Cellular — Corporate Spotlight

Trina Graham-Hodo
Director
Bolingbrook Customer Care Center
U.S. Cellular®

Trina Graham-Hodo is director of the flagship customer care center for U.S. Cellular®. As the center's leader, Trina is responsible for operations of U.S. Cellular's 450-seat customer service center. This location is primarily responsible for inbound customer service to Chicagoland and Northwest Indiana customers.

Her previous leadership experience and extensive background in telecommunications and customer service made her uniquely suited for the challenge of building the Bolingbrook Customer Care Center from the ground up.

Prior to joining U.S. Cellular® in 2005, Trina held leadership roles in customer service, operations, sales, and marketing for Comcast and with SBC/Ameritech.

She attended both Iowa State University and the University of Illinois. Trina is active in the community and is dedicated to grass roots organizations. She is a member of the National Coalition of 100 Black Women.

Trina lives in the Hyde Park/Bronzeville neighborhood with her husband and two children. In her free time, she is an avid reader and supporter of children's advocacy programs.

Noel Hornsberry
Area Sales Manager
U.S. Cellular®

Noel Hornsberry is an area sales manager at U.S. Cellular®. He is responsible for leading a staff of 200 retail associates in the Chicago market. Noel ensures the successful execution of the regional business plan, which includes U.S. Cellular's customer satisfaction strategy.

Prior to joining U.S. Cellular® in 2001, he held positions in retail sales management with emphasis on training, hiring, and team building.

Noel has received recognition for his outstanding performance as a leader and for his commitment to driving the dynamic organization culture. He received the U.S. Cellular® Expect It! Award and the coveted Midwest Region Leadership Award.

Noel earned a bachelor of science degree in criminal justice from Loyola University Chicago.

Active in the community through special projects for the United Way, Noel lives in the Plainfield area and enjoys spending quality time with his family. In his free time, he enjoys landscaping, bowling, bicycling, and attending sporting events.

Corporate Spotlight — **U.S. Cellular**

Ayesha (Amena) Karim
Field Marketing Manager
U.S. Cellular®

Tracey Banks Giles
Associate Relations Manager
U.S. Cellular®

Ayesha Karim is a field marketing manager at U.S. Cellular®. She is responsible for ensuring the successful execution of regional and corporate marketing programs that build brand equity, drive store traffic, and stimulate line and product sales.

Ayesha has held positions in both the newspaper and radio industries. She won the Silver Award at the 2000 Omni Intermedia Awards for best television commercial/public service announcement campaign and the Gold Award from the 2000 Aurora Awards, along with other marketing-related awards.

Ayesha earned a bachelor of arts degree in broadcast journalism from Roosevelt University and a master of science degree in integrated marketing communications from Northwestern University.

One of her guiding principles is to reach out to youth. Ayesha has served as a mentor for Jobs for Youth and the Chicago Youth Center. She is a member of the Fatimah Khan and Khayriyyah Khan International Dance Company, committed to teaching urban youth international dances.

Ayesha is rooted in family values and community volunteerism. She enjoys African-Cuban dancing, traveling, and conservative talk radio.

Tracey Banks Giles is an associate relations manager within the human resources community of U.S. Cellular®. U.S. Cellular's human resource community is comprised of four regions, West, Central, East, and Midwest. As associate relations manager within the Midwest region, Tracey is responsible for human resources leadership as well as partnering efforts with leadership throughout the organization to plan, design, and execute company-wide initiatives, business strategies, and programs.

Prior to joining U.S. Cellular® in 2003, Tracey held positions with Tellabs and Advocate Health Care.

Tracey holds a bachelor of arts degree in human resources development from Northeastern Illinois University and a master of business administration degree from DeVry University.

When not working, she enjoys traveling and spending time with her husband, daughter, and other family members. Tracey is committed to the Christian faith. Her guiding principle in life is helping others, "If I can help someone as I pass this way, then my living won't be in vain."—Author unknown

U.S. Cellular — Corporate Spotlight

William R. Isaac
Customer Service Manager
U.S. Cellular®

Erika Madison Williams
Associate Relations Manager
U.S. Cellular®

William Isaac is a manager at the flagship customer care center for U.S. Cellular®. As a customer care center leader, Bill is responsible for coaching and developing front-line leaders and helping to further shape the Bolingbrook culture.

Bill joined the company in 2000 as a customer service representative and held various roles within the customer service department. He successfully completed leadership training and was promoted to a coaching role. Bill received recognition for his outstanding performance as a leader and his contributions in driving the dynamic organization business model by being awarded a coveted Coach Award.

Before joining U.S. Cellular®, he held various leadership roles within the railroad industry for more than 23 years.

Bill is married with four children and two grandsons. In his free time, he enjoys all outdoor activity, and his favorite hobbies include cooking, camping, fishing, and bike riding.

Erika Madison Williams is an associate relations manager at the flagship customer care center for U.S. Cellular®. As the leader of associate relations, Madison Williams is responsible for human resources leadership as well as ongoing partnering efforts with cross-functional leaders throughout the organization to plan, design, and execute company-wide initiatives, business strategies, and programs within a 450-seat customer service center.

Prior to joining U.S. Cellular® in 2003, Madison Williams held positions with Sprint, Carson Pirie Scott, and Target.

She holds a graduate degree in human resource management from Loyola University Chicago, and has more than a decade of progressive human resource experience.

During her free time, Madison Williams enjoys cooking and outdoor activities with her husband and two children.

Corporate Spotlight — **U.S. Cellular**

Carlton Simmons
Manager
Customer Service/Data Tech Support
U.S. Cellular®

Carlton Simmons is the manager of the customer service/data tech support teams at the flagship customer care center, located in Bolingbrook, Illinois, for U.S. Cellular®. He is responsible for the coaching and development of seven customer care center coaches and approximately 84 associates. The national data tech support team provides technical support for U.S. Cellular's BlackBerry® product/service for the entire enterprise.

Carlton has designed and facilitated leadership trainings in the areas of teamwork, conflict resolution, managing diversity, and The Art of Sales Coaching.

Prior to joining U.S. Cellular® in 2005, he held various roles in sales, customer service, and retention. He previously served as area sales performance manager for Comcast Cable Corp.

Carlton attended both The University of Texas at Arlington and Northlake College.

He lives in Naperville with his wife and four children. In his free time, Carlton enjoys spending quality time with his family, and he is an avid sports fan, voracious reader, and disc jockey. Carlton takes great pride in his family and career.

Marc A. Smith
Customer Service Manager
U.S. Cellular®

Marc Smith is a manager at the flagship customer care center for U.S. Cellular®. As a customer care center leader, Smith is responsible for the operations of U.S. Cellular's 450-seat customer service center with more than 100 direct reports. This location is primarily responsible for inbound customer service to Chicagoland and Northwest Indiana customers.

Smith joined U.S. Cellular® in 2003, leading the customer care business to business teams.

Prior to joining U.S. Cellular® Smith held leadership roles at Ameritech Cellular and Cingular Wireless.

He attended The Ohio State University.

Smith lives in the west suburb of Lombard and has a daughter. In his free time, Smith enjoys photography and is an avid bowler. He is also active in the community and enjoys working with young people.

KRAFT

Kraft Foods is the world's second-largest food and beverage company. For more than 100 years, we've been dedicated to helping people around the world eat and live better. Hundreds of millions of times a day, in more than 150 countries, consumers reach for their favorite Kraft brands including *Kraft* cheeses and dinners, *Jacobs*, *Gevalia* and *Maxwell House* coffees, *Oscar Mayer* meats, *DiGiorno* pizzas, *Oreo* cookies, *Ritz* and *Wheat Thins* crackers and chips, *Philadelphia* cream cheese, *Milka* and *Côte d'Or* chocolates, *Honey Bunches of Oats* cereals, *Good Seasons* salad dressings and *Tang* refreshment beverage. They've also started adding our *Tassimo* hot beverage system, *South Beach Diet* line and a growing range of better-for-you *Sensible Solution* products to their shopping baskets, continually expanding their list of Kraft favorites.

Diversity critical to Kraft's success

Kraft consumers around the world span ages and ethnicities, nationalities and gender, beliefs and experiences. This is the world in which our future success or failure as a business will be achieved. Simply stated, we think that diversity among our own employees makes us a stronger company, contributes to a winning work climate, and connects us more closely with our diverse consumer base. We value the differences among us and seek to learn from them.

Our Diversity Vision

Our vision is about leadership. We want Kraft Foods to be recognized as the leading company in its ability to attract, develop and retain the highest-caliber talent and to fully leverage that talent to achieve consistently superior business results.

We strive to accomplish this by:
- Treating "effective diversity management" as a core competency and business priority
- Requiring accountability, including rewards and consequences, for diversity at all management levels
- Creating a workforce that reflects, at all levels, the diversity of our consumers and the population at large
- Respecting differences in life experiences, cultural backgrounds and work and life styles that add value to our business
- Recognizing and responding to employees' diverse needs for work life solutions that enable them to meet personal and business priorities
- Providing development that enables each person to reach his or her full potential
- Creating measurement systems to monitor progress, ensure accountability and identify issues
- Assuring equal opportunity and fair employment practices

Our People

Attracting the highest-caliber talent is an integral part of achieving our visions. We are convinced that our company is made more effective through a representation of diverse experiences, education, lifestyles, and cultural and geographic differences. To help build that breadth of perspective, we actively recruit talented employees for positions across the spectrum of expertise, experience and career stage.

Our Communities

At Kraft, we want to be more than the company that provides quality products at fair prices. We have the responsibility -- and the commitment -- to give back in support of the communities where we live and do business. It's been an important part of our heritage. We believe in sharing our resources to substantively contribute to building better communities.

Last year, we gave more than $84 million in food and financial support to non-profit organizations throughout the world.

We have two main focus areas for our contributions around the world: hunger and healthy lifestyles. As the second-largest food company in the world, we have a stake in addressing hunger and in advancing the important role that physical activity and a balanced diet play in healthy lives.

Through various volunteer programs and a dynamic workplace-giving program, our employees take an active role in building better communities where they live and work.

Supplier Diversity Develops Communities

We recognize that how we operate our business has an impact on the economic development of communities. This impact extends to companies from whom we purchase the goods and services that are essential to our operations.

Through our Supplier Diversity Program in the US, we consider the best and widest possible selection of supplier companies by ensuring the inclusion of minority-owned and women-owned suppliers in our purchasing decisions.

Our commitment to Supplier Diversity is based on the following beliefs:

- It makes good business sense to explore every source when making a purchasing decision for the company
- Working with diverse suppliers is an investment in local communities
- Our suppliers should be as diverse as the consumers who buy our products
- Considering a broad group of potential suppliers will lead to competition and ultimately, a better value for our business

In 1994, we purchased approximately $200 million in goods and services from diverse suppliers. The program has experienced significant growth since then, reaching more than a half billion dollars in 2003.

Whether it be our workplace, our communities or our suppliers - at Kraft we are committed to building strong and healthy relationships that are good for Kraft and the communities where we live and work around the world.

Chicago's
MOST INFLUENTIAL

"I am where I am because of the bridges I have crossed. Sojourner Truth was a bridge. Harriet Tubman was a bridge. Ida B. Wells was a bridge. Madame C.J. Walker was a bridge. Fannie Lou Hamer was a bridge."

OPRAH WINFREY
ENTERTAINMENT EXECUTIVE

Chicago's MOST INFLUENTIAL

Celebrating African-American Achievements

Carol L. Adams is secretary of the Illinois Department of Human Services. Appointed by Governor Rod Blagojevich in February of 2003, Adams directs the state's human services programs with a staff complement of more than 13,000 people and a $4 billion budget. The agency offers services at more than 300 locations statewide. Its major components are: alcoholism and substance abuse, community health and prevention, developmental disabilities, human capital development, mental health, and rehabilitation services.

A career public servant and public policy innovator, Adams has, for more than 30 years, made substantial contributions to human services, community development, sociological research, and African-American education and culture.

Adams is a native of Louisville, Kentucky, and the mother of one daughter.

Carol L. Adams, Ph.D.
Secretary of Human Services
State of Illinois

The Honorable Patricia Banks, a native of Marianna, Arkansas, earned bachelor, juris, and doctorate degrees from the University of Illinois at Chicago and the University of Wisconsin Law School, respectively. After serving as a civil rights lawyer for several years, Banks joined Sears Roebuck in 1974 as its first African-American attorney. Upon leaving Sears, she maintained a general civil practice until her election to the bench in 1994. Banks presides over medical malpractice, personal injury, and complex litigation trials in the Law-Jury Division.

Banks is a former chairperson of the Judicial Council of the National Bar Association (NBA), an organization that represents more than 1,800 black judges. In 2004, Banks chaired the *Brown v. Board of Education* 50th Year Anniversary Commemoration for the NBA. She is a faculty member for the Illinois Judicial Conference and an adjunct professor at DePaul University College of Law. Banks is a member of Delta Sigma Theta Sorority, Inc. and serves on many professional boards.

In addition to Exceptional Juris and Meritorious Service, Banks has received numerous other awards and recognition. Her motto is, "Nothing is beyond me."

The Honorable Patricia Banks
Judge, Law-Jury Division
Circuit Court of Cook County

Celebrating African-American Achievements

Chicago's
MOST INFLUENTIAL

The Reverend Willie Barrow, nicknamed "The Little Warrior," is best known for her tireless work as a social and spiritual activist. In the 1940s, she got her start in Burton, Texas when she led a demonstration against a segregated school system that refused to bus African-American children to school. During the 1950s, one of Barrow's key roles was as field organizer for Dr. Martin Luther King, Jr. She was responsible for the organization of transportation, shelter, meetings, and rallies for the demonstrators who came to participate in the marches and sit-ins during that era. During the 1960s, Barrow was among the founding members of Operation Breadbasket, a program that provided spiritual guidance and practical assistance to communities in need.

Currently, Barrow serves as chairperson emeritus of the RainbowPUSH Coalition, the organization that grew out of Operation Breadbasket. At the Coalition, she coordinates the activities of the national organization and serves as an aide to the Reverend Jesse Jackson, Sr.

In September of 1997, a street on Chicago's South Side was renamed in her honor. The legacy of Rev. Barrow continues to provide inspiration.

Rev. Willie Barrow
Chairperson, Emeritus
RainbowPUSH Coalition

Fran Bell is vice president of the YMCA of Metropolitan Chicago. She oversees four YMCA branches, and the organization's Community Schools Project. Ten thousand members and more than 2,500 youth are served in these urban YMCAs.

Bell sits on the executive committee of the African American Leadership Forum, dedicated to the recruitment, retention, and development of black professionals in the YMCA. The YMCA of the USA's creation of the Minority Executive and CEO Development Program is a direct result of her leadership.

Her background as an education major at West Chester University fueled her passion for teaching and mentoring youth. Bell's dedication is further demonstrated as a board member for the Support Group, an organization designed to help youth achieve academic goals through athletics; and a member of the Teen Advisory Council of Apostolic Church of God, where she worships.

The mother of two adult children, Bell spends her spare time ministering as one of the voices of gospel recording artists, JourneySong. The ensemble travels throughout the Midwest and Europe.

Fran J. Bell
Vice President
YMCA of Metropolitan Chicago

Chicago's MOST INFLUENTIAL

Celebrating African-American Achievements

**The Honorable
Patricia Martin Bishop**
Presiding Judge
Child Protection Division
Circuit Court of Cook County

Judge Patricia Martin Bishop is the presiding judge of the Child Protection Division of the Circuit Court of Cook County, Illinois.

Bishop is a member of the board of trustees for the National Council of Juvenile and Family Court Judges. She has chaired the Supreme Court of Illinois Judicial Conference Study Committee on Juvenile Justice, and has been a member of several other Illinois Supreme Court committees. In addition, Bishop has presented at local, national, and international conferences on child abuse/neglect topics, and has received numerous awards for her work.

Elected to the bench in 1996, Bishop was reelected in 2002. From 1986 to 1996, Bishop was an assistant Cook County public defender and rose to deputy chief for the Fifth District.

Earning a juris doctorate from Northern Illinois University College of Law in Dekalb, Illinois, Bishop received a bachelor of arts with honors from Middlebury College in Middlebury, Vermont. She has also studied at, and received honors from, the University of Nairobi in Kenya, East Africa.

Pamela Blackwell
President & Chief Operating Officer
Blackwell Consulting Services

Pamela Blackwell is president and chief operating officer (COO) of Blackwell Consulting Services, where she oversees the day-to-day operations and overall leadership of the company. With close to 20 years of experience in information technology services, Pamela has been with Blackwell for more than 12 years, most recently holding dual responsibilities as CFO and vice president of human resources.

Before becoming president and COO, Pamela was directly responsible for the financial stability and overall administration of the company. She managed revenues in excess of $35 million, and deployed human resource policies and procedures for a workforce of nearly 300 professionals.

Before joining Blackwell, Pamela spent several years with IBM where she held positions such as, systems engineer, education specialist, and marketing assistant. She first began her career, however, at United Airlines.

Pamela holds a bachelor's degree from Northern Illinois University, and is a graduate of the Kellogg Management Institute program at Northwestern University. She is also a member of the Committee of 200, the Executives Club of Chicago, the Kellogg Alumni Club of Chicago, and serves on the Christopher House board.

Celebrating African-American Achievements

Chicago's
MOST INFLUENTIAL

Robert "Bob" D. Blackwell, Sr. is chairman of Blackwell Consulting Services. A well-known leader in management and information technology, Bob's computer industry expertise spans more than 35 years. He is known in the industry as a visionary and dynamic leader.

In 1992, after working for more than 25 years with IBM, Bob founded Blackwell Consulting Services. Today, the company is a national full-service, full life-cycle management and information technology consulting firm, serving the Global 1,000 and middle market enterprises. With over 200 consultants and revenues of $43 million in 2005, Blackwell has grown to become one of the largest minority-owned management and IT firms in the U.S.

Holding a bachelor's degree from Wichita State University, Bob is a member of the Executives' Club of Chicago, the Economic Club of Chicago, and the Metropolitan Club of Chicago. Bob sits on the board for the Illinois Institute of Technology and is a trustee of the Museum of Science and Industry, and Lakeside Bank.

Bob passionately supports the Arts and Business Council, the Neighborhood Writing Alliance, and the ETA Creative Arts Foundation.

Robert D. Blackwell, Sr.
Chairman
Blackwell Consulting Services

William "Bill" Bonaparte, Jr. is owner, president, and chief executive officer of Bonaparte Corporation, the largest full-service, African-American-owned electrical contractor in Chicago. Under Bill's leadership, the company has grown to an average annual revenue base of $20 million, providing middle class jobs to more than 100 full-time employees.

He began his career in telecommunications as the first African-American PBX installer with Illinois Bell. Bill later retired from corporate America and formed Bonaparte Connection, supplying communication connectivity services.

Bonaparte is the proud recipient of many awards, honors, and recognitions, a few of which include his induction into the University of Illinois at Chicago Business Hall of Fame in 2002, and becoming archived by the HistoryMakers in 2003.

Bonaparte earned a bachelor of science degree from the Milwaukee School of Engineering, and a certificate from Massachusetts Institute of Technology.

He has two sons, William, III, and Jason, whom he hopes will succeed him in operating the company. Bill lives in metropolitan Chicago, has a special interest in sport fishing and history, and loves his mother's cooking.

William Bonaparte, Jr.
President & Chief Executive Officer
Bonaparte Corporation

Chicago's MOST INFLUENTIAL

Celebrating African-American Achievements

Barbara Bowles, CFA is vice chair of Profit Investment Management. In 1989, she founded The Kenwood Group, Inc., an equity investment advisory firm, which is a wholly owned subsidiary of Profit.

Barbara holds an MBA in finance from The University of Chicago Graduate School of Business, and a bachelor's degree from Fisk University. She received the chartered financial analyst designation in 1977.

She serves as a director for Black & Decker Corporation, Wisconsin Energy Corporation, Children's Memorial Hospital, the Chicago Urban League, Dollar General Corporation, and Hyde Park Bank. Barbara is an active member of the CFA Society of Chicago and the National Association for Securities Professionals. She is a trustee of Fisk University and serves on The University of Chicago Graduate School of Business advisory council.

In 2003, Barbara was honored with the Alumni of the Year Award from the African American MBA Association of The University of Chicago. She and her husband, Earl, are residents of the Hyde Park-Kenwood community.

Barbara L. Bowles, CFA
Vice Chairman
Profit Investment Management

Dr. Cynthia Boyd is chief compliance officer and associate vice president at Rush University Medical Center. In this position, she oversees implementation and operation of the compliance program. She is also responsible for investigating allegations of misconduct related to issues covered under the compliance program. Additionally, Cynthia is the assistant professor of medicine at Rush Medical College, and serves as director of medical staff operations at Rush.

A member of the board of directors for the Health Care Compliance Association, Cynthia is a fellow of the American College of Physicians. She has lectured and written widely on Medicare, health care reform, medical research compliance, and health disparities.

A native of Detroit, Michigan, Cynthia received a bachelor's in biology from the University of Colorado. Additionally, she earned her medical doctorate degree from the George Washington University School of Medicine and Health Sciences, and a master's from The University of Chicago.

Cynthia has over 13 years of clinical practice and teaching experience. She is the wife of Dr. William Gradishar, and the mother of two sons, Zachary and Nicholas. She enjoys traveling, reading, and watching old movies.

Cynthia E. Boyd, M.D.
Associate Vice President &
Chief Compliance Officer
Rush University Medical Center

Celebrating African-American Achievements

Chicago's
MOST INFLUENTIAL

Hailed as the "Queen of Gospel Music," Albertina Walker was born in 1929, in Chicago, Illinois. She has performed with gospel greats such as, professor Thomas A. Dorsey, Roberta Martin, Robert Anderson, Rosetta Thorpe, and personal friend, Mahalia Jackson. In 1951, Walker organized the world famous CARAVANS, and launched the careers of Pastor Shirley Ceasar, Inez Norwood, and the "King of Gospel," the Reverend James Cleveland.

Albertina founded The Albertina Walker Scholarship Foundation for the creative and performing arts. By spreading gospel music ministry for over six decades, Albertina has earned many awards, honors, and doctoral degrees. Among them include, a 1995 Grammy Award, five Gold Records, Gospel Music Workshop of America Excellence Award, and a Trumpet Award.

Inducted into the Gospel Music Hall of Fame in Detroit, Michigan and Nashville, Tennessee, Albertina received a Lifetime Legend Award by Chicago's city mayor, Richard M. Daley. She was also honored at a special ceremony by United States President, George W. Bush. In addition, Albertina was the recipient of the Pioneer in Music Award by the National Association of Black Owned Broadcasters (NABOB).

Albertina Walker Brooks
Gospel Singer
National Recording Artist

Marc Brooks is chairman and chief executive officer of MKMB Corporation, an investment firm that has placed capital in a wide range of industries. Some notable investments include an ownership stake in the nation's tenth largest cable television company, WOW Internet & Cable, and a national distribution partnership with U.S. Cellular through a sister company, Urban Media Group.

In addition to his responsibilities with MKMB, Brooks serves as vice chairman of Brooks Food Group (BFG), a food manufacturer with 300 employees and $100 million in revenue. Some of Brooks' other ventures include multiple partnerships with famed restaurateur Jerry Kleiner, including an upscale banquet facility and two restaurants in Chicago.

Some of Brooks' notable achievements include: Retail Firm of the Year recipient by the Minority Enterprise Development Council in 2003; recognition as one of Chicago's 100 Most Influential African-Americans by *N'DIGO* magazine in 2004 and 2005; and recipient of U.S. Cellular's Top Agent Award in 2006.

Brooks currently serves on the boards of WOW Internet & Cable, Brooks Food Group, Providence-St. Mel School, and De La Salle Institute.

Marc Brooks
Chairman &
Chief Executive Officer
MKMB Corporation

Chicago's MOST INFLUENTIAL

Celebrating African-American Achievements

The Honorable Dorothy Brown made history when she was elected clerk of the Circuit Court of Cook County in 2000, becoming the first African-American to hold that position. Reelected in 2004, she is the official keeper of records for all judicial matters brought into one of the largest unified court systems in the world. Brown is responsible for managing an annual operating budget of more than $100 million and has a workforce of more than 2,300 employees.

Brown graduated from Southern University in Baton Rouge, Louisiana. She also holds a master of business administration degree from DePaul University and a jurist doctorate from Chicago-Kent College of Law, and she is a certified public accountant.

Brown is the Cook County integrated criminal justice information system committee chair; the Illinois Integrated Justice Information System's vice chair and outreach committee chair; and the Illinois CPA Society vice chair.

Throughout the years, Brown has received numerous awards, including the National Association of Black Accountants' National Achievement in Government Award, the NAACP Medal of Freedom Award, and the Illinois Democratic Women's Hillary Rodham Clinton Leadership Award.

The Honorable Dorothy Brown
Clerk
Circuit Court of Cook County

Judge F. Keith Brown is a graduate of Drake University where he received both his bachelor of arts degree in economics and his law degree.

In July of 1991, Brown was appointed the first African-American judge for the 16th Judicial Circuit. As an associate judge, he served as the presiding judge of the traffic and family division. He has presided over matters relating to DUIs, mental health, small claims, juveniles, paternity, domestic violence, dissolution of marriage, and child support matters. In 1996, Brown was elected as a circuit judge for the 16th Judicial Circuit. Since that time, he has served as a felony trial judge, the presiding judge of the family division, and is currently hearing civil law jury cases.

Brown was past president of the Neighborhood Housing Service of Elgin, a board member of the Elgin YMCA, Literacy Volunteers of America, the local Head Start program, and a past member of the Elgin Planning Board. He was also instrumental in setting up a pro-se night court for divorce.

The Honorable F. Keith Brown
Circuit Court Judge
16th Judicial Circuit

Celebrating African-American Achievements

Chicago's
MOST INFLUENTIAL

Jeff Burns, Jr. is the associate publisher and senior vice president of Johnson Publishing Company, Inc. He is responsible for advertising sales and marketing the *Ebony* brand for Johnson Publishing Company, Inc. In addition, he creates special integrated marketing events for various sponsors associated with *Ebony*.

Burns is responsible for initiating the Ebony Outstanding Women in Marketing and Communications Award in 2000; the Ebony African-American Men's Day; Ebony Mother's & Daughters Empowerment Program; and the Ebony Film Festival Hollywood in Harlem. He initially joined Johnson Publishing Company, Inc., the world's largest black-owned publishing company, as an account sales representative.

Today, Burns serves on the board of trustees for Johnson C. Smith University, and is the vice chairman of the John H. Johnson School of Communications board of visitors at his alma mater, Howard University. In addition, he holds an honorary doctorate from Livingstone College.

Jeff Burns, Jr.
Associate Publisher &
Senior Vice President
Johnson Publishing Company, Inc.

ABC7's Cheryl Burton co-anchors Chicago's top-rated newscasts at 5:00 and 10:00 p.m. The Emmy-winning Chicago native joined ABC7 in 1992.

Burton has received many honors for her work including several Emmys. She was the first recipient of the 2005 Sisters in the Spirit Award, given by Chicago area gospel singers to persons who exemplify a faith-based life. She was honored in 2005 and 2004 with the Thurgood Marshall Award. The Chicago Association of Black Journalists (CABJ) presented Burton with the 2004 Russ Ewing Award for the emotional story of a mother to daughter kidney donation.

Burton is very active in the Chicago community and gives much of her time to nonprofit groups and charities. A volunteer for the Boys and Girls Club of America, she serves as a motivational speaker for Chicago Public Schools, among others. In addition, Burton is a member of the Society of Professional Journalists, the Association of Black Journalists, and the National Association of Black Journalists.

Burton graduated from the University of Illinois in Urbana-Champaign.

Cheryl Burton
News Anchor
WLS-TV ABC7

Chicago's
MOST INFLUENTIAL

Celebrating African-American Achievements

In 1992, the Honorable Bernetta D. Bush was elected as judge of the Circuit Court of Cook County. She was also assigned to the First Municipal District, and in January of 1995, she was assigned to the County Division. In March of 2000, Bush was assigned to the Chancery Division where she currently serves.

Bush is admitted to practice before the Illinois Supreme Court, the U.S. District Court for the Northern District of Illinois, and the Seventh Circuit of Appeals. A member of the Illinois Judges Association, Bush is a member of the Illinois Judicial Council, and other legal organizations.

Graduating from Northeastern Illinois University, Bush holds a bachelor's degree in history and a master's degree in education. In 1977, she received her juris doctorate degree from the DePaul University College of Law.

Bush has received numerous awards, and is often a speaker on issues related to the legal profession.

The Honorable Bernetta D. Bush
Judge, Chancery Division
Circuit Court of Cook County

Calvin Butler, Jr. began his career with RR Donnelley in 1999 as senior director of government affairs. Since then, he has lobbied all levels of government, led significant strategic initiatives across the company, and was selected in the company's executive management training program. Butler's selection into the company's executive management program began his process of learning manufacturing, and resulted in his managing both a direct mail (2002) and short run magazine plant (2004).

In 2005, Butler was promoted to corporate senior vice president of external affairs. He is responsible for the development and implementation of strategies in government and community relations, supplier diversity initiatives, alliance markets sales, and efforts to sell to the local, state, and federal government.

Very active in the community, Butler serves on the board of directors of Leadership Greater Chicago and the Illinois State Chamber, where he also serves on the executive committee. Additionally, he is active as a baseball coach, serving on the board of directors of the Greater Aurora Baseball Association. He has also served as past chairman of the Bradley University Alumni Association.

Calvin G. Butler, Jr.
Senior Vice President
External Affairs
RR Donnelley

Celebrating African-American Achievements

Chicago's
MOST INFLUENTIAL

Dr. Byrd is a full-time member of the radiology department at Rush University Medical Center (RUMC) in the section of neuroradiology. She is a fellowship director of the service, and maintains quality assurance of neuroimaging at RUMC for magnetic resonance imaging and computed tomography. Byrd performs daily interpretation of clinical neuroimaging studies.

A member of numerous radiological professional organizations, Byrd is a fellow of the American College of Radiology, a senior member of the American Society of Neuroradiology, and is a member of the National Medical Association.

Byrd received her undergraduate education and medical degree from Wayne State University in Detroit, Michigan. She completed her diagnostic radiology training at the University of California at Los Angeles (UCLA), with additional neuroradiology training at the Hospital for Sick Children in Toronto and UCLA.

She was chief of neuroradiology at King/Drew Medical Center in Los Angeles for eight years, and served as chief of neuroimaging at Children's Memorial Hospital in Chicago for 14 years.

Bryd is the wife of Gourmet Chef Richard Hadden.

Sharon E. Byrd, M.D.
Professor of Radiology &
Attending Neuroradiologist
Rush University Medical Center

William C. "Bill" Campbell is host/producer of ABC7's *Chicagoing*, a weekly program showcasing Chicago's rich history. He also served as the station's director of community services from 1978 until 2000. A three-time Emmy winner, Campbell was responsible for ABC7 editorials from 1978 to 1989.

Prior to joining ABC 7, he was director of communications for the Chicago Urban League and served as an assistant in the mayor's office.

Campbell was named a William Benton fellow in broadcast journalism, a select group of radio/television journalists chosen to participate in academic study at The University of Chicago.

Campbell's many honors, among others, include a Dr. Martin Luther King, Jr. Freedom Award from St. Sabina Church and a Communications Leadership Award from the Westside Branch NAACP. His alma mater, Harlan High School, made him the first inductee in their Hall of Fame. *Dollars & Sense* magazine named him one of America's Best and Brightest.

Campbell volunteers his time and serves on various boards including that of the Greater Chicago Food Depository. He is a graduate of Carleton College in Minnesota.

William C. Campbell
Host/Producer
WLS-TV ABC7

Chicago's MOST INFLUENTIAL

Celebrating African-American Achievements

Isaac "Ike" Carothers comes from a family with a strong background in public service. He is the grandson of the first African-American democratic committeeman of the 28th Ward and former state representative, and is the son of a former committeeman and alderman of the 28th Ward.

He received his bachelor's degree from DePaul University, and a master's in criminal justice from Chicago State University.

Carothers began his career in public service at the Cook County Public Defender's Office. He was appointed director of internal audit for the Chicago Park District in 1993, and in 1997, became deputy commissioner of the Chicago Department of Streets and Sanitation.

In 1999, Ike successfully ran for alderman of the 29th Ward. In 2001, he was appointed chairman of the City Council Committee on Police and Fire.

Since taking office in 1999, Carothers has garnered over $60 million in major projects in the 29th Ward, and has attracted millions of dollars in new residential development.

Carothers, and his wife Sharron, have two sons and are members of Original Providence Baptist Church.

The Honorable Isaac "Ike" Carothers
Alderman, Ward 29
City of Chicago

The Honorable Sharon Johnson Coleman was elected to the Circuit Court of Cook County in 1996. Since then, she has spent the bulk of her judicial career in the law division's trial section, where she currently sits. She has briefly served on two occasions in the child protection division.

Coleman is a member of the Illinois Bar (1984), the U.S. District Court for the Northern District of Illinois (1988), the Seventh Circuit Court of Appeals (1989), and the United States Supreme Court (1989).

She received her bachelor's degree from Northern Illinois University. After graduating from Washington University School of Law in St. Louis, Missouri, Coleman began her legal career as a criminal prosecutor and a civil litigator with the State's Attorney's Office in 1989.

Coleman has been a regular faculty member with the annual New Judges Training seminar for the office of the chief judge of the Circuit Court of Cook County since 1998, and for the Administrative Office of the Illinois Courts since 2001.

The Honorable Sharon Johnson Coleman
Judge, Law Division
Circuit Court of Cook County

Celebrating African-American Achievements

Chicago's
MOST INFLUENTIAL

The Honorable Annazette R. Collins-Langston is chairman of the House Committee of the Public Utilities. She is a member of the National Association for Female Executives; the Conference of Women Legislators; the Illinois Conference of Women Legislators; the Illinois Legislative Black Caucus; the National Caucus of State Legislators; and the National Caucus of Black State Legislators.

Collins-Langston received her honorary doctorate in March of 2006 from the Midwest Theological Institute, in addition to a Civil Service Award in April of 2006 from Northern Illinois University's Black Alumni Council. She also received the Women Making History Award in March of 2006 from the National Council of Negro Women, Chicago Midwest Section, and has been recognized in several Who's Who books since 2003.

Collins-Langston received a bachelor of science degree from Northern Illinois University in DeKalb and a master of science degree in criminal justice from Chicago State University. She has completed some post-graduate work in psychology counseling.

Collins-Langston is married to Keith Langston and is the parent of Angelique Nicole and Taylor Kourtnie.

**The Honorable
Annazette R. Collins-Langston**
Representative, Tenth District
Illinois House of Representatives

James Compton became executive director of the Chicago Urban League in 1972. In 1978, he was elected president and chief executive officer. He is also president and chief executive officer of the Chicago Urban League Development Corporation.

He serves on the board of The Field Museum of Natural History, the DePaul University board of trustees, and the Chicago Area Council of the Boy Scouts of America. A member of the Chicago Club, the Economic Club of Chicago, the Executives Club of Chicago, and the Commercial Club of Chicago, Compton's board affiliations include Ariel Mutual Funds, Onyx Capital Ventures, and Seaway National Bank.

He received an honorary doctorate from Aurora University; the 2002 National Urban League's Whitney M. Young, Jr. Leadership Award for Advancing Racial Equality; the City Club of Chicago's 2002 John A. McDermott Award for Civic Leadership; and the 2000 Illinois Action for Children Service Award.

A Morehouse College graduate, Compton received the Merrill Scholarship to study French literature at the University of Grenoble in France. He was awarded the doctor of humane letters honorary degree from Columbia College Chicago.

James W. Compton
President & Chief Executive Officer
Chicago Urban League

Chicago's MOST INFLUENTIAL

Celebrating African-American Achievements

Kevann M. Cooke is senior vice president, corporate secretary, and chief governance officer of Aon Corporation. In her role, she provides advice and counsel to the chairman and the board of directors on developing and implementing corporate governance best practices. In addition, she manages Aon Foundation and the department of community affairs.

Prior to joining Aon, Cooke was deputy chief of staff and special assistant to the president of the Cook County Board of Commissioners. She previously practiced law with the law firms of Phelan, Pope and John, Ltd. and Vedder, Price, Kaufman & Kammholz.

Cooke earned her law degree from Stanford University, and her undergraduate degree from Princeton University. She is vice chairman of 21st Century Urban Schools. She is also a member of the Economic Club of Chicago, Society of Corporate Secretaries and Governance Professionals, Chicago Bar Association, Black Women Lawyers Association, and a fellow of Leadership Greater Chicago.

Cooke resides in Chicago and enjoys traveling, reading, and outdoor sports.

Kevann M. Cooke
Senior Vice President &
Chief Governance Officer
Aon Corporation

Joy Cunningham is currently senior vice president, general counsel, and corporate secretary for the Northwestern Memorial HealthCare System. She is admitted to practice law before the Illinois, New York, Federal, and the Federal Trial Bars.

Before joining Northwestern, she served as a judge of the Circuit Court of Cook County. Joy was formerly associate general counsel for Loyola University of Chicago, and a trial attorney with the law firm of French, Rogers, Kezelis, et al. In addition, Joy was an assistant Illinois attorney general and judicial clerk to Illinois Appellate Justice Glenn Johnson.

She was the first African-American woman president of the Chicago Bar Association (2004-2005). Joy serves on several nonprofit boards, has authored professional publications, and is a member of several professional and civic associations. She has been recognized for her volunteer service to community and civic organizations. A member of the Economic Club of Chicago and The Chicago Network, Joy will join the Illinois Appellate Court in December of 2006.

Joy Virginia Cunningham
Senior Vice President, General
Counsel & Corporate Secretary
Northwestern Memorial
HealthCare System

Celebrating African-American Achievements

Chicago's
MOST INFLUENTIAL

Robert J. Dale is president and chief executive officer of RJDale Advertising & Public Relations, a 26-year old marketing communications agency currently at $51 million in billings. RJDale is one of the fastest growing agencies in the country, and is ranked among the leading black-owned agencies by *Black Enterprise* magazine. DiversityBusiness.com recently ranked RJDale among the nation's top 100 minority-owned businesses. The agency's clients include both general market and African-American targeted clients.

Dale, a native Chicagoan, is active in the community and an advocate for education. He is board president of the Institute of Positive Education, and board member of the Black Ensemble Theatre and Betty Shabazz International Charter School. Dale is a member of the Association of Business Leaders and Entrepreneurs (ABLE), Chicago's premier African-American business organization; the National Black Chamber of Commerce; the NAACP; RainbowPUSH Coalition; and the National Black United Front.

Dale earned his bachelor of science degree from Arizona State University, and his MBA from Stanford University. He has four sons and resides in Chicago's Bronzeville community with his wife, Cathy, and their youngest son, Damon.

Robert J. Dale
President & Chief Executive Officer
RJDale Advertising & Public Relations

The Honorable Danny K. Davis (D-IL07) was chosen by the people of the Seventh Congressional District of Illinois as their representative in Congress in 1996. He has been reelected by large majorities to succeeding Congresses.

Davis serves on the Government Reform, Small Business, and Education and the Workforce Committees. He is chair of the House Postal Caucus and is a member of numerous other caucuses, including the Black Caucus and the Progressive Caucus.

Davis has distinguished himself as an articulate voice for his constituents and an effective legislator who is able to move major bills to passage. He practices a unique style of communication and interaction with his constituents through advisory task forces, town hall meetings, weekly television and radio shows featuring audience call-in, periodic written public reports, and regular attendance at other community events.

Prior to his election to Congress, he served on the Cook County Board of Commissioners and the Chicago City Council. Before seeking public office, Davis had productive careers as an educator, community organizer, health planner/administrator, and civil rights advocate.

The Honorable
Danny K. Davis
Congressman
Seventh District of Illinois
U.S. House of Representatives

Chicago's
MOST INFLUENTIAL

Celebrating African-American Achievements

Michael D. Davis
Group Vice President
Strategic Development
RR Donnelley

Michael D. Davis, group vice president of strategic development with RR Donnelley, is a seasoned professional with diverse management, operations, and manufacturing experience amassed throughout his business career. In his current role, Michael manages the development and growth strategies for multiple business units and is responsible for leading the formation of long term strategic plans for these businesses.

Prior to his current role, Michael was vice president of manufacturing finance at RR Donnelley, and previously held the position of vice president of purchasing with Moore Corporation Limited. In addition to his career with RR Donnelley, Michael held a variety of positions of increasing responsibility with World Color. He has several years of financial management and analysis experience, as well as purchasing and supply chain management experience with multi-plant and multi-billion dollar corporations in the printing industry.

Michael graduated with a bachelor's degree in finance from Murray State University. He currently resides in Aurora, Illinois.

Photo by DAVE BUSTON /AFP/Getty Images

Shani Davis
Olympic Champion
Ice Speed Skating

Speed skater Shani Davis won two Olympic medals at the 2006 Winter Games in Turin, Italy, a gold medal in the 1,000-meter event and a silver medal in the 1,500-meter event. He is a two-time world allround champion (2005, 2006), and is the current world record holder for fastest time in both the 1,000- and 1,500-meter events.

Born in Chicago in 1982, Davis was raised by his mother on the South Side. He started roller-skating at local rinks at age two but was quickly bored with it. At six, Davis switched to ice and joined the Evanston Speedskating Club, where he began competing locally after two months. At eight, Davis was winning regional competitions in his age group.

He won five National Age Group Championships (1995, 1997, 1999, 2000, 2003) and a North American Championship (1999). Davis made history at 17 when he became the first U.S. skater to earn spots on both the short and long track junior world teams three years in a row (2000-2002). His first international medals came at the 2002 Junior Country Match and 2002 Junior World Championships.

Celebrating African-American Achievements

Chicago's
MOST INFLUENTIAL

The Honorable William "Will" Quincy Davis began serving in the Illinois House of Representatives on January 8, 2003.

Davis currently serves on the Higher Education Appropriations, Child Support Enforcement, International Trade and Commerce, and Labor Committees. He also serves as vice chairman of the Elementary and Secondary Education Appropriations Committee.

Since taking office, Davis worked to restore $12 million to the Illinois Student Assistance Commission for the Monetary Award Program (MAP); helped secure more than $57 million in additional state funding for schools in the 30th District; and passed legislation that provides affordable prescription drugs for all senior citizens in Illinois.

He graduated from Southern Illinois University Carbondale in 1989, earning a bachelor of arts degree in political science. Davis is currently completing a master of public administration degree at Governors State University.

Davis is a member of Kappa Alpha Psi Fraternity, Inc., a founding member of the Better Funding for Better Schools Coalition, and serves on the Foundation Board of South Suburban College.

**The Honorable
William Quincy Davis**
Representative, 30th District
Illinois House of Representatives

Dr. R. Martin Earles is a practicing dermatologist in Chicago and a pioneer in hair-transplants among African Americans. He was the first to publish a paper on hair transplants in black women, "Hair Transplants in Black Women," in the *Journal of Dermatologic Surgery and Oncology* (1986).

Earles developed an acne treatment line and treatment products for razor bumps. He also developed dandruff treatment products, for one of which he holds a U.S. patent. His son, Robert, is chief executive officer of Dr. Earles, LLC and is directing placement of products in the general marketplace. Andrea Earles, his daughter, is marketing director, and the children's mother, Eve Earles, is the media consultant.

He holds bachelor's and master's degrees from Howard University and completed his residency in dermatology at Rush Medical Center in Chicago.

Earles has appeared in many popular magazines including *Ebony*, *Jet*, *Essence*, and *Vogue*. He is a member of the National Medical Association, Sigma Pi Phi Fraternity, Inc., and Kappa Alpha Psi Fraternity, Inc.

Dr. Earles' hobbies include golfing and writing poetry.

R. Martin Earles, M.D.
Dermatologist & President
Dr. Earles, PC

THE INAUGURAL EDITION *Who's Who In Black Chicago*

Chicago's MOST INFLUENTIAL

Celebrating African-American Achievements

Dr. Barbara Eason-Watkins was appointed chief education officer of Chicago Public Schools in August of 2001.

She received a bachelor's degree in elementary education, with honors, from the University of Michigan, a master's degree in educational administration and supervision from Chicago State University, and a doctorate in education from Loyola University Chicago.

Before her appointment, Eason-Watkins was a nationally recognized school principal from the Chicago Woodlawn community. Her experience in education includes teaching in Highland Park, Michigan, and serving as principal of two elementary schools in Chicago. She has spent her entire 30-year professional career working to improve the quality of public education.

Her awards include the Whitman Award for Excellence in Educational Leadership (1989); CPS Principal of Excellence Award (1990 and 1995); Phi Delta Kappa Educator of the Year (1995); CPS Principal Leadership Award (1997); Telly Award for the Virtual Pre-K Project (2002); Tsunami Foundation Storm Award (2004); and recognition as the Most Powerful Woman in Education by the *Chicago Sun-Times* (2004). She is also co-author of the highly successful book *On Common Ground: The Power of Professional Learning Communities* (2005).

Dr. Barbara Eason-Watkins
Chief Education Officer
Chicago Public Schools

Nyambi Ebie, M.D., is president of the Cancer Medicine Group, consultants in cancer treatment in Chicago. He is also a medical-legal consultant. He earned his medical doctor degree from Northwestern University Medical School and his juris doctor degree from DePaul University.

Ebie is a fellow of the American College of Physicians and the American College of Legal Medicine. He is a member of the National Medical Association, the American Medical Association, and the American Trial Lawyers Association.

He has served on the board of The Latin School of Chicago, and on the governing council of Trinity Advocate Hospital. Ebie is also an assistant professor of public health at the University of Illinois. His favorite subject is cancer prevention, about which he speaks frequently and for which he has made television appearances.

Ebie is married to Marie Ebie, a psychologist. They have three children: Jeremy, Kenneth, and Jennifer.

Nyambi Ebie, M.D., F.A.C.P.
President
Cancer Medicine Group

Celebrating African-American Achievements

Chicago's
MOST INFLUENTIAL

Don Elligan, Ph.D., M.M. is a clinical psychologist in private practice, and a professor of psychology at Harold Washington City College. His clinical practice specializes in the treatment of depression, anxiety related disorders, and marital therapy.

Elligan is a licensed psychologist in Illinois, Massachusetts, and Indiana. In addition, he is the author of *Rap Therapy: A Practical Guide for Communicating with Youth and Young Adults through Rap Music* (Kensington, 2004).

A member of the American Psychological Association, Elligan is also active in the Association of Black Psychologists. He holds both a master's and a doctorate degree in clinical psychology, a master's in management degree in organizational development, and a bachelor's degree in psychology.

Currently, Elligan lives in Chicago with his wife, Tracey Lewis-Elligan, Ph.D., and son.

Don Elligan,
Ph.D. Clinical Psychologist &
Professor of Psychology
Harold Washington City College

James Essex, a senior vice president for Jones Lang LaSalle, is retail director for HSBC. He is responsible for Household Finance Corporation's retail operations, and HSBC's real estate portfolios.

Previously, he worked as a program manager dedicated to retail network distribution expansion (new stores, relocation, and ATMs) for Bank of America. Before that, Essex served as senior asset manager for Exelon, where he oversaw the financial and operational aspects of 5,056,729 square feet of office space throughout Illinois. Additionally, Essex has managed the financial and operational aspects of Ameritech's real estate portfolio. He has also managed office buildings and portfolios, creating operating budgets and overseeing project and construction management.

Essex received a bachelor of science degree in business administration from Chicago State University, and an MBA from Northwestern University's J.L. Kellogg Graduate School of Management.

Essex serves on the board of Heartland Alliance, a nonprofit organization dedicated to providing human services for the underprivileged and those in need of a second chance.

A Chicago native, Essex is married to Camille. They have two sons, Gregory and Christopher.

James Essex
Senior Vice President
Corporate Solutions
Jones Lang LaSalle Americas, Inc.

Chicago's MOST INFLUENTIAL

Celebrating African-American Achievements

The Honorable Timothy C. Evans
Chief Judge
Circuit Court of Cook County

Timothy C. Evans serves as the chief judge of the Circuit Court of Cook County, the largest of the 22 judicial circuits in Illinois. Evans oversees the circuit's approximately 400 judges who he assigns throughout the court's eight divisions and six geographic districts. He also oversees an annual budget of $166.4 million, and more than 2,700 employees who work in 14 non-judicial offices.

Evans was first elected chief judge in 2001, and was reelected to a second, three-year term in 2004. Only the fourth person to serve as chief judge of the Circuit Court of Cook County, he is the first African-American to serve in this position.

Evans has expanded opportunities for women and minorities, appointing the first Hispanic American as presiding judge of the Fourth Municipal District, and the first woman as presiding judge of the Chancery Division. His efforts also led to the creation of a new, state-of-the art court facility for domestic violence cases in Chicago.

A 1965 graduate of the University of Illinois, Evans received his juris doctorate from The John Marshall Law School in 1969.

© Photo by Kenneth Muhammed

The Honorable Minister Louis Farrakhan
Nation of Islam

Born Louis Eugene Walcott in 1933, Minister Louis Farrakhan was reared by his mother in a highly disciplined, spiritual household in Roxbury, Massachusetts. Known as "The Charmer," he achieved fame in Boston as a vocalist, calypso singer, dancer, and violinist. He joined the Nation of Islam in 1955 and decided to dedicate his life to the teachings of the Honorable Elijah Muhammad.

Farrakhan became the leader of the Nation of Islam in 1977. In 1979, he founded *The Final Call*, an internationally circulated newspaper. In 1991, Minister Farrakhan penned *A Torchlight for America*. He led 2,000 blacks from America to Accra, Ghana for the Nation of Islam's first International Saviours' Day in October of 1994.

In 1995, Farrakhan led the Million Man March on the Mall in Washington, D.C., which drew nearly two million men. He returned to the Mall in 2000 with the Million Family March.

Additionally, Farrakhan launched a prostate cancer foundation in his name in 2003. First diagnosed with prostate cancer in 1991, he survived a public bout with the disease and currently maintains a rigorous work schedule.

Celebrating African-American Achievements

Chicago's
MOST INFLUENTIAL

State Representative Mary E. Flowers was first elected to the Illinois House in 1984. She has devoted her career to the needs and rights of children, and fights for working families in Illinois.

Currently, Flowers serves as chairperson for the Health Care Availability Access committee, and is a member of several appropriations, initiatives, and committees. Flowers introduced legislation that created the state's first in-school daycare at a Chicago public high school, was the architect and original sponsor of the Illinois Managed Care Act of 1999, and was lead sponsor of renaming Calumet Expressway after Bishop L. Ford.

Additionally, Flowers sponsored the first low-income energy assistance program; African-American sensitivity training for all Illinois police officers; legislation encouraging the state treasurer to deposit funds in banks in minority communities; and further reformed Illinois health care by introducing the Hospital Report Card Act in 2003.

A few of her many awards and honors include, Democratic Legislator of the Year-Illinois State Crime Commission, and the Black Pearl Award.

Flowers attended Kennedy King Community College and the University of Illinois at Chicago. She resides in Chicago with her husband and daughter.

**The Honorable
Mary E. Flowers**
State Representative
Illinois House of Representatives

Lula M. Ford presently serves as a commissioner for the Illinois Commerce Commission. She is the first African-American woman appointed as a commissioner in the agency's 90-year history. Prior to her appointment, Ford was the assistant director of central management services for the State of Illinois. For nearly 35 years, she served as an elementary school teacher, principal, assistant superintendent, instruction officer, and school leadership development officer for the Chicago Public Schools.

Ford has received numerous awards for her dedicated work as an educator, child advocate, and public servant. She has won accolades from former President Bill Clinton and Chicago Mayor Richard M. Daley for her excellent job performance and contribution to Chicago's inner city schools.

An active participant in many civic organizations, Ford is a member of Delta Sigma Theta Sorority, Inc., LINKS (Chicago Chapter), Crusade of Mercy, the Chicago Urban League, and the United Negro College Fund.

She received a bachelor of science degree from the University of Arkansas-Pine Bluff, and was awarded master's degrees from Northeastern University and the University of Illinois at Urbana-Champaign.

Lula M. Ford
Commissioner
Illinois Commerce Commission

THE INAUGURAL EDITION *Who's Who In Black Chicago®*

Chicago's
MOST INFLUENTIAL

Celebrating African-American Achievements

Justice Charles E. Freeman graduated from Virginia Union University with a bachelor of arts degree in 1954. He received his juris doctor degree from The John Marshall Law School in 1962. He engaged in the general practice of law from 1962 to 1967, and then served as assistant attorney general, assistant state's attorney, and attorney for the Board of Election Commissioners.

Freeman was appointed arbitrator for the Illinois Industrial Commission in 1965 by Governor Otto G. Kerner. Later, he was a commissioner on the Illinois Commerce Commission, appointed by Governor Walker and confirmed by the Senate.

Freeman was elected to the Cook County Circuit Court in 1976 and to the Illinois Appellate Court in 1986. In 1990, he was elected to the Supreme Court of Illinois. In 1997, Freeman was selected chief justice and served in that capacity until 2000, when he was retained for another ten-year term. He is a member of many bar association and has received numerous awards.

Freeman and his wife, Marylee, have one son, Kevin Lyle Freeman, a partner with the law firm of Gardner, Carton & Douglas.

**The Honorable
Charles E. Freeman**
Justice
Supreme Court of Illinois

Leslie A. Hairston, a Chicago native who grew up in the Fifth Ward's Hyde Park and South Shore communities, comes from a family rich in the tradition of community and civic service. Her community and civic values led her to run for alderman of Chicago's city council.

Hairston graduated from the University of Wisconsin and Loyola University School of Law. She is a former assistant attorney general for the State of Illinois, where she handled litigation for the Office of the Illinois Attorney General, Consumer Protection Division. Hairston was also staff attorney and special prosecutor for the State Attorney's Appellate Prosecutor's Office, where she argued before the Illinois Supreme Court.

Hairston was elected to office in 1999, and reelected in 2003, where she has worked to attract new businesses, create new jobs, and stabilize the community by making sure there is a mix of affordable, moderate, and market rate housing stock in the ward.

As Fifth Ward alderman, Hairston serves on the following committees: buildings, rules and ethics, human relations, parks and recreation, and special events, and cultural affairs.

**The Honorable
Leslie A. Hairston**
Alderman, Ward #5
City of Chicago

Celebrating African-American Achievements

Chicago's
MOST INFLUENTIAL

As president and CEO of the Chicago-based Hartman Publishing, Inc., Hermene Hartman is one of the most significant and influential black women in American publishing.

Her flagship publication, *N'DIGO*, was founded in 1989, and has since become the largest African-American newspaper circulation in the nation, and the largest alternative newspaper circulation in Chicago. The weekly publication has an audited circulation of 150,000, and a readership of 600,000.

In 1995, *N'DIGO PROFILES* was established as a special annual publication, with a targeted insert in the *Chicago Tribune* and *Crain's Chicago Business* magazine with a circulation of 325,000.

Hartman is founder and president of the N'DIGO Foundation, a 501c3 nonprofit organization, which began in 1995. It sponsors an annual black tie gala to raise funds for educational purposes.

In 2004, Hartman became the president of the Alliance of Business Leaders and Entrepreneurs (ABLE), a business group dedicated to entrepreneurial pursuits with 70 members with revenues of nearly one billion in collective annual revenues.

She has received over 200 awards for outstanding achievement in media, business, community services, education, and communication.

Hermene Hartman
President & CEO
Hartman Publishing, Inc.

Ron Hawkins is vice president and national ombudsman for McDonald's Corporation. Ron is the first African American to ever hold this position at McDonald's. In this role, Ron evaluates the application of policies, practices, procedures, and fundamental values to reach equitable solutions with the U.S. franchisees and corporate employees.

Hawkins joined McDonald's in 1971 as a crew person behind the counter while attending school. In 1973, he moved up to restaurant management in the Washington, D.C. region. Ron has worked in every level of restaurant management, mid management, and various regional operations department head positions.

At McDonald's, Ron has received numerous awards including the prestigious President's Award, the highest award of excellence awarded to the top 1% of the corporation.

Hawkins received his business degree from Prince George Community College in Largo, Maryland. He resides in Naperville, Illinois with his wife of 25 years, Santá, and two daughters, Tanisha and Sharday.

Ron works actively in his church and community serving on several boards and choirs to serve where there is a need.

Ron Hawkins
Vice President &
National Ombudsman
McDonald's Corporation

Chicago's MOST INFLUENTIAL

Celebrating African-American Achievements

Jacquelyn Heard has been press secretary to Chicago Mayor Richard M. Daley since August of 1997. She advises the mayor on issues of public policy and media relations; serves as his chief liaison with local and national media; and oversees the writing of mayoral speeches and press releases for the mayor's office and the city's 48 departments.

Born in Chicago, Heard graduated from Lane Technical High School in 1984. She earned a bachelor's degree, magna cum laude, from Northwestern University's Medill School of Journalism in 1988.

Immediately after graduation, she joined the *Chicago Tribune* as a general assignment reporter. She was an education writer from 1991 to 1994, and a city hall reporter from 1994 to 1997.

Heard has received many awards including the *Chicago Tribune*'s Edward Scott Beck Award and the Travelers and Immigrant Aid Society's Reporter of the Year in 1990. She also received a certificate of appreciation from the Interfaith Organizing Project of Greater Chicago, the Phenomenal Woman Award from the Annual Expo for Today's Black Woman, and was featured in the *Crain's Chicago Business* 40 Under 40.

Jacquelyn L. Heard
Mayoral Press Secretary
City of Chicago

Robert Higgins, M.D., joined Rush University Medical Center in February of 2003 as professor and chairman of cardiovascular-thoracic surgery.

Higgins earned his bachelor's degree from Dartmouth College in 1981 and his medical degree from Yale University School of Medicine in 1985. He completed a residency in general surgery at the University Hospital in Pittsburgh and a fellowship in cardio-thoracic surgery at Yale University. In 1993, Higgins went to England as a senior registrar in transplantation at Cambridge University's Papworth Hospital.

Higgins has been appointed to the advisory committee on organ transplantation by the secretary of the Department of Health and Human Services. His expertise lies in the area of heart and lung transplantation and mechanical circulatory support; off-pump, minimally invasive cardiac surgery; and outcome assessment and improvement for heart failure and cardiac surgery patients.

Higgins has written more than 100 peer reviewed papers and book chapters and has made dozens of presentations throughout the United States. He has provided high-level leadership skills, combining proven expertise in administration, education, and research as one of the country's few African-American academic chairman in cardiac surgery.

Robert Higgins, M.D., MSHA
Mary & John Bent
Professor & Chairman
Dept of Cardiovascular
Thoracic Surgery
Rush University Medical Center

Celebrating African-American Achievements

Chicago's
MOST INFLUENTIAL

Greg Hinton joined U.S. Cellular® in 2002, where he is currently senior director of strategic sourcing talent and diversity. He has responsibility for sourcing talent, staffing strategies, EEO compliance, and diversity program development for U.S. Cellular®.

He began his human resources career in 1978 and worked for major corporations like RR Donnelley, Amtrak, Pepsi-Cola, and Abbott Laboratories before joining U.S. Cellular®.

Greg sits on various boards including the League of Black Women, the Hispanic Alliance for Career Enhancement, the Chicago Minority Business Development Council, the Employment Management Association, staffing.org, the Black Data Processing Association, and the Recruiting Roundtable.

In addition to his professional achievements, Greg founded a local human resources organization called the Chicago Association of Minority Recruiters, designed to meet the development needs of minority human resources professionals.

Greg finished his bachelor of science degree from the University of Illinois and his master of science degree from Loyola University of Chicago. He has three children, and when they are not keeping him busy, he enjoys cooking, reading, and sporting activities. He is currently finishing a cookbook entitled "Tales of Two Cooks."

Gregory T. Hinton
Senior Director
Strategic Sourcing & Diversity
U.S. Cellular®

Raymond Hodges is senior vice president in Jones Lang LaSalle's public institutions group. He provides real estate consulting and advisory and management services to public sector clients such as federal, state, and municipal government agencies. Primarily, he heads development of the firm's public sector facility management practice.

He joined Jones Lang LaSalle in 1997 and has served clients such as Bank of America, Harris Bank, and Citigroup during his tenure with the firm. Previously, Raymond was an officer in the U.S. Air Force, serving honorably as an F-111 weapon system officer, civil engineering officer, and air liaison officer.

Raymond earned a master of business administration degree from Tarleton State University and a bachelor's degree in architecture from Illinois Institute of Technology. He is an adjunct professor of decision sciences at DeVry University's Keller Graduate School of Management, and is an active member of the Chicago chapter of CoreNet.

Raymond is a native of Chicago's south suburbs, where he currently resides with his wife, Jeanmarie, and two children, Grace and Jacob. He enjoys music, the arts, reading, cooking, and traveling.

Raymond S. Hodges
Senior Vice President
Public Institutions
Jones Lang LaSalle

Chicago's MOST INFLUENTIAL

Celebrating African-American Achievements

Louis Holland is the managing partner and chief investment officer of Holland Capital Management, L.P., where he oversees the management of the firm's equity and fixed income investment strategies. Prior to founding Holland Capital, he formed the investment advisory firm of Hahn Holland & Grossman, where he was responsible for security and industry research and portfolio management.

Holland's investment experience was augmented by 15 years at A.G. Becker Paribas Inc. There, he was vice president specializing in asset and portfolio management for corporations, endowments, foundations, public funds, Taft-Hartley, and high net worth individuals. He has been a special guest and a 20-year veteran panelist on *Wall $treet Week With Louis Rukeyser*, and *Louis Rukeyser's Wall Street*. Holland has also appeared on *The MacNeil/Lehrer NewsHour*, CNN's *Moneyline*, CNBC, and is a frequent guest on *Chicago Tonight Show*. The National Association of Securities Professionals honored him with the 2004 Maynard Jackson Entrepreneur of the Year Award.

Holland received his bachelor of science degree in economics from the University of Wisconsin and attended the Loyola University Chicago's Graduate School of Business.

Louis A. Holland
Managing Partner &
Chief Investment Officer
Holland Capital Management, L.P.

Robert Howard is president and chief executive officer of Boys & Girls Clubs of Chicago. He oversees a budget of $16 million. The Clubs serve a diverse population of 18,000 youth, ages five to 19, providing structured after-school and summer programming at 28 clubs and ten childcare centers.

Howard was a "Club kid" while growing up on Chicago's South Side. He credits the Clubs for the positive values and guidance he received from caring adult professionals, which contributed to his success in corporate America (senior vice president at Payless Shoes). He holds an MBA from Harvard and a master's degree in history from Roosevelt University.

Howard is an active member of several civic institutions including the capital improvement advisory committee of the City of Chicago. He was featured in Crain's Chicago Business; inducted into the University of Illinois at Chicago's Alumni Leadership Academy and Phi Alpha Theta's historical honors society at Roosevelt University; and recognized for outstanding community service by the Association of Collegiate Business Schools and Programs. Additionally, Howard has appeared on numerous television programs stressing mentorship and community involvement.

Robert Howard
President & Chief Executive Officer
Boys & Girls Clubs of Chicago

Celebrating African-American Achievements

Chicago's
MOST INFLUENTIAL

Senator Mattie Hunter, a native Chicagoan, has represented the Third Legislative District in the Illinois Senate since 2003. She presently serves as chairperson of the Appropriations III Committee.

Hunter worked for the Human Resources Development Institute, Inc., where she developed and managed a shelter for battered women and children, and was managing director for the Center for Health and Human Services in Johannesburg, South Africa. She participated, coordinated, and presented lectures at joint health and human services conferences in Zimbabwe, Nigeria, and Zambia.

Hunter received a bachelor's degree (government) from Monmouth College and a master's degree (sociology) from Jackson State University. In 2004, she attended the John F. Kennedy School of Government at Harvard and received a certificate in Leadership for the 21st Century: Chaos, Conflict, and Courage, and she attended a Salzburg Seminar on multicultural healthcare in Salzburg, Austria.

Some legislation passed by Hunter includes SJR31, a Slave Trade Commission to study the slave trade and its consequences on the black community, and SB1, "Ticket for the Cure," a scratch-off lottery ticket with all proceeds going to breast cancer awareness and treatment.

**The Honorable
Mattie Hunter**
Senator, Third District
Illinois Senate

Don Jackson is the founder, chairman, and chief executive officer of 35-year-old Central City Productions, Inc. (CCP), a national television production, sales, and syndication company based in Chicago, Illinois.

Jackson earned his bachelor of science degree in radio, television, and film from Northwestern University in 1965. After graduating from Northwestern, Jackson became the youngest and first African-American sales manager at WVON, the top radio station in the Chicago market at the time.

In 1970, Jackson founded Central City Marketing, Inc. For over three decades, the company has specialized in marketing, promotion, sales, and the production of media and television programs for African Americans.

Today, CCP is the full-service company that produces, syndicates, and manages advertising sales for all of the company's local and national television programs. Under his guidance, CCP has launched many new and unique television programs to African Americans nationwide. Many of these programs have more than 25 years of consecutive airing over local and national television.

Jackson is married to Rosemary Jackson, and they have two adult children and two grandsons.

Don Jackson
Chairman & Chief Executive Officer
Central City Productions, Inc.

Chicago's MOST INFLUENTIAL

Celebrating African-American Achievements

Rev. Jesse L. Jackson, Sr.
Founder & President
RainbowPUSH Coalition, Inc.

Born in Greenville, South Carolina, Jesse Jackson, Sr. graduated from North Carolina A&T State University in 1964 and earned his master of divinity degree in 2000.

In 1965, he became a full-time organizer for the Southern Christian Leadership Conference (SCLC). Shortly thereafter, Dr. Martin Luther King, Jr. appointed him to direct SCLC's Operation Breadbasket program. Jackson went on to found Operation PUSH (People United to Serve Humanity) and the National Rainbow Coalition, which eventually merged in 1996 to become the RainbowPUSH Coalition.

Jackson's 1984 presidential campaign registered more than one million new voters and won 3.5 million votes. His 1988 campaign registered two million-plus new voters and won seven million votes.

A renowned orator and activist, Jackson has received the prestigious NAACP Spingarn Award, more than 40 honorary doctorate degrees, and the Presidential Medal of Freedom. Additionally, he has written two books, *Keep Hope Alive* and *Straight from the Heart*.

Jackson married his college sweetheart, Jacqueline Lavinia Brown, in 1963. They have five children: Santita Jackson, Congressman Jesse L. Jackson, Jr., Jonathan Luther Jackson, Yusef DuBois Jackson, Esq., and Jacqueline Lavinia Jackson, Jr.

Valerie B. Jarrett
Managing Director &
Executive Vice President
The Habitat Company

Valerie B. Jarrett is a managing director and the executive vice president of The Habitat Company. The Habitat Company is one of the nation's premier developers and managers of residential apartments. Habitat has developed more than 25,000 housing units and currently manages more than 30,000 units.

Before joining The Habitat Company in 1995, Jarrett served for eight years in the City of Chicago government as deputy corporation counsel for finance and development, and deputy chief of staff for Mayor Richard M. Daley. She also served as commissioner of the department of planning and development for the city. Prior to her city government service, Jarrett practiced law with two private law firms, specializing in the area of commercial real estate.

From 1995-2003, Jarrett served as chairman of the Chicago Transit Board. She is currently chair of the Chicago Stock Exchange Board. Jarrett serves as a director of several corporate and nonprofit boards, including USG Corporation, the Federal Reserve Bank of Chicago, The Joyce Foundation, and The University of Chicago.

Celebrating African-American Achievements

Chicago's
MOST INFLUENTIAL

The Honorable Lionel Jean-Baptiste has served as alderman of Evanston's second ward since 2001. He is a husband, father of three, and grandfather of one. After coming from Haiti at the age of 14, Lionel earned a degree in political science from Princeton University in 1974.

In Brooklyn, New York, he taught on the elementary and collegiate levels, served as director of special housing for the New York City Housing Preservation and Development Department, and organized for jobs and worker's rights and against police brutality.

Lionel earned his law degree from Chicago-Kent College of Law. He went into private practice working in the areas of immigration, personal injury, real estate, and probate. Likewise, he worked on political cases such as the reparations case that is being litigated against several U.S. corporations.

He was a member of the African Liberation Support Committee and the Durban 400. Lionel is co-founder of the Haitian Relief Fund of Illinois and the Haitian Congress to Fortify Haiti. A member of the Governor's Task Force on Racial Profiling, he is listed in *Who's Who Among American Lawyers*.

**The Honorable
Lionel Jean-Baptiste**
Alderman, Ward 2
City of Evanston

William A. Johnson, M.D., is medical director of the Chicagoland Central program for VITAS Innovative Hospice Care®, and he is medical director of the Luck Care Center, an HIV/AIDS primary care clinic in Chicago.

Concerned with the devastation caused by HIV, Johnson dedicates much of his time to HIV/AIDS-related organizations and to the relief efforts of organizations such as the Foundation for Hospices in Sub-Saharan Africa. In recognition of his and his wife's many contributions to the cause, they were named Provider Advocates of the Year in 2002 by the AIDS Legal Council in Chicago. Johnson also lectures frequently around the country on topics related to HIV and pain management for terminally ill patients.

Board certified in internal medicine and in hospice and palliative medicine, Johnson completed a medical degree at The University of Chicago Pritzker School of Medicine, where he attained honor status. He was the recipient of the Monarch Award in Medicine in 2001, and was named a Trailblazer in Healthcare by the RainbowPUSH Coalition in 2005.

William A. Johnson, M.D.
Medical Director, Chicagoland Central
VITAS Innovative Hospice Care®

Chicago's
MOST INFLUENTIAL

Celebrating African-American Achievements

The Honorable Emil Jones, Jr.
President
Illinois Senate

The Honorable Emil Jones, Jr. has been a member of the Illinois General Assembly since 1973. He is an independent-minded and progressive legislator with a solid reputation of fairness and advocacy. He is a strong proponent of social justice, and fair and adequate funding of public education in Illinois.

Jones has served as Senate president since 2003, receiving the unanimous support of his caucus in 2003 and 2005.

A 1953 graduate of Chicago's Tilden Technical High School, Jones graduated from Loop Junior College. He also attended Roosevelt University, which awarded him a doctorate of humane letters degree, *honoris causa*, in 2004. He received an honorary doctor of humane letters degree at Chicago State University. In 2004, he was named to the board of directors of the Forum of Senate Presidents. In addition, he serves on the board of directors of the State Legislative Leaders Foundation. Also in 2004, Jones was inducted into the Phi Theta Kappa International Honor Society of Harold Washington College.

Jones has four children and is married to Dr. Lorrie Jones.

Karen Jordan
Co-Anchor
WLS-TV ABC7

ABC 7's Karen Jordan co-anchors the number one-rated weekend newscast in Chicago. Jordan, who grew up in Evanston, Illinois, joined ABC 7 Chicago in 2003.

Previously, Jordan served as weekend anchor at WPHL-TV in Philadelphia, Pennsylvania. Jordan began her career in Rockford, Illinois as a general assignment reporter for WIFR-TV. She gained early experience at WMAQ-AM in Chicago, where she worked through the Medill News Service as a radio reporter.

Being recognized for excellence throughout her career, Jordan was most recently named a 2003 Rising Star by *Today's Chicago Woman*. She was honored with the YMCA Black Achiever Award, and received the Bethune Recognition for women in the media from the National Council of Negro Women. She is a member of the National Association of Black Journalists.

Jordan graduated from Spelman College in Atlanta, Georgia with a bachelor's degree in English. She earned a master's degree in broadcast journalism from Northwestern University's Medill School of Journalism.

Born in Nashville, Tennessee, Jordan is married to broadcast journalist Christian Farr. Her father, Robert Jordan, is a long-time anchor and reporter at WGN-TV in Chicago.

Celebrating African-American Achievements

Chicago's
MOST INFLUENTIAL

Born in Brooklyn, New York in 1963, Michael Jordan grew up in Wilmington, North Carolina. He attended Emsley A. Laney High School where he participated in football, baseball, and basketball, and was named to the McDonald's All-American Team as a senior. After earning a scholarship to the University of North Carolina at Chapel Hill, he led the team to a national championship in 1982.

His 13 seasons with the Chicago Bulls were monumental: six NBA championships; ten league scoring titles; five-time league Most Valuable Player; NBA Finals MVP six times; and All-Star Game MVP three times. Following his second retirement, he returned to basketball for two seasons with the Washington Wizards. Jordan is the NBA's all time leader in most points per game (30.1) and is third on the NBA's list of all-time scorers (32,292 points). He also won two Olympic gold medals.

In addition to his triumphs on the court, Jordan is one of the most marketed athletes in history. He has served as a spokesperson for numerous brands, and is a successful restaurateur and businessman. Jordan is married and has three children.

Photo by TANNEN MAURY /AFP/Getty Images

Michael Jordan
NBA Basketball Legend
Chief Executive Officer
Jumpman, Inc.

Jeanette Newton Keith, M.D. is an assistant professor of medicine and an attending physician at The University of Chicago Hospitals in the section of gastroenterology/nutrition, department of internal medicine.

She is a fellow of the American College of Nutrition, and a member of the American Medical Association and National Medical Association. Likewise, Keith is a member of the American College of Gastroenterology, American Society for Bone and Mineral Research, and the American Society of Parenteral and Enteral Nutrition.

Keith attends on the Nutrition Support Service at The University of Chicago Hospital. Her main clinical interest is the medical management of obese patients, especially those with nutritional complications following bariatric surgery with a specific focus on calcium and vitamin D metabolism. Other interests include lactose maldigestion, women and minority health, nutritional aspects of colorectal cancer prevention, and general gastroenterology.

She earned her degree in medicine from the Indiana University School of Medicine in Indianapolis. Keith trained in general internal medicine at Indiana University Medical Center. She completed fellowships at the University of Missouri-Columbia in gastroenterology, and the University of California-Davis in clinical nutrition.

Jeanette Newton Keith, M.D.
Assistant Professor of Medicine &
Attending Physician
The University of Chicago Hospitals

THE INAUGURAL EDITION *Who's Who In Black Chicago®*

Chicago's MOST INFLUENTIAL

Celebrating African-American Achievements

Avis LaVelle is president and founder of A. LaVelle Consulting Services, LLC, a strategic communications consulting company founded in 2003. A LaVelle Consulting Services seeks to provide government and corporate clients with guidance on public affairs, public relations, government relations, and crisis communications.

LaVelle formerly served as an assistant secretary of the U.S. Department of Health and Human Services during the Clinton administration. Likewise, she was press secretary to Chicago Mayor Richard M. Daley. In the private sector, LaVelle was the vice president of communications and government relations for The University of Chicago Hospitals, and was vice president of community relations and communications for Waste Management, Inc.

LaVelle is a graduate of the University of Illinois at Urbana-Champaign and Keller Graduate School of Management. With a commitment to public education, LaVelle served six years as vice president of the Chicago School Reform Board. She is a member of Apostolic Church of God and Delta Sigma Theta Sorority, Inc.

She and husband, Osekre D. Hoes, are the parents of one son, Robert.

Avis LaVelle
President
A. LaVelle Consulting Services, LLC

Adorn Lewis has worked in various management positions for Flowers Communications Group since 1994. As senior vice president, she is responsible for agency client services.

Prior to joining FCG, Lewis was the national director of the National Council of Negro Women's Black Family Reunion Celebration. Before this position, she was the president and CEO of ALD Communications, a Chicago-based public relations and special events firm. She previously served as an account group supervisor at Burrell Public Relations. Lewis also has worked as a brand public relations supervisor at Milwaukee-based Miller Brewing Company. She launched her public relations career in 1985 as an associate editor at ShopTalk Trade Publication.

With a bachelor's degree in mass communications from Drake University in Des Moines, Iowa, Lewis currently serves as a board member for Muntu Dance Theater of Chicago and Little Brothers Friends of the Elderly. She is a member of the National Association of Black Journalists, Chicago Association of Black Journalists, and Alpha Kappa Alpha Sorority, Inc.

She has garnered more than 25 industry awards for excellence in communications and public relations.

Adorn L. Lewis
Senior Vice President
Flowers Communications Group

Celebrating African-American Achievements

Chicago's
MOST INFLUENTIAL

Corey Lewis is the chief financial officer for the corporate solutions business at Jones Lang LaSalle. Corey oversees financial and business matters for a diverse group of real estate service lines, including tenant representation, facility management, project management, and consulting.

Corey is a member of the National Association of Black Accountants and an active participant in the Executive Leadership Council, a Washington, D.C.-based organization providing African-American executives at Fortune 500 companies with a networking and leadership forum. Lewis also serves on the board of directors of the Partnership for Quality Childcare, a nonprofit organization aiming to improve the quality of childcare available to Chicago's low-income families.

Corey earned his master's of business administration degree from The University of Chicago and a bachelor of science degree from Hampton University.

A native of Milwaukee, Corey is the husband of Raishon Lewis and is the proud father of two children, James Bryton and Raina Devyn.

J. Corey Lewis
Chief Financial Officer
Jones Lang LaSalle Americas, Inc.

Irwin Loud oversees the development of Muller & Monroe's private equity investment programs and serves on the investment committee. A private equity innovator, Irwin was named one of "25 to Watch" over the next 25 years by *Pensions and Investments* in 1999.

Previously, Irwin was senior portfolio manager and private equity investor for the Florida State Board of Administration (FSBA), which manages the state's $110 billion pension fund. While at FSBA, Irwin played a prominent role in launching the industry's first partnership focused exclusively on private equity co-investments. He also was the architect of the formal structuring and growth of the portfolio to $3.2 billion in commitments.

Irwin began his career at Chase Manhattan Bank, N.A., New York, where he served as a loan officer in the international and investment banking divisions.

Irwin received his bachelor of science (summa cum laude) and MBA degrees from Florida A&M University, School of Business & Industry.

Irwin C. Loud, III
Chief Investment Officer
Muller & Monroe Asset
Management, LLC

THE INAUGURAL EDITION   *Who's Who In Black Chicago*

Chicago's MOST INFLUENTIAL

Celebrating African-American Achievements

The Honorable Freddrenna M. Lyle
Alderman, Ward 6
City of Chicago

Freddrenna M. Lyle was appointed as the Sixth Ward Alderman of the City of Chicago in 1998. She was elected in 1999, and reelected in 2003.

Before her appointment, Lyle practiced law for 18 years achieving many professional accomplishments including: president, Cook County Bar Association, board member of the National Bar Association, Supreme Court Committee member on character and fitness, and co-chair of the Lawyer's Committee for Harold Washington.

She is a homeowner in Park Manor where her family has resided for more than 45 years. Lyle attended Park Manor Elementary, South Shore High School, the University of Illinois at Chicago, and John Marshall Law School.

Lyle is committed to enhancing the quality of life for her Sixth Ward residents. From assisting seniors, to providing supervised recreation for young people, Lyle for Kids, a foundation she created, runs a full schedule of programs.

Lyle serves on the parks and recreation, economic development, traffic and public safety, and rules and ethics committees. She is a serious legislator and advocate for the citizens of the Sixth Ward.

Haki R. Madhubuti
Founder & Publisher
Third World Press

Author, educator, and poet Haki R. Madhubuti is founder and publisher of Third World Press in Chicago. He is the distinguished university professor at Chicago State University. Madhubuti is a professor of English, founder and director emeritus of the Gwendolyn Brooks Center for Black Literature and Creative Writing, and director of the MFA in creative writing program at Chicago State.

Madhubuti has published 27 books (some under his former name, Don L. Lee) including *Black Men: Obsolete, Single, Dangerous?: The African American Family in Transition*; *GroundWork: New and Selected Poems 1966-1996*; *HeartLove: Wedding and Love Poems*; *Tough Notes: A Healing Call for Creating Exceptional Black Men*; *Run Toward Fear*; and *YellowBlack: The First Twenty-One Years of a Poet's Life, A Memoir*.

He is a recipient of the National Endowment for the Arts, the National Endowment for the Humanities Fellowships, and the Illinois Arts Council Award. Madhubuti earned his master of fine arts degree from The University of Iowa, and he holds two honorary doctoral degrees.

An avid cyclist, he is married to Safisha Madhubuti and is the father of five children.

Celebrating African-American Achievements

Chicago's
MOST INFLUENTIAL

Commissioner of the Chicago Department of Public Health Terry Mason, M.D., is a urologist by training. He is assistant professor of urology at the University of Illinois, and is on the faculty at the University of Illinois School of Public Health. A graduate of the University of Illinois College of Medicine, he completed his residency in urology at Michael Reese Hospital. He is affiliated with Mercy and Illinois Masonic Hospitals and is a regional chair of the National Black Leadership Initiative on Cancer Control Network.

To help Americans understand that preventative medicine is essential to healthy living, he created the Center for New Life and co-founded the Health Solutions Institute. It uses core musculoskeletal rehabilitation and optimized food resources for the treatment of diabetes, elevated cholesterol, obesity, and other chronic medical conditions.

His awards include the Outstanding Young Doctor Award from *Dollars & Sense*, Nigerian-American Forum's Distinguished Persons Award, and the Monarch Awards Foundation Men in Medicine Award. He is a lifetime member of the NAACP and a board member of the Saltpond Redevelopment Institute of Ghana, West Africa.

Terry Mason, M.D., FACS
Commissioner
Chicago Department of Public Health

Pamela McElvane is chief executive officer of P&L Group, Ltd., a Chicago-based business of specialty companies offering an innovative approach to diversity recruiting business solutions. Pamela received the 2005 Media Ambassador Award from Boardroom Bound; the 2005 Media Cornerstone of the Year Award from the Chicago Minority Business Development Council and Minority Business Enterprise; and 2005 Woman of the Year honors from the American Society Institute. She is currently on the boards of directors for Legacy Bancorp, the American Cancer Society, Boardroom Bound, and the Gamaliel Foundation.

Pam is co-founder of *Black MBA Magazine*, the official publication of the National Black MBA Association, Inc. She also owns *Black IT Professional* magazine and founded Diversified Recruitment, Inc., which provides online branding and permanent/temporary staffing.

Pam received her bachelor's degree in English, sociology, and social welfare; her MBA in finance and international marketing; and her master's degree in public policy from University at California, Berkeley.

Josh, six, and Cameron, three, are her two boys. She attends Triedstone Full Gospel Baptist Church (Bishop Simon Gordon presiding), where she leads their strategy team.

Pamela A. McElvane, MBA
Chief Executive Officer
P&L Group, Ltd.

THE INAUGURAL EDITION *Who's Who In Black Chicago*®

Chicago's
MOST INFLUENTIAL

Celebrating African-American Achievements

Barbara J. McGowan
Commissioner
Metropolitan Water Reclamation
District of Greater Chicago

Barbara J. McGowan was first elected commissioner in November of 1998, and reelected to a six-year term in December of 2004.

The mission of the Metropolitan Water Reclamation District of Greater Chicago is to keep sewage pollution out of Lake Michigan, while properly treating sewage to avoid contamination of the Cook County area's water system. McGowan has been the chair of the district's committee on affirmative action for seven years.

A few of her numerous accomplishments include the deposit of more than $40 million of district funds in minority-owned banks, and revising the district's affirmative action ordinance to include fines and penalties for contractors who violate the program. In addition, McGowan continues to lend her strong support of the Apprentice Training Program, requiring contractors to have minority and women apprentices.

McGowan created the opportunity for the district to appoint the first African-American lobbyist, the first African-American female head attorney, and the first African-American director of information technology.

Recently, McGowan received the 2006 Outstanding Public Service Award from the African-American Contractors Association.

Cheryl Mayberry McKissack
Founder, President &
Chief Executive Officer
Nia Enterprises, LLC

Cheryl Mayberry McKissack is the founder, president, and chief executive officer of Nia Enterprises, LLC, a Chicago-based research, systems integration, and marketing services firm founded in January of 2000. Nia Enterprises, LLC provides opt-in, permission-based marketing data solutions for the growing and specialized market of African-American women and their families.

Prior to founding Nia Enterprises, McKissack enjoyed a successful 23-year corporate career in technology. In 2005, she was named an associate adjunct professor of entrepreneurship at the Kellogg School of Business, Northwestern University. McKissack recently co-edited The Nia Guide series of books for black women focusing on career, work-life balance, and health and wellness.

McKissack, a native of Seattle, Washington, received her bachelor of science degree from Seattle University, and in two-and-one-half years, earned her MBA from Northwestern's J.L. Kellogg School of Management.

McKissack serves on the board of directors of The PrivateBanCorp (NASDAQ: PVTB), and as a director of the Deluxe Corporation (NYSE: DLX).

Celebrating African-American Achievements

Chicago's
MOST INFLUENTIAL

Ms. Deryl McKissack is president and chief executive officer of McKissack & McKissack, an architectural, engineering, and program management firm. The firm was established in 1990 with $1,000, no clients, and no employees. Today, McKissack & McKissack has 150 employees with four office locations. In 2002, McKissack expanded to Chicago, Illinois, building on the successes she had established; she recently opened offices in Miami, Florida and Baltimore, Maryland. The firm was recently recognized in *Engineering News-Record* as the 54th largest construction management firm.

McKissack & McKissack provides quality service to health care, environmental, government, education, residential, sports and recreational, commercial, and transportation related construction projects. Notable projects include the National Institutes of Health, restoration of the Thomas Jefferson and Lincoln Memorials, the renovation of the main Treasury Building, the Chicago and D.C. Public Schools, the Chicago Housing Authority, the New Washington Convention Center, RFK Stadium, O'Hare International Airport Modernization Program, and Chicago's McCormick Place expansion.

McKissack holds a bachelor's degree in civil engineering from Howard University.

Deryl McKissack
President & CEO
McKissack & McKissack

The Honorable Reverend Meeks is the senior pastor of Salem Baptist Church of Chicago. Under his leadership, the church has served the Roseland Community since 1985 and has more than 22,000 members. Serving in the Illinois Senate since 2003, Meeks has supported legislation to improve the lives of underserved people in Illinois, particularly in his fight for education funding reform.

In 1998, Meeks led the rally to "dry up" Roseland by collecting votes to close 26 area liquor stores in oversaturated areas. He also established the House of Hope, a $50 million, 10,000-seat worship and community activity center.

In addition to serving the 15th Illinois Senatorial District, Meeks is chairman of the Illinois Legislative Black Caucus, and serves as the executive vice president of the National RainbowPUSH Coalition.

A native of Chicago, Meeks is a graduate of Bishop College in Dallas. He and Jamell, his wife of more than 25 years, have four children.

**The Honorable
Rev. James T. Meeks**
Senator, District #15
Illinois State Senate

Chicago's MOST INFLUENTIAL

Celebrating African-American Achievements

Marquis D. Miller is executive director of the Chicago State University Foundation. He is responsible for all institutional advancement activities, including fundraising and resource development, public and media relations, and alumni programs for the University.

A member of Omega Psi Phi Fraternity, Inc., he is a proud graduate of The Ohio State University. Currently, Miller is a member of the board of directors of the Association of Fundraising Professionals (AFP) Chicago chapter, and co-chair of the diversity and fellows committee. He is also a member of the board of directors of the Trinity Higher Education Corporation, and chair of the program development committee.

Miller is a member of the Leadership Council of Chicago United, Inc., and serves as a member of the audience diversity and development committee of the Museum of Contemporary Art. He has also served on the boards of Lakefront Supportive Housing; The Harvard School of Chicago; Prevent Blindness America and Prevent Blindness Ohio; the Columbus Speech & Hearing Center; and as a member of the Mid-Ohio Regional Planning Commission.

Marquis D. Miller
Executive Director
Chicago State University Foundation

Alderman Emma Mitts has championed the cause of uniting the people of the 37th Ward to get things accomplished in the community. Her vision of "Unity In The Community" is designed to strengthen the community by everyone working together, block-by-block and shoulder-to-shoulder. Through her commitment, Mitts has provided affordable housing, increased senior housing, improved education, reduced crime, increased economic development with job opportunities and training, and brought a thriving economy to the community.

Mitts' mission to rebuild the 37th Ward is in full bloom. She is overseeing many projects since taking office, including the opening of San Miguel Catholic School, the Ronald McNair Elementary School, and the Washington Square Mall. The 37th Ward will have its first Chicago Public Library in April and a Wal-Mart in July. The future looks even brighter as Menards, Coca-Cola, and CVS/pharmacy are coming into the 37th Ward.

Some of Mitts' personal achievements include being the first African-American female alderman of the 37th Ward and the founder of the Community Action Council.

**The Honorable
Emma Mitts**
Alderman, Ward 37
City of Chicago

Celebrating African-American Achievements

Chicago's
MOST INFLUENTIAL

Eugene Morris is a 38-year veteran of the advertising industry. Under his stewardship, E. Morris Communications, Inc. (EMC) has emerged as one of the most respected in the industry. The company has attracted a blue chip client roster that includes Wal-Mart, American Family Insurance, Tyson Foods, and the Illinois Department of Transportation. Gene has been profiled in a number of publications, authored several articles, and is much sought after as a speaker on the national level.

As chairman and chief executive officer for EMC, Gene manages day-to-day agency operations with a staff of 45 team members who provide creative marketing, sales promotion, public relations, media planning, special events, and market research services.

Gene is a member of several associations and boards including, the national board of directors of AAAA, Alliance of Business Leaders and Entrepreneurs, and the *American Legacy* magazine. He also serves for Junior Achievement, Roosevelt University Alumni board of governors, and is vice chairman of the Sickle Cell Disease Association of Illinois.

Gene earned his bachelor of science and MBA degrees from Roosevelt University in Chicago, Illinois.

Eugene "Gene" Morris
Founder, Chairman &
Chief Executive Officer
E. Morris Communications, Inc.

Yvette Moyo, president and chief executive officer of Resource Associates International, Ltd., is a marketing authority with nearly 30 years' experience. She is best known for creating two brands, Real Men Cook® and Marketing Opportunities in Business and Entertainment™ (MOBE). She is also co-founder of Real Men Charities, Inc., a nonprofit committed to building healthier families and communities.

Real Men Cook®, the largest annual national urban family-focused Father's Day celebration, generated close to $1 million for nonprofits and has attracted nationwide media coverage. The Real Men Cook® brand product offshoots include Real Men Cook Sweet Potato Pound Cake®, sold in grocery stores nationwide; and the Simon & Schuster published book, *REAL MEN COOK: Rites Rituals and Recipes for Living*.

Moyo co-founded the conference series, MOBE, which generated over $200 million in business to registrants through associations conceived at MOBE symposiums. In 2000, MOBE created the first White House briefing on African-American business and technology.

Moyo conceived "Bonus Living for Families," an initiative renaming blended, adoptive and foster families. She has helped to raise eight bonus children and one biological son.

Yvette J. Moyo
President & Chief Executive Officer
Resource Associates
International, Ltd.

THE INAUGURAL EDITION *Who's Who In Black Chicago*®

Chicago's MOST INFLUENTIAL

Celebrating African-American Achievements

In 1964, Ishmael was born in Albuquerque, New Mexico to the leader of the Nation of Islam, The Most Honorable Elijah Muhammad and to the multi-talented Tynnetta Muhammad. Ishmael enjoys the distinct honor of serving as the assistant minister to The Honorable Minister Louis Farrakhan and the Nation of Islam's headquarters in Chicago.

Ishmael served as one of the principal coordinators of the historic Million Man March that drew over a million black men to Washington, D.C. He has planned and organized events and conferences throughout the U.S., and has been featured in local, national, and international print and broadcast media.

His travels have taken him to Egypt, Saudi Arabia, Jerusalem, Pakistan, West Africa, Europe, New Zealand, and South America. Ishmael studied in Cuernavaca, Mexico for 17 years. He is bilingual, speaking both fluent Spanish and English.

Loving husband and father of seven, Ishmael is an outstanding spokesman for the upliftment of blacks throughout the world in the new millennium. "My greatest desire is to help my father in the mission of resurrecting, redeeming, and restoring black people in America and throughout the world."

Minister Ishmael R. Muhammad
Assistant Minister to
The Honorable Louis Farrakhan
Nation of Islam

Bob Nash is vice chairman of ShoreBank Corporation and serves as chairman of ShoreBank Enterprise Detroit and the Detroit Bank Advisory Committee. He is also chairman of the board for ShoreBank Neighborhood Institute and ShoreBank Enterprise Cleveland.

Bob served as under secretary of the U.S. Department of Agriculture for small community rural development. He then served as director of presidential personnel to former President Bill Clinton.

Prior to working for the Clinton Administration, he worked for Governors Bumpers, Pryor, and Clinton in Arkansas, and joined Winthrop Rockefeller Foundation as its vice president.

Bob Nash
Vice Chairman
ShoreBank Corporation

Celebrating African-American Achievements

Chicago's
MOST INFLUENTIAL

Martin Nesbitt is president and chief executive officer of The Parking Spot. He founded and conceptualized the company in 1997 in partnership with Chicago's Pritzker family and is responsible for running all strategic and operating aspects of the business, which generates $70 million in revenue and has 15 locations and 850 employees. The company has been featured in *The New York Times*, *USA Today*, and *Entrepreneur* magazine for its innovative approach to an old-line business.

Prior to creating The Parking Spot, Nesbitt was an equity partner at Jones Lang LaSalle, one of the nation's leading corporate real estate firms. Before that, he was employed by General Motors Acceptance Corporation in the area of financial planning, where he became a GM fellow.

Nesbitt is currently a trustee of Chicago's Museum of Contemporary Art, and serves on the boards of the Chicago Housing Authority, the Illinois Finance Authority, and The University of Chicago Laboratory Schools.

Nesbitt received a master of business administration degree from The University of Chicago and a bachelor's degree in economics and management from Albion College.

Martin H. Nesbitt
President & Chief Executive Officer
The Parking Spot

Professor of medicine and human genetics Dr. Olufunmilayo (Funmi) Olopade directs a multidisciplinary clinical and laboratory research program at The University of Chicago Medical Center. Olopade is internationally renowned for her expertise in cancer genetics and has published extensively in the area of genetics of breast cancer predisposition.

Olopade received her medical degree with distinction from the University of Ibadan in Nigeria. She came to the United States as a resident in internal medicine at Cook County Hospital, Chicago, where she was named chief medical resident. She completed her postdoctoral fellowship training in the joint section of hematology/oncology at The University of Chicago and was appointed to the faculty in 1991.

Olopade is the recipient of numerous honors and awards including the ASCO Young Investigator Award, the James S. McDonnell Foundation Scholar Award, the Doris Duke Distinguished Clinical Scientist Award, and a 2005 MacArthur Fellowship "genius" grant.

Olufunmilayo Olopade
M.D., FACP
Professor, Medicine & Human Genetics
The University of Chicago
Medical Center

Chicago's
MOST INFLUENTIAL

Celebrating African-American Achievements

Javette C. Orgain, M.D., MPH, a family physician, is chair of the Illinois State Board of Health, the advisory board to the Illinois Department of Public Health. At the University of Illinois Medical Center, she has been a teacher, researcher, student advisor, and mentor since 1991. She also practices as a hospice physician with Vitas Healthcare Corporation.

Orgain served as the 100th president of the National Medical Association in 2000. She is second vice president of the Illinois Academy of Family Physicians, chairs the community affairs committee of the Cook County Physicians Association, and serves on the advisory board of the Daniel Hale Williams Preparatory School of Medicine.

Orgain received her doctor of medicine and public health degrees from the University of Illinois at Chicago.

A native Chicagoan, she has been featured in numerous publications nationally and internationally. In 2001, *Black Enterprise* magazine named her one of America's Leading Black Doctors. In 2003, Orgain was recommended by Congressman Jesse Jackson, Jr., honored by the National Library of Medicine, and named "Local Legend" by the American Medical Women's Association.

Javette C. Orgain, M.D., MPH
Chair, Illinois State Board of Health &
Associate Professor of
Clinical Family Medicine
University of Illinois at Chicago

Dr. Mary K. Palmore is a board certified obstetrician/gynecologist (OB/Gyne) in private practice on Chicago's Southside. Her practice includes, but is not limited to obstetrics, family planning, surgery, infertility, and new options in weight management. As chair of the section of OB/Gyne at Advocate Trinity, she works with nursing, administration, and her colleagues to make the female healthcare experience an outstanding one.

Dedicated to community service, Palmore is president of the Hyde Park auxiliary of Children's Home and Aid of Illinois. She is an active member of Trinity UCC Women's Chorus, Chicago Top Ladies of Distinction, and Alpha Kappa Alpha Sorority, Inc. Palmore was chosen to participate with a select group of 100 women in the 2006 Leadership Fellows class of Leadership America.

She graduated from Hampton Institute (University) and Rush Medical College where she was the only African-American woman in her class. When she moved to Dallas, Texas, she became the first and only African-American female in OB/Gyne, and was honored as such.

In her spare time, Palmore enjoys reading, spending time with family, shopping, and travel.

Mary K. Palmore, M.D., F.A.C.O.G.
Obstetrician & Gynecologist
Mary K. Palmore, MD, SC

Celebrating African-American Achievements

Chicago's
MOST INFLUENTIAL

Allison Payne joined WGN-TV News in March of 1990 as co-anchor of *WGN News at Nine*. The five-time Emmy award-winning anchor also co-anchors WGN's bi-weekly program *People to People* with Steve Sanders. In August of 2005, she joined the *The Real Show* with Ramonski Luv and Joe Soto on V103 as headline reader.

Before WGN-TV, Payne anchored the nightly news for WNEM-TV in Saginaw, Michigan. Her career as a television journalist began at WNWO-TV in Toledo, where she was an intern but quickly moved up to anchor the station's late news.

Recognized by *Today's Chicago Woman* in its 1999 special edition of "100 Women Making a Difference in the City," she was also featured in *Essence* for her work at the anchor desk.

A Richmond, Virginia native, Payne grew up in Detroit. She graduated magna cum laude from the University of Detroit and earned a master's degree from Bowling Green State University.

In 1995, Payne established the Kathryn Payne Memorial Scholarship fund in honor of her late mother. An avid traveler, Payne has traveled to Kenya, South Africa, Egypt, and much of Europe.

Allison Payne
News Anchor
WGN-TV

The Honorable Toni Preckwinkle has served as alderman/committeeman of the Fourth Ward in Chicago since 1991. She represents approximately 60,000 residents. Toni serves on several city council committees, including the finance; rules and ethics; energy, environmental protection and public utilities; parks and recreation; and landmarks committees. She also consults with developers and other business entities on the building of new housing in the ward.

In 2003, Toni formed Quad Communities Development Corporation with a diverse group of neighborhood leaders. She has received more than 25 awards from government, civil rights, religious, business, and community organizations for her innovative ideas and service.

Toni is a past president of Disabled Adult Residential Enterprises (1985-1987). She serves on the board of directors of the Illinois Council Against Hand Gun Violence; is political director of the South Side chapter of the Independent Voters of Illinois; and is executive director and coordinator for economic development for the Chicago Jobs Council.

Toni holds bachelor's and master's degrees from The University of Chicago. Her husband of 37 years is Zeus Preckwinkle, a schoolteacher. They have two children.

**The Honorable
Toni Preckwinkle**
Alderman, Ward 4
City of Chicago

THE INAUGURAL EDITION *Who's Who In Black Chicago*

Chicago's MOST INFLUENTIAL

Celebrating African-American Achievements

Quintin E. Primo, III is chairman and chief executive officer of Capri Capital Advisors, a real estate investment management firm headquartered in Chicago. The firm has over $2.7 billion in real estate assets currently under management, representing pension funds, governmental agencies, and other institutional investors. He co-founded the firm in 1992. Quintin is also chairman of Capri Select Income, a real estate mezzanine investment fund.

Recieving an MBA from Harvard University Graduate School of Business Administration, Quintin also holds a bachelor of science degree in finance from Indiana University. He is a voting member of the Pension Real Estate Association, the Urban Land Institute, and is a board member of the Real Estate Roundtable.

Quintin is a member of the Federal Reserve Bank of Chicago, Seventh District Advisory Council, and The Economic Club of Chicago. He serves as a board trustee of the Chicago Community Trust, (Episcopal) Church Pension Group, and the University of Chicago Hospitals. He is chairman of the Primo Center for Women and Children, and founder and chairman of the Real Estate Executive Council.

Quintin E. Primo, III
Chairman & Chief Executive Officer
Capri Capital Advisors

The Honorable Judith C. Rice, 48, was elected city treasurer of the City of Chicago on February 25, 2003. She has held that office since her appointment by Mayor Richard M. Daley in November of 2000.

Preceding her appointment as city treasurer, Rice served as the first woman commissioner of two of the biggest infrastructure agencies in City of Chicago government. She headed the Chicago Department of Transportation, and was commissioner of the Chicago Department of Water.

Earlier, Rice was managing deputy director, then director of the Department of Revenue. She began her city career in 1989 as an assistant corporation counsel. From 1982 to 1989, Rice worked in the Cook County State's Attorney's Office, where she rose to assistant state's attorney.

She graduated, cum laude, in 1981 from Loyola University with a bachelor of arts degree in communication.

Rice is also very active in community affairs. She sits on the boards of BBF Family Services, the March of Dimes, Uhlich Children's Home, and the United Negro College Fund.

The Honorable Judith C. Rice
City Treasurer
City of Chicago

Celebrating African-American Achievements

Chicago's
MOST INFLUENTIAL

Linda Johnson Rice is president and chief executive officer of Johnson Publishing Company, Inc., publishers of *Ebony* and *Jet* magazines, and the number one African-American publishing company in the world. Rice oversees the corporation's domestic and international business operations, which include Fashion Fair Cosmetics and the EBONY Fashion Fair.

Rice is the recipient of the Robie Award for Achievement in Industry from the Jackie Robinson Foundation; the Tower of Power Award of The Trumpet Awards from Turner Broadcasting; the Alumni Merit Award from the University of Southern California; and the Alumni of the Year Award from Northwestern University's Kellogg Graduate School of Management's Black Management Association.

Rice serves on the boards of directors of Bausch & Lomb, Inc.; Kimberly-Clark Corp.; Omnicom; MoneyGram International, Inc.; The Art Institute of Chicago; the United Negro College Fund; the University of Southern California; and several others. She is also a member of the Magazine Publishers Association.

Rice holds a bachelor's degree in journalism from the University of Southern California's Annenberg School of Communication, and an MBA from Northwestern University's J.L. Kellogg Graduate School of Management.

Linda Johnson Rice
President & Chief Executive Officer
Johnson Publishing Company, Inc.

Desiree Rogers was elected president of Peoples Energy's utilities, Peoples Gas and North Shore Gas, in July 2004. She oversees field operations, customer service functions, and gas supply management. She also serves as a senior vice president of Peoples Energy Corporation. Since joining Peoples Energy in 1997, Rogers' responsibilities have included customer care, marketing, and sales and rates for the utilities. Likewise, she is responsible for communications, contributions, and government relations for the corporation.

Previously, Rogers was the director of the Illinois Lottery between 1991 and 1997.

Rogers serves on the boards of the Lincoln Park Zoo, Museum of Science and Industry, and the Northwestern Memorial Foundation. She holds memberships in The Commercial Club of Chicago, The Economic Club of Chicago, and the Wellesley Business Leadership Council. Rogers also serves on the corporate boards of Equity Residential and Blue Cross Blue Shield of Illinois.

Rogers has been featured in *Black Enterprise*, *Ebony*, *Chicago Tribune*, and *Vogue*.

Receiving a bachelor's degree from Wellesley College, Rogers holds a master's degree from Harvard Business School.

Residing in Chicago, Rogers has a daughter, Victoria.

Desiree Glapion Rogers
President
Peoples Gas and North Shore Gas

Chicago's
MOST INFLUENTIAL

Celebrating African-American Achievements

As founder of Ariel Capital Management, LLC, John Rogers, Jr. is the father of the investment and business philosophy that guides the firm today. As the firm's chief investment officer, he manages Ariel's small- and mid-cap institutional portfolios as well as the Ariel Fund and the Ariel Appreciation Fund. Moreover, since Ariel's founding, John has shepherded the growth of assets under management to more than $19 billion.

At Princeton, John studied economics and served as captain of the varsity basketball team his senior year. John serves on the boards of directors of Aon Corporation, Bally Total Fitness Holding Corporation, Exelon Corporation, and McDonald's Corporation. His civic affiliations include roles as director of the Chicago Urban League; trustee of The University of Chicago; board member of the Chicago Symphony Orchestra; and board member of the John S. and James L. Knight Foundation.

In addition, he is the former president of the board of the Chicago Park District, and a former trustee of Princeton University.

John W. Rogers, Jr.
Chairman & Chief Executive Officer
Ariel Capital Management, LLC

Jim Rose is the sports anchor/reporter for the top-rated ABC7 weekday newscasts at 4:00 and 6:00 p.m. He joined ABC7 Chicago in 1982.

Previously, Rose served as a weekend sports anchor and play-by-play reporter at WIXT-TV in Syracuse, New York from 1977-82. During this time, he also hosted and produced *Sportsweek Nine*, a weekly sports magazine, and WIXT's *The Halftime Report*.

During his college years, he worked as a sports anchor at WPRO-TV in Providence, Rhode Island. Rose began his career in sports broadcasting while serving in the U.S. Army, acting as sports director for AFN-TV in Berlin, West Germany in 1973.

He has won several awards for his work, including the 1981 Best Sports Story Award from the Syracuse Press Club for his *Sportsweek Nine* segment on the Sugar Ray Leonard/Larry Bonds title fight. The Syracuse Press Club also honored him in 1980 for Best Reporting under Deadline Pressure, and in 1979 for Best Sports Story.

Rose serves on the board of directors for the Boys and Girls Clubs of Chicago, and is a 1977 graduate of Rhode Island College.

Jim Rose
Sports Anchor & Reporter
WLS-TV ABC7

Celebrating African-American Achievements

Chicago's
MOST INFLUENTIAL

The Honorable Bobby L. Rush was elected a member of Congress in the U.S. House of Representatives on November 3, 1992. In this role, Rush sits on the powerful House Committee on Energy and Commerce, and serves on the Subcommittee on Commerce, Trade, and Consumer Protection; the Subcommittee on Telecommunications and the Internet; and the Subcommittee on Health. He is also a co-chairman of the Congressional Biotech Caucus.

Rush has brought nearly $2 billion of federal funding to the First Congressional District of Illinois since his election.

A co-founder of the Illinois Black Panther Party in 1968, Rush operated the Party's Free Breakfast for Children program.

He received a bachelor's degree from Roosevelt University and a master's degree in political science from the University of Illinois at Chicago. He holds a second master's degree in theological studies from McCormick Seminary.

In addition to his congressional duties, Rush is pastor of Beloved Community Christian Church in Chicago. He and his wife, Carolyn, are the parents of six children.

The Honorable Bobby L. Rush
Congressman, First District of Illinois
U.S. House of Representatives

Kwame's responsibility includes human resources management of Kraft's global manufacturing, customer service, logistics, procurement, engineering, snacks, beverages, and cheese and dairy. He joined Kraft 20 years ago as manager of affirmative action compliance at Oscar Mayer. There, he held a number of positions, most notably vice president of human resources sales and customer service, and vice president of global human resources, HQ functions, talent acquisition, and diversity.

Before Kraft, Kwame was an elected official and executive director of the Dane County Parent Council, Inc. in Madison, Wisconsin.

Kwame's accomplishments include Outstanding Contribution to Human Rights in Madison from the Equal Opportunity Commission, and the Outstanding Recent Alumni Award from the University of Wisconsin-Whitewater. President Reagan appointed him chairperson of Wisconsin's Civil Rights Commission, and he served two terms on the University of Wisconsin-Madison's Graduate School of Business board of visitors.

Kwame holds a bachelor's degree, magna cum laude, and a master's degree in educational administration from the University of Wisconsin-Madison.

Kwame resides in Oak Park with his wife and two children. He enjoys reading, exercise, and travel. He also has two adult children.

Kwame S. Salter
Senior Vice President
Human Resources
Global Supply Chain
Kraft Foods, Inc.

Chicago's
MOST INFLUENTIAL

Celebrating African-American Achievements

Hosea Sanders is the co-anchor of *ABC7 News This Morning*. He joined ABC7 in 1994, and plays a major role in both the news and programming areas. Sanders hosts important local specials such as *Operation Save-A-Life*, a salute to John Johnson, and is a featured reporter on ABC7's Emmy Award-winning *People, Place, and Things* program.

Winning six Emmy Awards for live coverage, spot news, entertainment reporting, news writing, and overall news achievement, Sanders has received more than 100 awards from various civic and community organizations.

A national motivational speaker, Sanders is dedicated to mentoring and helping young people. He is active in the Alpha Phi Alpha Big Brothers program, the Chicago Public Schools Mentoring Program, and the NAACP Mentoring Program. He serves on the board of the Open Book Literacy Program, and is a member of the National Association of Black Journalists, the Chicago Association of Black Journalists, and the National Academy of Television Arts and Sciences.

A former state champion sprinter, Sanders graduated from Henderson State University in Arkansas, where he received his bachelor's degree in communications and journalism.

Hosea Sanders
Co-Anchor
WLS-TV ABC7

Chicagoan Warner Saunders, anchor of NBC 5's six p.m. and ten p.m. newscasts, celebrated 38 years in broadcasting in 2006. He has earned two of Chicago broadcasting's most prestigious awards: induction into the Chicago Journalism Hall of Fame and the Chicago Television Academy's Silver Circle. Saunders has also received 19 Chicago Emmy Awards.

A past president of the Chicago Association of Black Journalists, he received the 1999 Hull House Jane Addams Award for community service. In February of 1990, Saunders delivered reports from South Africa on the release of Nelson Mandela. While a member of the NBC 5 sports team, he filed many interesting stories, including a salute to the outstanding athletes of the Negro Leagues. His *DuSable, The Uncrowned Champions* won the 1984 Chicago Association of Black Journalist's Media Award.

Saunders is a graduate of Xavier University in New Orleans, and he holds a master's degree from Northeastern Illinois University.

He and his wife, Sadako, live in Chicago, and have one adult son, Warner Jr. Saunders' favorite quote is, "Never use race as a reason for success nor an excuse for failure."

Warner Saunders
News Anchor
NBC 5 Chicago, WMAQ-TV

Celebrating African-American Achievements

Chicago's
MOST INFLUENTIAL

Michael W. Scott is president of the Board of Education for the City of Chicago, and of MS& Associates, LLC.

A product of the Lawndale community of Chicago's Westside and the Chicago Public School system, Scott graduated from Fordham University earning a bachelor's degree in urban planning. He serves as the commissioner on the Public Building Commission of Chicago and on the PBC administrative operations committee. Additionally, he serves on the boards of directors for the Community Bank of Lawndale, Mount Sinai Hospital, Better Boys Foundation, and the Chicago Historical Society.

Former vice president of regulatory affairs for Comcast Corporation, Scott was also vice president of Pyramid West Development Corporation. He was instrumental in the rehabilitation of 1,500 housing units, building a 250-unit senior citizen center, a nursing home, and the establishment of the Community Bank of Lawndale. Special assistant to Mayor Harold Washington, director of special events, and chief cable administrator, Scott was also a CPS board member from 1980-1981. Likewise, he was recognized for marshaling support for the student desegregation plan, and chairing the Committee on Real Estate.

Michael W. Scott
President
Chicago Board of Education

Dr. Horace E. Smith received his medical degree from the University of Illinois Medical Center. He is director of the Comprehensive Sickle Cell/Thalassemia Program at Children's Memorial Hospital. He is also an assistant professor of pediatrics at Northwestern Medical School.

Smith became pastor of the Apostolic Faith Church in 1980. In 2004, he was elected presiding bishop of the Pentecostal Assemblies of the World, an organization of more than 7,000 churches worldwide.

He serves on the boards of the historic Wabash YMCA board, the Family Institute at Northwestern University, and World Vision International.

Smith and the Apostolic Faith Church partnered with World Vision to sponsor orphaned children in Africa whose parents have died as a result of HIV/AIDS. To date, more than 1,000 have been adopted.

Husband to Susan Davenport Smith, they have been married since 1976 and are the parents of three daughters. Susan Smith is an AIDS clinical trials pharmacist at Children's Memorial Hospital.

Among his numerous honors and awards in print media, Smith was featured in the *N'DIGO* Diamond Anniversary of 2005.

Horace E. Smith, M.D.
Director
Comprehensive Sickle Cell
Thalassemia Program
Children's Memorial Hospital

Chicago's MOST INFLUENTIAL

Celebrating African-American Achievements

Stephanie's current scope of responsibilities includes human resource management of Kraft's global category development and North America commercial units. Together, these units drive the total revenues for Kraft's premier brand portfolio, totaling approximately $33 billion.

During her 16 years with Kraft, Stephanie has held numberous generalist positions of increasing responsibility. Prior to her current position, she was vice president of human resources, North America businesses and corporate headquarters; and vice president of human resources, midwest business divisions. Likewise, she was senior director of human resources, Madison site; director of human resources, field sales and customer service; director of human resources, Kraft cheese division; and associate director of human resources, marketing services. She has held specialist positions in the human resources disciplines of employee relations, staffing, compensation, benefits, and HRIS within Kraft's corporate headquarters and the former frozen products group.

Before joining Kraft in 1990, Stephanie held a variety of human resources positions in the headquarters and field operations of two major Chicago retailers for nine years.

Stephanie received her undergraduate and graduate degrees from Northwestern University in Evanston, Illinois.

Stephanie B. Smith
Senior Vice President,
Human Resources
Global Category Development &
North America Commercial
Kraft Foods, Inc.

Paula A. Sneed is executive vice president of global marketing resources & initiatives. As a member of Kraft's executive team, she is responsible for worldwide leadership and oversight of marketing resources, including consumer insights & strategy, media, advertising, digital and consumer relationship marketing, packaging and brand design, consumer promotions, marketing alliances, kitchens, consumer relations, and other marketing disciplines for more than 100 major food brands.

Paula held numerous leadership roles at Kraft and has been recognized by *Ebony*, *Black Enterprise*, *Working Mother*, and *Fortune* magazines. She was the recipient of Harvard Business School's African-American Alumnus of the Year.

A trustee of Simmons College, Teach for America, and the Chicago Children's Museum, Paula is a director of Airgas Inc. and Charles Schwab Corporation. She is a member of the Executive Leadership Council and The Chicago Network.

Receiving her bachelor's from Simmons College, Paula holds an MBA from Harvard Business School. She also received an honorary doctorate of business administration from Johnson & Wales University.

A native of Malden, Massachusetts, she is married to Lawrence P. Bass. Their daughter, Courtney Bass, lives in Beijing.

Paula A. Sneed
Executive Vice President
Global Marketing
Resources & Initiatives
Kraft Foods, Inc.

Celebrating African-American Achievements

Chicago's
MOST INFLUENTIAL

Pervis Spann, "The Blues Man" is owner of radio station WVON in Chicago, the only African-American-owned station in the city. His award-winning station has a talk show format covering all the latest news, current events, and other pertinent issues that affect not only the black population, but everyone.

Spann, whose career in radio spans (pun intended) 50-plus years, is still the all night blues man on WVON. He attended Midwest Broadcasting School in Chicago, and was first a disc jockey on WVON before becoming owner.

He has written a bestselling novel, entitled *The 40 Year Spann of WVON*, along with co-author Linda C. Walker. Their collaboration was so successful that they have embarked on a second book, "The Spann of The Original Regal Theater," due out this summer.

Spann's daughter, Melody is station president, and along with her dad, has taken WVON from being the voice of the Negro to the voice of the nation.

Pervis Spann
Owner
WVON Radio Station

Melody Spann-Cooper is president of WVON 1450 AM. The station is a subsidiary of Midway Broadcasting Corporation, the oldest African-American-oriented radio station in the Chicago area and the only African-American-owned-and-operated talk radio station in the third-largest media market in the country.

Considered a visionary, Spann-Cooper purchased the company's controlling interest in 1999, thereby, joining an elite list of female broadcast owners. She is the only female to hold this coveted position in the third largest broadcast market in the country, and has used her media vehicle as an agent of change, addressing the social issues that affect society.

The *Chicago Sun-Times* recognized Spann-Cooper as one of the 10 Most Powerful Women in Media, and *Crain's Chicago Business* ranks her one of the 100 Most Influential Women in Chicago.

Spann-Cooper holds a bachelor of science degree in criminal justice from Loyola University Chicago. She is married and is the daughter of legendary radio personality, Pervis Spann, "The Blues Man."

Melody Spann-Cooper
President
Midway Broadcasting Corporation

THE INAUGURAL EDITION *Who's Who In Black Chicago*®

Chicago's
MOST INFLUENTIAL

Celebrating African-American Achievements

Soul and gospel artist Mavis Staples possesses one of the most recognizable and treasured voices in contemporary music. From her early days sharing lead vocals with her groundbreaking family group, The Staple Singers, to her powerful solo recordings, Mavis Staples is an inspirational force in modern popular culture and music.

A 40-year-plus veteran of the music scene, Staples is a Rock and Roll Hall of Fame and Museum inductee. She is also one of VH1's 100 Greatest Women of Rock and Roll. Staples, both with The Staple Singers and on her own, is responsible for blazing a rhythm and blues trail while never relinquishing her gospel roots.

Her voice has influenced artists from Bob Dylan to Prince, who dubbed her "the epitome of soul." Staples has appeared with several dignitaries, some of which include, the Reverend Dr. Martin Luther King, Jr., Bill Cosby, Presidents Kennedy, Carter, and Clinton, Janis Joplin, Pink Floyd, Santana, and Tom Petty & The Heartbreakers. She has also recorded with Bob Dylan, Los Lobos, Aretha Franklin, Marty Stuart, and many others.

Mavis Staples
National Recording Artist

Dana V. Starks was appointed first deputy superintendent, which is the second position within the Chicago Police Department, by superintendent Philip J. Cline on October 6, 2003. Currently entering into his 29th year with the department, he began his career on November 1, 1977.

Prior to his current position, Starks held several positions throughout the department as a patrolman, sergeant, lieutenant, commander, and deputy chief.

Starks has been awarded two department commendations, 22 honorable mentions from the Chicago Police Department, and more than 50 complimentary letters from community groups, churches, and block clubs. He has also been awarded the Fitness, Appearance, Special Service, Problem Solving, and Special Commendation awards.

He is a member of the Black Star Project, Safer Foundation, Prevention Partnership, Federal Initiative to Reduce Violence by Ex-offenders, and Fight Crime: Invest In Kids Illinois. He also serves on the steering committee of Project Safe Neighborhoods.

Dana V. Starks
First Deputy Superintendent
Chicago Police Department

Celebrating African-American Achievements

Chicago's
MOST INFLUENTIAL

Dr. Howard T. Strassner, Jr. received his undergraduate and medical degrees from The University of Chicago and The University of Chicago Pritzker School of Medicine. His postdoctoral clinical training includes a four-year residency in obstetrics and gynecology at Columbia-Presbyterian Medical Center and The Sloan Hospital for Women in New York. Likewise, Strassner fulfilled a two-year fellowship in maternal-fetal medicine at the Women's Hospital, The University of Southern California/Los Angeles County Medical Center.

He is a professor and the chairman of the department of obstetrics and gynecology. He is also the director of the maternal-fetal medicine section at Rush University Medical Center. Additionally, Strassner is co-director of the Rush Perinatal Center and the Rush Regional Perinatal Network.

He has received two gubernatorial appointments to statewide bodies: the Infant Mortality Reduction Advisory Board and the Governor's Task Force on AIDS in Healthcare. In 2001, *Chicago* magazine featured Strassner as one of Chicago's Top Doctors.

His clinical and research interests include premature rupture of membranes, preterm labor, cervical ripening, medical disorders in pregnancy, and preconception counseling.

Dr. Howard T. Strassner, Jr.
Chairman & Professor
Department of
Obstetrics & Gynecology
Rush Medical College

Michael W. Stuttley is presiding judge of the Sixth Municipal District, Juvenile Justice Section. With more than 27 years of legal experience, his trial and legal experience includes administrative, criminal defense, family, personal injury, real estate, probate, and juvenile law.

As presiding judge of the juvenile court in Markham, Illinois, Judge Stuttley is working to meet the needs of offenders, victims, and residents so that our communities are enhanced, rather than torn apart by the crimes of our youth. He has developed countless programs that allow offenders to rehabilitate. Stuttley stands by his basic principles that tend to work: "If offenders realize there is a victim that has been impacted by their actions, it is my hope that the offender will take accountability for their actions and attempt to right their wrong."

Judge Stuttley serves on the boards of numerous civic and professional organizations including the Illinois Supreme Court Special Committee on Child Custody, Illinois Judges Association, and the Supreme Court Committee of Judicial Performance. He has received countless honors and awards for his service.

**The Honorable
Michael W. Stuttley**
Judge
Juvenile Division
Circuit Court of Cook County

Chicago's MOST INFLUENTIAL

Celebrating African-American Achievements

Sam Sylk
Radio Personality
WGCI 107.5 FM

Known as the "Sylkiest Man n Radio," Sam is a television/radio show host and on-air personality for WGCI 107.5 FM Chicago. His unique style and attractive vocal tone can be heard and seen all over his hometown of Chicago. He is the number one weekday radio show host from 2 p.m. to 6 p.m., on WGCI in Chicago.

Previously, Sam was weekend personality for WAKS, Cleveland. His "Sylky Style" has made him famous in the city of Chicago with his ever-popular cable show, the *Sam Sylk Show*, which can be seen on Chicago's Comcast Cable Channel 25. The show consists of music videos and celebrity appearances. It is the only Chicago cable show where audience members can find their favorite actors, singers, athletes, along with special events. The *Sam Sylk Show* is an all access pass to the entertainment industry. The show also includes a special feature segment entitled the "Radio View," which shows entertainers live in the radio station with Sam Sylk during on-air interviews.

Sam Sylk has become a household name and an avenue used by successful local business organizations.

Cedric D. Thurman
Senior Vice President
HSBC Bank Team
Jones Lang LaSalle

Cedric D. Thurman is senior vice president of retail transaction management for Jones Lang LaSalle's HSBC Bank team. He is responsible for managing a tenant representation team that consults, advises, and executes retail transactions on behalf of HSBC's retail branch and consumer-finance portfolio on a national basis.

Thurman is a board member of the following organizations: the Museum of Science and Industry, Junior Achievement of Chicago, INROADS/Chicago, Inc., University of Illinois College of Business Alumni, the MSI African-American Outreach Committee, Jones Lang LaSalle's civic committee, Jones Lang LaSalle's African-American Employee Resource Group, and Wright Insurance Group.

He has been named to the Outstanding Men in America, selected as a Jones Lang LaSalle Club Award honoree, and twice named INROADS/Chicago Alumnus of the Year.

Thurman received a bachelor of science degree in finance from the University of Illinois and a master of business administration degree from the Kellogg Graduate School at Northwestern University.

A native Chicagoan, Thurman has been married to Michelle Speller-Thurman for 12 years. They are the proud parents of one son, Cedric Alexander.

Celebrating African-American Achievements

Chicago's
MOST INFLUENTIAL

Life safety has been Cortez Trotter's first priority throughout his 32 years of public service. In May of 2006, he became Chicago's first chief emergency officer (CEO), following his retirement from the Chicago Fire Department (CFD). As CEO, he will oversee the long-range planning strategy for manmade and natural disasters, and coordinate preparedness, response, and recovery activities for the Chicago Police Department, CFD, Chicago Department of Public Health, and Office of Emergency Management and Communications.

As fire commissioner, Trotter managed 5,000 sworn members and a $430 million budget. He also positioned the department as a leader in the fire service industry by implementing several best practices, including changes to the department's high-rise incident command policies.

Trotter was a business major at Dominican University, and appeared on the cover of *Fire Chief* magazine for his progressive leadership style. He was recognized by Jones Lang LaSalle for effective incident command at the LaSalle Bank fire, and by the Apartment Building Owners and Managers of Illinois for his life safety education efforts. Trotter is a board member for the Chicago Metropolitan Division of The Salvation Army.

Cortez Trotter
Chief Emergency Officer
City of Chicago

Jason is a member of Ariel's portfolio management team. More specifically, he leads the firm's research analysis of banks, information services, office equipment and supplies, office furnishings and fixtures, and telecommunications industries. He also oversees the team's day-to-day activities, including the supervision and development of Ariel's research associates and administrative staff.

In 2006, Jason was appointed to oversee Ariel's client restriction monitoring. In this capacity, he manages the team that ensures adherence to specifications for client contracts. Prior to joining Ariel in 2003, he worked at Bank One/American National Bank for ten years, most recently as a finance manager in the planning and analysis group.

Jason received his master of business administration degree from The University of Chicago and his bachelor of arts degree in politics from Princeton University. He serves as president of the board of directors for both the Emergency Fund for Needy People and After School All Stars. In addition, he serves as treasurer of the board of directors for the Joffrey Ballet.

Jason J. Tyler
Senior Vice President
Portfolio Management
Ariel Capital Management, LLC

Chicago's MOST INFLUENTIAL

Celebrating African-American Achievements

As corporate secretary of Ariel Capital Management, LLC (Ariel), Roxanne is an active liaison with the firm's external directors. Additionally, she is the corporate secretary to the office of the president, Ariel's senior management group. In this capacity, she is responsible for facilitating this leadership group's functioning and accountability.

Prior to joining Ariel, Ward spent four years working as the first assistant general counsel/board liaison for the Chicago Park District.

Roxanne earned her master's of administration and bachelor of arts degrees from The University of Chicago, and her juris doctorate from Harvard Law School.

Beyond Ariel, Ward is actively involved in the community, serving on the boards of the Illinois Facilities Fund, the Safer Foundation, and the Congo Square Theater Company.

Roxanne M. Ward
Vice President and
Corporate Secretary
Ariel Capital Management, LLC

The Honorable Eddie Washington, state representative of the 60th District, has already made history by becoming the first African American to represent the Waukegan/North Chicago area in the General Assembly.

Washington hails from East St. Louis, but has lived in the Waukegan area for almost 20 years. Since his arrival, he has been active in efforts to improve the community by working with local organizations. He is the founder of the activist group P.O.W.E.R. (People Organized Working for Equal Rights). Washington has worked with the Lake County Urban League as former director of employment and economic development, and he was director for the Waukegan Township Staben Center. He is also an active member of Lake County's NAACP and John Howard Association.

A friend of the labor community, Washington is a Metra conductor and a member of the United Transportation Union. He is also host of *The Eddie Washington Journal*, a radio talk show on WKRS on Saturday evenings. Prior to winning the state representative race, Washington served as a trustee for the North Shore Sanitary District.

**The Honorable
Eddie Washington**
Representative, 60th District
Illinois House of Representatives

Celebrating African-American Achievements

Chicago's
MOST INFLUENTIAL

Mary Beth Stone West is group vice president for Kraft Foods, Inc. and president of the North American grocery sector. The $2.7 billion sector includes brands such as Jell-O, Cool Whip, Kraft Salad Dressing, Miracle Whip, and A.1.

In 1986, Mary Beth joined General Foods Maxwell House division. In 1998, she was appointed vice president of new business development, and in 1999, she became vice president of marketing and strategy, enhancers division. In 2001, she was appointed executive vice president of Kraft Foods, and general manager of its meals division.

Mary Beth was acknowledged by *Crain's Chicago Business'* 40 Under 40, and *Minority MBA's* Next Generation of Business Leaders. In 2005, she was named to *Black MBA Magazine's* Top 50 Under 50. A member of the Executive Leadership Council and Foundation, she was appointed to the board of directors for J.C. Penney in 2005.

Mary Beth, her husband, Hiry, and two children reside in Evanston. She actively volunteers with Off The Street Club, Junior Achievement, and her church. She received a bachelor's degree from Nazareth College and an MBA from Columbia University.

Mary Beth Stone West
Group Vice President, Kraft Foods
President, Grocery Segment
Kraft Foods, Inc.

In 2003, Governor Rod Blagojevich asked Dr. Eric Whitaker to serve as director of the Illinois Department of Public Health. Whitaker oversees an agency comprising more than 1,100 employees, three laboratories, and seven regional offices that impacts the health of 12 million Illinois citizens.

Before his appointment, Whitaker co-founded Project Brotherhood: A Black Men's Clinic, a weekly clinic for African-American men housed in the Woodlawn Adult Health Center, and one of the first of its kind in the country. Among his awards and recognition, *Crain's Chicago Business* named Whitaker to its prestigious 40 Under 40 rising stars in business and government in 2003.

He received an undergraduate degree in chemistry from Grinnell College, a master's degree in public health from the Harvard School of Public Health, and a medical degree from The University of Chicago Pritzker School of Medicine. Whitaker has completed most of the coursework towards an MBA at Northwestern University's Kellogg School of Business. Additionally, he is an assistant professor at the University of Illinois at Chicago School of Public Health and Rush Medical College's department of medicine and preventive medicine.

Eric E. Whitaker, M.D., MPH
Director
Illinois Department of Public Health

Chicago's MOST INFLUENTIAL

Celebrating African-American Achievements

The Honorable Jesse White
Secretary of State
State of Illinois

The Honorable Jesse White was elected the 37th Illinois secretary of state in November of 1998. In November of 2002, he was reelected by winning all 102 counties and garnering more than 2.3 million votes—the largest vote total by any candidate for Illinois statewide office in 25 years.

Previously, White was the Cook County recorder of deeds, where he was first elected in 1992 and reelected in 1996. Before that, he served 16 years in the Illinois General Assembly.

White also served as a paratrooper in the U.S. Army's 101st Airborne Division and as a member of the Illinois National Guard. He played professional baseball with the Chicago Cubs and had a 33-year career with Chicago's public school system as a teacher and administrator.

White earned his bachelor of science degree from Alabama State College (now Alabama State University) in 1957, where he was a two-sport athlete earning all-conference honors in baseball and basketball. He has been inducted into the Southwestern Athletic Conference and the Alabama State University Sports Halls of Fame.

Born in Alton, Illinois, he now lives on Chicago's near-north side.

Rufus Williams
President & CEO
Olympus, LLC

Rufus Williams heads Olympus, LLC as its president and CEO. Olympus, LLC was incorporated in 2000, providing business and financial management, contract negotiation, negotiation strategy, and career development to athletes and entertainers.

A certified public accountant, Williams spent ten years at the HARPO Entertainment Group, having held several positions, including chief financial officer, controller, and vice president of financial planning and strategic development. Likewise, he managed Oprah Winfrey's extensive philanthropic endeavors and other special projects. Williams began his career at Arthur Andersen & Co., and later worked at Baxter Healthcare Corporation.

He graduated magna cum laude from Southern University in Baton Rouge, Louisiana with a degree in accounting.

Williams is a member of the Chicago Public School Board of Education, a member of the board of trustees of the Chicago Teachers Pension Fund, and president of the Fund for Inner City Athletic Equipment. He also serves as treasurer of the board of trustees of Providence-St. Mel School. Williams is a past president of the Better Boys Foundation, and past treasurer of the board of trustees of Francis W. Parker School.

Celebrating African-American Achievements

Chicago's
MOST INFLUENTIAL

Ruth Theresa Prudeaux Williams is employed at Unity Funeral Parlors, Inc. as part owner, chair of the board, and a licensed funeral director. She volunteers at Church of St. Edmund, where she is an ordained Episcopal priest.

Williams graduated from Xavier University, St. Louis University, and Chicago Theological Seminary where she holds a doctorate of ministry degree, a doctorate of divinity, and is a Ph.D. candidate.

Williams is active in the Bishop's Associates, the Episcopal Church Women, and the Society for the Companions of the Holy Cross. She formed The LaRuth Club to assist widows in being independent. Her memberships include the Chicago Chapter of The Links, Inc., the Chicago Network, the Child Welfare League of America, and Alpha Kappa Alpha, Inc. and Alpha Gamma Mu, Inc. sororities.

Williams was featured in the *Chicago Tribune* in 1985; in *N'DIGO* magapaper as one of the "N'Fluential Black Chicagoans" in 2003; and in *The HistoryMakers* in September of 2004.

She enjoys theater, symphony, ballet, opera, and a good book.

Rev. Dr. Ruth "Teena" Williams
Funeral Director
Unity Funeral Parlors, Inc.

Through the power of media, Oprah Winfrey has created an unparalleled connection with people around the world. As supervising producer and host of the top-rated, award-winning *The Oprah Winfrey Show*, she has entertained, enlightened and uplifted millions of viewers for the past two decades. Produced by her own production company, Harpo Productions, Inc., the show is seen by an estimated 49 million viewers a week in the U.S. and is broadcast internationally in 122 countries.

Oprah began her broadcasting career at WVOL radio in Nashville while still in high school. At the age of 19, she became the youngest person and the first African-American woman to anchor the news at Nashville's WTVF-TV.

Oprah's commitment to use her life to make a difference in the lives of others has extended beyond the realm of television into film, print, radio, education and philanthropy. Together, her accomplishments have established her as one of the most respected and admired public figures today. In addition to numerous daytime Emmys, other awards and honors, she was named one of the 100 Most Influential People in the 20th Century by *Time* magazine.

Photo by Brad Barket/Getty Images
Oprah Winfrey
Chairman
Harpo, Inc.

www.boeing.com

SOME SEE A WALL. OTHERS, A BRIDGE.

It takes vision to empower a community and courage to enact change. We salute those who understand the passion of possibility. Boeing is proud to support individuals and organizations that inspire betterment for minority communities everywhere.

BOEING
Forever New Frontiers

"I want to be remembered as the guy who gave his all whenever he was on the field."

WALTER PAYTON, 1954-1999
CHICAGO BEARS RUNNING BACK

Celebrating African-American Achievements

Lovie Smith
Head Coach
Chicago Bears

Lovie Smith is in his third year as the head coach of the Chicago Bears. Smith led the Bears to the 2005 NFC North Division title and earned NFL Coach of the Year honors in his second season.

The 13th head coach in Bears history effective January 15, 2004, Smith previously served three seasons as the defensive coordinator of the St. Louis Rams. He helped the Rams to the Super Bowl in 2001 and became assistant head coach in 2003. He also coached linebackers with the Tampa Bay Buccaneers from 1996 to 2000.

Smith coached 13 years at six different colleges after beginning his coaching career in 1980 at his hometown high school in Big Sandy, Texas. Smith was a two-time All-American and three-time all-conference defensive back in college at Tulsa.

Smith and his wife, MaryAnne, have three sons, Mikal, Matthew, and Miles, and twin grandsons, Malachi and Noah. An active contributor to the American Diabetes Association, he and his wife also started a foundation to help qualified high school students from low socio-economic backgrounds afford and attend college.

Gill Byrd
Defensive Quality Control Coach
Chicago Bears

Gill Byrd is in his first season as the Bears' defensive quality control coach. Hired on February 20, 2006, Byrd came to Chicago after beginning his coaching career over three seasons in St. Louis. His first two seasons were spent as the Rams' defensive assistant before being promoted to assistant secondary coach in 2005.

Playing his entire ten-year NFL career with the San Diego Chargers, Byrd retired after the 1993 season. He remains the team's all-time leader in interceptions (42) and interception return yards (546). A first-round draft pick by the Chargers in 1983, Byrd was a two-time Pro Bowler and led all NFL cornerbacks in interceptions from 1989 to 1991. He was inducted into the Chargers Hall of Fame in 1998.

Byrd returned to the NFL with the Green Bay Packers in 1999, serving as the team's executive director of player programs and community affairs for two seasons (1999-2001).

Byrd graduated from San Jose State University with a degree in finance. He and his wife, Marilyn, have two sons playing college football, Gill II at New Mexico State, and Jairus at Oregon.

Celebrating African-American Achievements

Darryl Drake
Wide Receivers Coach
Chicago Bears

Darryl Drake is in his third season as the Bears' wide receivers coach. Hired on February 6, 2004, Drake came to Chicago after six seasons (1998-2003) as the receivers coach at the University of Texas, adding the title of associate head coach in 2003.

A veteran of 21 seasons of collegiate coaching, Drake began his coaching career at Western Kentucky as a graduate assistant. He spent nine seasons with the Hilltoppers (1983-1991) before moving on to Georgia for five years and then to Baylor for one.

Drake was an all-conference wide receiver at Western Kentucky University (WKU) during his three-year career (1975, 1977-1978) and helped the Hilltoppers to a conference championship as a senior. He spent time in the NFL and the CFL while earning his bachelor's and master's degrees from WKU.

Drake was an all-state performer in football and an All-American in both track and field and basketball at Flaget High School in Louisville. He and his wife, Sheila, have three daughters, Shanice, Felisha, and Marian. Drake is an investor in Hilltoppers, Inc., which owns several restaurants in Texas.

Harold Goodwin
Assistant Offensive Line Coach
Chicago Bears

Harold Goodwin is in his third season as the Bears' assistant offensive line coach. He joined the organization on January 27, 2004 after spending four seasons as the offensive line coach at Central Michigan from 2000 to 2003.

Goodwin began his coaching career in 1997 as a graduate assistant at the University of Michigan, his alma mater. There, he helped the Wolverines win a national title while working with an offensive line that featured four future NFL performers. He moved on to a full-time position at Eastern Michigan in 1998, where he coached tight ends and tackles for a year before being promoted to offensive line coach.

Goodwin went to high school in Columbia, South Carolina, where he earned two letters in basketball and football. An offensive lineman for the University of Michigan from 1992 to 1994, he spent two seasons as a student assistant before earning his degree in management/communications.

Goodwin and his wife, Monica, have two daughters, Kylee and Miya, and are expecting their third child. His brother, Jonathan, played with the New York Jets from 2002 to 2005.

THE INAUGURAL EDITION *Who's Who In Black Chicago*®

Celebrating African-American Achievements

Don Johnson
Defensive Line Coach
Chicago Bears

Don Johnson is in his second season as the Bears' defensive line coach. Hired on February 16, 2005, Johnson came to Chicago after five seasons at UCLA where he was the Bruins' defensive line coach and recruiting coordinator.

A 20-year veteran of college coaching, Johnson began his coaching career at Santa Ana Valley High School (SAVHS) in California from 1976 to 1982. He returned to SAVHS in 1986 after coaching at Jersey City State College from 1984 to 1985. Johnson coached at Riverside Community College for six years, interrupted by two years at Cal State Fullerton. He coached at Nevada-Reno from 1995 to 1999, during which time he spent two off-seasons in the NFL minority coaching internship program with the San Francisco 49ers.

Johnson was a defensive lineman at Butler Community College (1973) and Jersey City State (1974-1976). He spent 25 years as a high school and college basketball official, including eight years at the Division I level.

He and his wife, Deborah, have two daughters, Denise and Leanna, and one son, Don Jr. A fourth son, Duane, died in an automobile accident in 2002.

Tim Spencer
Running Backs Coach
Chicago Bears

Tim Spencer is in his third season as the Bears' running backs coach. Hired on January 27, 2004, he came to the NFL following ten seasons of coaching at his alma mater, The Ohio State University (OSU), where he contributed to a Heisman Trophy-winning running back and a national championship.

Spencer helped Chicago to its first 2,000-yard rushing season in 15 years as the Bears totaled 2,099 rushing yards in 2005 while rushing for 100 or more yards in 13 regular season games. Spencer was part of three Big Ten championship teams as a coach at OSU and helped produce a 1,000-yard rusher in six of those ten years.

Spencer had a nine-year professional career highlighted by six years with the San Diego Chargers from 1985 to 1990. The third-leading rusher in OSU history with 3,553 yards, he led the team in rushing yards his final two seasons and was the Buckeyes' co-captain and MVP as a senior. Spencer returned to OSU in 1993 to finish his degree requirements. Spencer and his wife, Gilda, have two sons, Cole and Evan.

Celebrating African-American Achievements

Steven Wilks
Defensive Backs Coach
Chicago Bears

Steven Wilks is in his first season as the Bears' defensive backs coach after being hired on February 16, 2006. Wilks came to Chicago after two seasons as the defensive backs coach under Ty Willingham at Notre Dame in 2004 and the University of Washington in 2005.

Wilks coached at eight different schools during his 11-year college coaching career. He began his career as the defensive coordinator at Johnson C. Smith University from 1995 to 1996. Wilks then served in the same position from 1997 to 1998 at Savannah State before becoming their head coach for the 1999 season. He coached defensive backs at Illinois State in 2000 and Appalachian State in 2001. Wilks was the co-coordinator of the defense at East Tennessee State in 2002 before coaching at Bowling Green State in 2003.

A defensive back at Appalachian State from 1987 to 1991, Wilks went to training camp with the Seattle Seahawks and played one season for the Charlotte Rage of the Arena Football League. The native of Charlotte, North Carolina holds a bachelor's degree in communications. He and his wife, Marcia, have a daughter, Marissa.

Morocco Brown
Assistant Director of Pro Personnel
Chicago Bears

Morocco Brown is in his sixth season as the Bears' assistant director of pro personnel. Hired to his current position in 2001, Brown's primary responsibilities are scouting individual players on AFC teams as well as players in other professional leagues.

Brown came to Chicago after serving as an assistant scout with the Washington Redskins in 2000. He had a short stint as an intern with the Indianapolis Colts in 1999 after serving a yearlong internship with the Atlantic Coast Conference working in the administration of championship events.

A two-time honorable mention all-conference selection as a linebacker at North Carolina State from 1994 to 1998, Brown was a senior captain and the first player in Wolfpack history to lead the team in tackles for three straight years. He was a three-sport prep performer at Kecoughtan High School in his hometown of Hampton, Virginia. An all-state selection in football, Brown was named the outstanding prep athlete in the Tidewater area his senior year.

He and his wife, Kendra, are expecting the birth of their first child, a son, in May of 2006.

THE INAUGURAL EDITION *Who's Who In Black Chicago*

Celebrating African-American Achievements

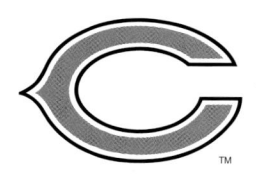

Bobbie Howard
Director of Player Development
Chicago Bears

Bobbie Howard is in his third season as the Bears' director of player development. A veteran of three seasons as a player with Chicago, Howard returned to the team in his current capacity in 2004.

Howard implements the NFL's player assistance programs for the Bears, paramount among those being continuing education and internships. Howard also organizes the team's rookie education seminars and provides services to help new players relocate and become acclimated to life in Chicago.

Playing in 35 games with the Bears at linebacker from 2001 to 2003, Howard totaled 46 special teams tackles during that time with a career-high 22 in 2001. He started nine games at linebacker in 2002 and totaled a career-high 57 tackles.

A college linebacker at Notre Dame from 1995 to 1998, Howard started his final two years and compiled 245 tackles during his career. A native of Rand, West Virginia, he graduated from Notre Dame in 1999 with a double major in finance and computer applications. A three-sport prep star, Howard was a two-time all-state performer while helping DuPont High School to a pair of state football titles.

Tony Medlin
Head Equipment Manager
Chicago Bears

Tony Medlin is in his 20th season with the Chicago Bears and his tenth as the team's head equipment manager. He is responsible for ordering and organizing the team's inventory of apparel and equipment and serves as the team's liaison with the NFL's sole apparel provider, Reebok.

After the 2000 season, Medlin was recognized as the NFL's top equipment manager. Two seasons earlier, he was selected to coordinate the game ball operations for Super Bowl XXXIII and has done so for the last eight years.

Named one of the NFL's first African-American head equipment managers in 1997, Medlin initially joined the Bears as an assistant equipment manager in 1987. He previously served as athletic equipment manager at North Carolina Central University from 1982 to 1987, after he graduated from there with a bachelor of science degree in therapeutic recreation.

Medlin and his wife, Chandra, have one daughter, Brandy. Medlin is the older brother of Ron Medlin, head athletic trainer for the Atlanta Falcons. Involved in numerous charitable endeavors, he is chairman of the annual Chicago Bears Coat Drive.

Celebrating African-American Achievements

Kevin Turks
Assistant Pro Scout
Chicago Bears

Kevin Turks is in his sixth season in Chicago and his fifth as the Bears' assistant pro scout. Hired to his current position in 2002 after one season as a scouting intern, Turks handles advance scouting of individual players and teams across the NFL as well as players in other professional leagues.

Turks came to Chicago after serving a yearlong internship in 2000 with Walt Disney's Wide World of Sports in Orlando, Florida working in event management.

A four-year letter-winner as a linebacker at North Carolina State from 1994 to 1998, Turks was a senior captain while earning the team's 12th Man of the Year award. He is an active member of the Wolfpack Alumni Association.

Turks was a prep performer in football, basketball, and track at Tucker High School in his hometown of Tucker, Georgia. A three-time all-state selection in football, he was also a member of the 400-meter relay team that won the state championship his senior year.

Turks and his wife, Lakeisha, reside in Beach Park, Illinois.

Jacinta Williams
Stadium Sales & Fan Services Assistant
Chicago Bears

Jacinta Williams is in her fourth season with the Chicago Bears. After two seasons as a fan services assistant, Williams added similar duties in the stadium sales department to her title in 2006. In her dual role, she handles administrative duties for both departments on a daily basis and manages 50 fan services representatives at home games.

Williams graduated from the University of Illinois at Urbana-Champaign with a bachelor of science degree in kinesiology. During her final two years at Illinois, she served as a volunteer Illini recruiter and program coordinator, assisting in the on-campus visits of football recruits and the annual post-season banquet.

A student of physical fitness, Williams is a certified personal trainer and is studying to become a clinical massage therapist.

Born and raised in Chicago, Williams attended Thornwood High School in South Holland, Illinois. She currently resides in Calumet City, Illinois where she dedicates free time to serving as a role model for children. She volunteers in a variety of roles for the Dolton Bears youth football team as well as in several church youth groups.

THE INAUGURAL EDITION *Who's Who In Black Chicago*®

COMMEMORATE YOUR APPEARANCE IN WHO'S WHO IN BLACK Chicago®

THE INAUGURAL EDITION
With A Beautiful Handcrafted Plaque.

Your picture and biographical data will be mounted on a 16"x 20" rich, hand stained 3/4" birch wood plaque and sealed with a non-glare finish.

Order Your Commemorative Plaque Now!

Only $149.95 • Plus Shipping & Handling
Call (614) 481-7300 Now!
www.whoswhopublishing.com

Chicago's
CORPORATE BRASS

"Success doesn't come to you...you go to it."
MARVA COLLINS
EDUCATOR

Chicago's CORPORATE BRASS
Celebrating African-American Achievements

Yasmin Bates
Executive Vice President
Chicagoland - South Division
Harris N.A.

Yasmin T. Bates began her banking career in 1976 when she joined Harris N.A., as a commercial banking trainee.

Serving as executive vice president at Chicagoland's South Division of Harris N.A., Yasmin's division encompasses more than half of the bank's 200 branches. Among her myriad responsibilities, Yasmin oversees development and implementation of the division's growth strategies, including increasing market share and customer loyalty.

Yasmin is a board member of the Chicago Equity Fund, Community Investment Corporation, Glenwood School for Boys, and The Network of Real Estate Professionals. She is a member of the University of Illinois Business Advisory Council, The University of Chicago's Visiting Forum, and the Urban Bankers Forum of Chicago. She also served on the special allocations committee of the United Way of Chicago. Mayor Richard M. Daley appointed Yasmin to serve on the first Comprehensive Housing Affordability Strategy committee for the City of Chicago. Additionally, she served on the Fannie Mae National Advisory Board and the American Bankers Association community development committee.

A graduate of the University of Illinois, Yasmin holds a bachelor of science degree in business administration.

Monica Armstrong Billinger
Manager, Corporate
Supplier Diversity
Health Care Service Corporation

Monica Armstrong Billinger is the manager of corporate supplier diversity for Health Care Service Corporation, a mutual legal reserve company, and an independent licensee of the BlueCross BlueShield Association. Monica promotes enterprise-wide procurement opportunities with M/WBE and other diverse businesses, while increasing outreach activities throughout Illinois, Texas, New Mexico, and Oklahoma.

An active member of the Chicago Minority Business Development Council, Chicago United, and the Women's Business Development Council, Monica serves on the Women's Business National Enterprise Council.

The former supplier diversity manager for the State of Missouri, Monica has several years of experience in M/W/DBE certification and business development. She served as the vice president of the Jefferson City Graduate Chapter of Alpha Kappa Alpha Sorority, Inc. Monica appeared in the 2004-2005 premier publication of *Who's Who in Black St. Louis*, and received the President's Choice Award by the Mid-Missouri chapter of the NAACP.

Raised in Maywood, Illinois, Monica earned a bachelor's degree in marketing and an MBA from Lincoln University. The wife of Chicago native Anthony Billinger, they are the proud parents of one son, Julian.

Celebrating African-American Achievements

Chicago's
CORPORATE BRASS

Ty Bonds is vice president of human resources manufacturing, U.S. convenient meals sector. He has overall human resources responsibility for the U.S. convenient meals manufacturing facilities. His primary focus is providing the human resources strategic direction, the execution of employee and organizational excellence strategy, and talent management. Ty joined General Foods Corporation in 1984 at the Chicago Kool-Aid facility.

He has received several awards, most notably the General Foods President Award, the Oscar Mayer President Award, and the YMCA Black Achiever in Industry Awards in Chicago and New York City. Ty also received the INROADS Business Advisor of the Year Award; the Benedict College Charter Day Award; the Kraft Diversity Leadership Award; and the Most Influential African-American Martin Luther King, Jr. Award in Lake County, Illinois. A board trustee for Benedict College, he is a lifetime member of the National Association of African Americans in Human Resources.

Ty holds a bachelor of science degree in human resources and operations management from Northern Illinois University.

Ty lives in the Chicago area with his wife, Denise, and three daughters, Octavia, Ashley, and JonTayé.

Ty Bonds
Vice President
Human Resources Manufacturing
U.S. Convenient Meals Sector
Kraft Foods North America

Julian E. Brown is corporate contributions manager for Nicor Gas. He is responsible for corporate contributions, memberships, volunteerism, scholarships, matching gifts, and community programs.

Julian currently serves on the boards of the leadership council for Metropolitan Open Communities and Illinois Dollar for Scholars. He is also chairman of United Way's Strength Through Diversity initiative, and was recently presented with the Professional Grant Maker of the Year award by the West Suburban Philanthropic Network. Likewise, he was noted as "Someone You Should Know in Philanthropy" by *The Business Ledger*.

An instructor for the Academy for Non-Profit Excellence at the College of DuPage, Julian is one of the founding members of the Corporate Volunteer Council of Metropolitan Chicago. He is also one of the founding fathers of the African American Management Network – known at Nicor Gas as "En Rapport."

Holding a bachelor's degree in business administration from Bradley University in Peoria, Julian received an MBA from Benedictine University in Lisle.

A Special Olympics basketball coach, Julian and his wife, Carla, have two sons, Darren and Andrew.

Julian E. Brown
Corporate Contributions Manager
Nicor Gas

Chicago's CORPORATE BRASS

Celebrating African-American Achievements

At The University of Chicago, Susan Campbell serves to advance community and city government relations, develop partnerships, and build programs that enhance the quality of life in mid-south side communities. She works internally on campus, planning initiatives and neighborhood real estate projects.

Before joining The University, Susan was a partner in Chicago's oldest African-American-owned architectural, planning, and construction management firm, Campbell Tiu Campbell (CTC). At CTC, Susan was responsible for business development and the firm's urban planning practice. Over the past 20 years, she was involved in several important urban planning and redevelopment projects in Chicago.

Susan holds a bachelor's degree in economics and sociology from Tufts University, a master's in architecture from the Illinois Institute of Technology, and a master's in urban planning and policy from the University of Illinois at Chicago.

Susan has served on the board of directors of the National Organization of Minority Architects, American Institute of Architects Chicago Chapter, Women in Planning and Development, and Chicago's Near South Planning board.

A Chicago resident, Susan is married to Don, and they have a daughter, Lauren.

Susan M. Campbell
Associate Vice President
Community & Government Affairs
The University of Chicago

Jerry Carpenter was born and raised in Philadelphia. He graduated from Indiana University of Pennsylvania in 1987 and began a lengthy sales career with Johnson & Johnson, relocating him to Chicago. Jerry's achievements included winning the President's Trophy, Sales Representative of the Year, Balanced Performer, and 100% Club. Those achievements allowed him to be promoted up the sales ladder.

After ten outstanding years with J&J, Jerry went to Ameritech where he managed solution consultants, successfully increasing sales in corporate accounts. He was recruited from SBC/Ameritech to Advo, where he served as area sales manager. He managed sales teams to quarterly awards, as well as the President's Club.

In 2004, Jerry moved to RR Donnelley, the largest print corporation in North America, with annual sales of $8.3 billion dollars. He was hired as the director of sales in the Premedia Technologies business unit and promoted to vice president of sales.

Jerry is married with three children, and serves as treasurer and trustee board member at Greater Open Door Baptist Church. Jerry is a lifetime member of Alpha Phi Alpha Fraternity, Inc.

Jerry Carpenter
Vice President of Sales
RR Donnelley

Celebrating African-American Achievements

Chicago's
CORPORATE BRASS

Eva Chess is a director in external affairs at RR Donnelley where she is responsible for developing strategies to accelerate the inclusion of minority- and woman-owned businesses into the company's supply base. Her role is to design, develop, and oversee a corporate-wide process to increase RR Donnelley's involvement in the economic development of minority and women-owned businesses. A lawyer by training, she also has had careers in investment banking and corporate social responsibility.

Chess holds a bachelor of arts degree from the University of North Carolina, and a juris doctorate from the University of Virginia, where she is a member of the Alumni Council board.

She serves on the Chicago Board of the Jackie Robinson Foundation and on the advisory board of Leadership Illinois. Chess has served as a member of the boards of directors of the United Way of Stamford, Connecticut, the Midwest Women's Center, and the American Association of University Women Educational Foundation. Her professional affiliations include the International Association of Business Communicators, and the American, National, and Virginia Bar Associations.

Chess is an alumna of Leadership America.

Eva Chess
Director, External Affairs
RR Donnelley

During the four years Frank Clark has been with RR Donnelley, he has had a major impact within the marketplace concerning the commercial sales organization. Through his executive relationships, he has been able to expand the company's range of customers. The Alliance Markets Group, that Frank heads, is an innovative business that focuses on driving incremental growth to the integrated print communications businesses of RR Donnelley via forging strategic alliances with MBEs across the country.

He is on the board of the Primo Center for Women and Children and the Chicago Multicultural Dance Center (CMDC) nonprofit board. Additionally, he is a member of the NextGen Network, an organization for future African-American leaders in corporate America, sponsored by the Executive Leadership Council in Washington, D.C. Frank is also a fellow of the Leadership Greater Chicago organization. Additionally, he is a member of the Union League Club in Chicago.

Frank is a native Chicagoan, graduate of Eisenhower High School, and received a bachelor's degree in economics from Northern Illinois University. He also holds an MBA from the Illinois Institute of Technology.

Frank M. Clark III
Corporate Vice President
Alliance Markets Group
RR Donnelly

Chicago's CORPORATE BRASS
Celebrating African-American Achievements

Alfonso "Al" Cobb began his career with Harris in 2002. He now serves as managing director and head of retail brokerage sales at Harris Investor Services.

In this role, Al oversees all of the sales and marketing activities of Harris' retail brokerage division. He supervises teams of recruiting specialists, regional sales managers, brokerage operations managers, and marketing and compliance managers.

Earning his bachelor's degree from Mercer University in Macon, Georgia, he received an MBA from Kennesaw State University in Kennesaw, Georgia.

Al is currently a candidate for his Certified Financial Planner (CFP) designation at DePaul University in Chicago. In addition, he holds his Chartered Estate Planning Practitioner (CEPP) designation and his National Association of Securities Dealers Series 6, 7, 8, 24, 63, and 66 licenses.

Al is a member of the Beta Gamma Sigma Honor Society for AACSB Accredited Business Programs, the National Black MBA Association, and Rotary International.

Alfonso Cobb
Managing Director &
Head of Retail Brokerage Sales
Harris Investor Services

Angela L. Coley is chief operating officer and vice president of sales for Almae Publisher's Representatives, Inc., an independent advertising sales rep company for nationally distributed magazines. A few of which include, *American Legacy*, *American Legacy Woman*, *Being Single*, *Sophisticate's Black Hair Styles and Care Guide*, and the book publication, *Who's Who in Black Chicago*.

As a business partner with her sister, Beverly Coley-Morris, Angela is responsible for the daily operations of the company and manages Almae's national sales accounts and marketing activities for *Sophisticate's Black Hair Styles and Care Guide*.

Angela enjoys singing, is an active member of the Trinity United Church of Christ Women's Chorus, and a member of Alpha Kappa Alpha Sorority, Inc.

Attending Chicago State University, Angela received a bachelor of science degree in business administration. She earned a certificate in the Lawyer's Assistant program at Roosevelt University, and is currently working toward an MBA at Keller Graduate School of Management.

Angela L. Coley
Chief Operating Officer &
Vice President of Sales
Almae Publisher's
Representatives, Inc.

Celebrating African-American Achievements

Chicago's
CORPORATE BRASS

Lester Coney joined Aon as senior managing director in 1998. One of the company's top global producers, he co-led the team responsible for securing the largest human resources consulting account awarded in the history of the company. At Aon, he keeps the company connected to ethnic, minority, and community organizations by providing corporate support for key initiatives and events.

Coney holds a bachelor's degree from George Williams University. He is chairman of the Goodman Theatre; vice chair of the DuSable Museum of African Art and History board of trustees; chairman of City Year Chicago; founding chairman of the Congo Square Theatre's board; and a trustee at Aurora University and Roosevelt University.

Coney's countless honors include 100 Black Men for 2005, *Crain's Chicago Business*' Top 50 Minorities in Business in 2004, and Chicago United's 2003 Business Leaders of Color. He is also an appointed member of the Illinois State Treasurer's Office Business Roundtable and represents Aon on the leaders council for Chicago United. Coney resides in Chicago's West Loop and is the father of two children, Chanel and Javon.

Lester "Les" Coney
Senior Managing Director
Aon Risk Services, Inc.

Heather A. Davis is vice president of marketing and sales for Nia Enterprises, LLC. She is a sales and marketing professional with more than 20 years of media marketing and sales experience.

For three years, Davis was on the faculty of Columbia College in Chicago, where she taught core marketing courses in the advertising studies department. Before joining Nia Enterprises, Davis was vice president and director of sales for Central City Productions, an independent television production, sales, and syndication company that produces the annual *Stellar Gospel Music Awards* and the business weekly *Black Enterprise Report*. Servicing both agency and direct accounts, she boosted revenue from existing clients such as Coca-Cola, Johnson & Johnson, Toyota, General Motors, and McDonald's by creating promotions and exposure opportunities outside of the traditional media space.

Davis is a member of the Market Research Association, the Broadcast Advertising Club, and American Women in Radio & Television.

A graduate of Columbia College in Chicago, she received a bachelor's degree with honors in advertising. Davis enjoys sharing her outdoor sports interest with her adult daughter, Lauren Brooke.

Heather A. Davis
Vice President, Marketing & Sales
Nia Enterprises, LLC

Chicago's CORPORATE BRASS

Celebrating African-American Achievements

Amina J. Dickerson
Senior Director
Global Community Involvement
Kraft Foods

As senior director of global community involvement, Amina J. Dickerson is responsible for Kraft's philanthropic strategy worldwide, including programs in health and wellness, hunger and employee engagement.

Previously, Dickerson held executive posts with the Chicago Historical Society and the National Museum of African Art at the Smithsonian Institution. She was also president of Chicago's DuSable Museum of African American History. Named Distinguished Visitor with the John D. and Catherine T. MacArthur Foundation, Dickerson was appointed a Class XVI Kellogg fellow, and a Newberry Library fellow.

Dickerson is an advisor for Chicago's African American Legacy Fund, Department of Cultural Affairs, and for the Harris Theater at Millennium Park. She was also named to the International Committee of the Council of Foundations in 2005. Dickerson has received numerous honors for her work including Chicago's Professional Grantor of the Year.

She studied theater and arts management at Emerson College and Harvard University, and holds a master's in arts management from the American University in Washington, D.C. She resides in Chicago's South Shore community with her husband Julian Roberts.

Willard S. Evans, Jr.
Vice President
Gas Supply & Engineering
Peoples Energy Corporation

Willard S. Evans, Jr. is vice president of gas supply and engineering for Peoples Gas and North Shore Gas, the utilities of Peoples Energy. He has held this position since October of 2004.

After joining Peoples Energy in 1974 as an engineering intern, Evans rose through the ranks in the gas operations division. From October 2003 to October 2004, he was vice president of operations for Peoples Gas. From 1997 to 2003, he was vice president of information technology services.

Evans serves on the board of Chicago Commons and the advisory board of the Masters in Technology Program at Northwestern University. He is a member of the Chicago Chapter of the Society of Information Management (past chair and president), American Gas Association, Northwestern Club of Chicago, and the Kellogg Alumni Club of Chicago.

Evans holds a bachelor of science degree in electrical engineering and a master's degree in management from Northwestern University. He and his wife, Debra, live in Skokie, Illinois. They have a daughter and son.

Celebrating African-American Achievements

Chicago's
CORPORATE BRASS

Ernest Freeman is supplier diversity manager for QTG (Quaker Oats, Tropicana, and Gatorade), a division of PepsiCo. Responsible for increasing the effectiveness of supplier diversity efforts here in Chicago, QTG spent more than $238 million with minority and women businesses in 2005.

Before joining PepsiCo, Ernie held managerial positions with Federal-Mogul Corporation where he was the architect for the company's formal supplier diversity program. He began his career as a logistics officer in the U.S. Army's Third and Sixth Infantry Divisions and culminated his career at the rank of major with the Industrial Operations Command, Rock Island, Illinois.

Freeman is board president for the Chicago Minority Business Development Council and the 2006 recipient of the council's Andres C. Rasmussen, Jr. Award and the SBA 2006 Minority Small Business Champion of the Year.

A native of Chicago and a member of Omega Psi Phi Fraternity, Inc., Ernie has a master of science degree in management from the University of La Verne and a bachelor of science degree in business administration from Western Illinois University. He and his lovely wife of 23 years have two children.

Ernest V. Freeman
Manager, Supplier Diversity
PepsiCo

E. Morris Communications, Inc.'s (EMC) youngest executive, Sheila Y. Gordon, focuses on organizational design and development for "the only advertising agency that Talks To The Soul." With more than $40 million in billings, Wal-Mart and Tyson Foods topping the client roster, Sheila girds her staff by ascribing to a holistic management approach that requires understanding the professional and social side of each employee. Sheila's human resource activity spans 15 years across various industries.

A dual-degreed alumna of the University of Illinois, Sheila earned a bachelor of science in psychology, and a master's in human resources and organizational development.

An active member of her community, she is passionate about mentorship and philanthropy. A few of her affiliations include the American Association of Advertising Agencies (Chicago, HR chapter), Society for Human Resource Managers, Notaries Association of Illinois, and Alpha Kappa Alpha Sorority, Inc.

Sheila is the proud recipient of EMC's highest employee honor, The Soul of Excellence Award. Her drive is contagious as she is endearingly called, HR Lady. Her motto is, "Always have a pulse on what matters to your staff."

Sheila Y. Gordon
Human Resources Director
E. Morris Communications, Inc.

Chicago's CORPORATE BRASS

Celebrating African-American Achievements

Deborah Gray-Young is vice president and director of media services for E. Morris Communications, Inc. (EMC), a full-service advertising agency specializing in connecting premium brands and services to African-American consumers. Relying on more than 25 years of experience, Deborah is responsible for overseeing the planning and placement of advertising budgets for EMC's Fortune 500 clients.

Deborah, who is currently the chairperson of the Multicultural Media Committee for the Association of American Advertising Agencies, is frequently quoted in business and trade publications including *Black Enterprise, USA Today, The Washington Post,* and *Advertising Age*. She is also a frequent presenter at industry conferences including, the Target Market News African American Research Summit, The Power of Urban Radio, and the Multicultural Media Expo. Likewise, she contributed to the Cabletelevision Advertising Bureau's annual Multicultural Marketing Guides.

A member of Christ Universal Temple, Deborah is a facilitator of spiritual empowerment classes. She also serves on the board of directors of the Universal Foundation for Better Living.

A published author of inspirational booklets, Deborah is an avid reader and amateur photographer.

Deborah Gray-Young
Vice President &
Director of Media Services
E. Morris Communications, Inc.

Bobbie Gregg is vice president and global chief compliance officer of Aon Corporation, with responsibility for compliance risk management and business conduct across the Aon enterprise. She also oversees compliance with the requirements of the Aon Regulatory Settlement Agreement, which requires Aon to implement certain business reforms in the U.S. and abroad. Bobbie held similar positions at Sears, Roebuck and Co., and Bank One prior to joining Aon.

Bobbie was identified as a leader to watch in "Minority Corporate Counsel Association Spotlights In-House Women-of-Color: 15 Leaders to Watch," published in *Diversity & The Bar* (March/April 2003). Likewise, she was recognized for her leadership role at Sears in "Women at the Top in Corporate America," published in *Ebony* (March 2001).

Earning a juris doctorate, cum laude, from Northwestern University School of Law in Chicago, Bobbie received a bachelor's from the University of Illinois.

She is married to David Gregg, and they are the parents of three lovely daughters.

Bobbie Gregg
Vice President &
Global Chief Compliance Officer
Aon Corporation

Celebrating African-American Achievements

Chicago's
CORPORATE BRASS

Charles Horn III began his career with BMO Financial Group, parent company of Harris, 18 years ago. Today, he serves as managing director and head of the direct business development team for the U.S. cash management sales division of BMO's investment banking arm, Harris Nesbitt.

Charles leads a specialized team of professionals that cover the global insurance industry, securitization and equity sponsors, and diversified financial services market segments. He has an ongoing mandate to develop new revenue sources for the bank, targeting the above industries, as well as managing several of the firm's largest clients.

Charles earned his bachelor's degree from the Illinois Institute of Technology, with concentrations in information technology management and accounting. Additionally, he serves on the executive board of the Have a Heart for Sickle Cell Anemia Foundation.

Charles Horn III
Managing Director
Harris Nesbitt/BMO Nesbitt Burns

Richard D. Jackson, a Chicago native, has worked in the field of human services for 34 years. Earning a bachelor's degree in clinical social work and substance abuse from Northeastern Illinois University, Jackson holds a master's degree in human service administration from Spertus College. He has worked as a clinician, supervisor, college instructor, trainer, administrator, and policy advocate in all areas of human services.

In his current position, Jackson is responsible for the coordination, negotiation, and management of all human service agreements with governmental funding sources and endowment entities. Additionally, he provides executive leadership, policy direction, and the coordination of the agency's community relations.

He currently serves on the Community Behavioral Healthcare Association of Illinois board (past president); the Chicago Drug and Enforcement Task Force; the Cook County State's Attorney African-American Advisory Council; and the Bristol-Meyer-Squibb Pharmaceuticals advisory board. Jackson is also a member of the Illinois Advisory Council on Alcoholism and Drug Dependency; the Chicago Community Development Advisory Council; and is the board chair of New Visions of Hope Foundation.

Richard is an avid boater, and enjoys spending his summer days on Lake Michigan.

Richard D. Jackson
Vice President, External Relations
Habilitative Systems, Inc.

Chicago's CORPORATE BRASS

Celebrating African-American Achievements

Elliott Jones is managing director of the Aon Chicago Service Center, located in Glenview, Illinois. He is responsible for a staff of more than 340 people whose job it is to provide service to 17 Aon offices, in support of their clients.

Before joining Aon in 1999, Elliott was employed by Willis and Alexander & Alexander, where he managed brokerage operations specializing in casualty insurance and alternative risks programs. He began his career in 1971 as an underwriter for CNA Insurance Company and later joined Zurich Insurance Company, where he managed a national account team focused on large corporate clients. While at Willis he was named president and CEO of the Chicago office of Willis' wholesale broker, Stewart Smith.

Elliott was recently named vice president of the Chicago chapter of the National African American Insurance Association.

Elliott received a bachelor's degree in economics and business administration from Wheaton College in 1969. He earned the associate in risk management (A.R.M.) designation in 1988.

A native of Chicago, Elliott has six children ranging in age from 17 to 31.

Elliott Jones, A.R.M.
Managing Director
Aon Client Services
Aon Risk Services, Inc.

Anedra Kerr is vice president of development at Advocate Charitable Foundation, the philanthropic arm of Advocate Health Care, which is the largest health care delivery system in metropolitan Chicago and is recognized as one of the top ten systems in the country. Anedra is responsible for helping raise $24 million annually in philanthropic support for Advocate.

Under Anedra's leadership, Advocate's special events doubled in revenue and attendance over four years. In her efforts to generate philanthropic support for Advocate South Suburban Hospital and Advocate Trinity Hospital, she increased giving by 49%. In 2005, she was named an Advocate Star Performer.

Committed to community enrichment, Anedra serves as a board member of the Peoples Jazz Theatre and is a member of Alpha Kappa Alpha Sorority, Incorporated. She is an instructor in the Undergraduate Leadership Program at Northwestern University. She has served as a speaker for the Association of Fundraising Professionals and at the Expo for Today's Black Woman.

Anedra received a bachelor of science degree in marketing from Hampton University and a master of science degree in communication from Northwestern University.

Anedra Kerr
Vice President of Development
Advocate Charitable Foundation

Celebrating African-American Achievements

Chicago's
CORPORATE BRASS

Paul D. King began his career with Harris in 2004. He currently serves as vice president and senior portfolio manager with Harris Private Bank, which provides comprehensive financial services to affluent clients. Paul specializes in developing customized asset management programs for large and complex trust and investment relationships.

Paul earned a bachelor's degree from Butler University in Indianapolis, Indiana and an MBA from the Kellstadt Graduate School of Business at DePaul University.

He is a Certified Financial Analyst Charterholder (CFA), a member of the Association of Investment Management Research, and a member of the Investment Analysts Society of Chicago.

Paul D. King
Vice President &
Senior Portfolio Manager
Harris Private Bank

LaTretta Long-Hill began her career with Harris in 1982. Today, she serves as vice president of PCCG product operations U.S., service delivery and business loan servicing team at Harris N.A.

In this role, LaTretta oversees the delivery of support services related to North American Item Processing (NAIP) and business loan operations for Harris.

LaTretta is currently pursuing her business degree at DePaul University in Chicago. She is an active member of the Business Administration Institute (BAI), and has served as a member of Harris' Diversity Council. In addition, she works with the bank's African-American affinity group, known as AALPs (African American League of Professionals).

LaTretta Long-Hill
Vice President
PCCG Product Operations
Harris N.A.

Chicago's CORPORATE BRASS

Celebrating African-American Achievements

Anthony McCain is vice president of distribution for Nicor Gas. In this role, he is responsible for the distribution of natural gas throughout Nicor Gas' 32,000-mile pipeline system, which serves more than two million customers across the Nicor Gas service territory, encompassing the upper third of Illinois.

Anthony is a member of the American Gas Association, Center for Economic Development, and the American Association of Blacks in Energy. He also serves on the board of directors of Voices for Illinois Children and the Midwest Energy Association. Anthony is a fellow of Leadership of Greater Chicago, a think tank for developing community leaders and a network for executing civic and community action.

Earning a bachelor's degree from Benedictine College in 1984, Anthony also received a master's degree in business administration from Benedictine College in 1993.

A resident of Bolingbrook, Anthony is married with five children.

Anthony McCain
Vice President, Distribution
Nicor Gas

Lena McClinton is a manager within the production planning division of the Cintas Corporation. Cintas designs, manufactures, and implements corporate identity uniform programs, and provides entrance mats, restroom supplies, promotional products, first aid and safety products, fire protection services, and document management services for approximately 700,000 business.

McClinton is responsible for the purchasing and managing of all stock and exclusive raw materials for the national accounts sales division of Cintas. She also manages the new centralized maintenance team for Chicago.

Joining Cintas in 1985, McClinton spent the last ten years in production planning. Prior to that, her other areas of responsibility included, but was not limited to, internal auditor, western zone care team leader, production planning auditor, collection manager, and accounts receivable.

McClinton attended the University of Illinois at Chicago. She and her husband Emmanuel, are the proud parents of a daughter, Tanika, a son, Emmanuel, and a grandson, Letroy.

Lena McClinton
Manager
Cintas Corporation

Celebrating African-American Achievements

Chicago's
CORPORATE BRASS

Richelle Parham is senior vice president and general manager of Digitas Chicago. As general manager of the Chicago office, Richelle oversees day-to-day operations with responsibility for finance, staffing, human resources, technology, and facilities. She also guides strategy and execution for key client relationships and helps drive new business development.

Promoted through a series of positions since joining Digitas in 1994, Richelle previously managed Digitas' relationship with InterContinental Hotels Group. Her experience base spans relationship and interactive marketing, content management, and Web platforms/eCommerce across diverse clients. Some of which include Bayer Pharmaceuticals, AT&T Wireless, and American Express.

Prior to joining Digitas, Richelle was with Citicorp units for several years.

Richelle, who has served on the steering committee for the United Way Young Leaders Society, received bachelor's degrees in both marketing, and design and merchandising, from Drexel University.

Richelle Parham
Senior Vice President &
General Manager
Digitas Chicago

Cheryl Pearson-McNeil is a communications professional known for her unique ability to balance her business expertise with a creative flair. As an award-winning executive with more than 21 years of public relations, communications, and writing experience, Cheryl brings high energy and enthusiasm to every industry she has touched. Her expertise spans a diverse number of industries including advertising, television, public affairs, the nonprofit sector, and the continually changing world of politics.

She served as the press secretary for city treasurer Miriam Santos, the first Latino elected official in the City of Chicago. Cheryl also established the first marketing and public relations departments for the multimillion dollar nonprofit organizations in the Chicago area including: the Girl Scouts, the YWCA, and Boys & Girls Clubs. As a former director of station relations for WMAQ, the NBC affiliate in Chicago, Cheryl is a familiar and welcome face in the diverse and multicultural communities in and around Chicago.

Cheryl holds a bachelor of arts degree in public relations from Purdue University, and an MBA from the Keller Graduate School of Management.

Cheryl Pearson-McNeil
Vice President
Communications &
Community Affairs
Nielsen Media Research

Chicago's CORPORATE BRASS

Celebrating African-American Achievements

Wynona Redmond is public affairs director for Dominick's Finer Foods. She oversees the operations of the public affairs office including public relations, local and state government relations, community relations, special events, and the Dominick's Children's Foundation.

Wynona has strengthened Dominick's connection to the community through special events including the Dominick's annual Ministers' Breakfast. She participates in food drives with the Greater Chicago Food Depository, and awards scholarship dollars to the United Negro College Fund and to Dominick's employees.

Prior to Dominick's, Wynona served in a public affairs management capacity for the Illinois Department of Children & Family Services, the Chicago Housing Authority, and Cook County Hospital.

Active in the North Lawndale community, Wynona is a member of St. Agatha Catholic Church and serves as supervisor of the Lawndale Civic and Educational Jr. Girls and Boys Club. She is the newly elected president of the National Black Public Relations Society, and a member of several distinguished boards, councils, and committees.

A resident of Oak Park, Illinois, Wynona graduated from Loyola University of Chicago with a bachelor's degree in communications.

Wynona Redmond
Public Affairs Director
Dominick's Finer Foods

Lauri M. Sanders is director of public and governmental affairs for Jewel-Osco, the Midwest's largest food and drug retailer. Lauri has responsibility for community, government and media relations, and corporate contributions, and helps implement the company's strategic plan.

Prior to joining Jewel-Osco, Lauri served as director of public affairs and communications for Chicago State University. She has also served as director of news affairs for the Chicago Police Department, and director of media relations for Northwestern Memorial Hospital.

A graduate of Spelman College in Atlanta, Georgia, Lauri holds a master's degree in journalism from Roosevelt University, and is a member of Alpha Kappa Alpha Sorority, Inc. She currently sits on the board of directors for the Bottomless Closet, the Cosmopolitan Chamber of Commerce, and the National Black Public Relations Society.

She is a native Chicagoan, who resides in the city's South Side with her family.

Lauri M. Sanders
Director, Public & Government Affairs
Jewel-Osco

Celebrating African-American Achievements

Chicago's CORPORATE BRASS

Lemuel "Lem" Seabrook III began his career with BMO Financial Group, parent company to Harris, more than 20 years ago. Today, he serves as managing director of asset portfolio management for the bank's Investment Banking Group (IBG).

In this role, Lem is responsible for the Chicago-based optimization division of the bank's asset portfolio management team. This division engages in the buying and selling of credit exposures using credit derivatives and structured products, in order to actively manage the risk, return, and diversification of the IBG credit portfolio.

Lem is a graduate of The University of Chicago, holding both a bachelor's degree in business, and an MBA in finance.

He is a member of the International Association of Credit Portfolio Managers (IACPM), and of the Chicago Council of Foreign Relations.

Lemuel Seabrook III
Managing Director
Asset Portfolio Management
Financial Group

James Smith is the vice president of institutional marketing and client services for Ariel Capital Management, LLC. He specializes in business development and client servicing for Ariel's institutional and advisor accounts across the central region.

He joined Ariel in 2001 after working for Goldman Sachs & Company, where he provided customized wealth management services for high net worth individuals and families. Before Goldman, however, James was a management consultant with Deloitte Consulting, where he focused on supply chain optimization and organizational turnaround. In addition, James spent four years as a manufacturing department manager and process engineer with The Procter & Gamble Company.

Beyond Ariel, James is actively involved in the community, serving as a board member for the Chicago Children's Museum; a Trustee of Talladega College; a local school council community representative for Ariel Community Academy; as well as a Heartland Housing board member for The Heartland Alliance.

Graduating from Princeton University with a bachelor's degree in mechanical engineering, James received a dual master's degree in marketing and operations from Northwestern University's J.L. Kellogg Graduate School of Management, and the McCormick School of Engineering.

James Smith
Vice President
Institutional Marketing & Client Services
Ariel Capital Management, LLC

THE INAUGURAL EDITION *Who's Who In Black Chicago*®

Chicago's CORPORATE BRASS

Celebrating African-American Achievements

As general manager at 150 N. Michigan Ave. (previously known as the Smurfit-Stone Container Building), Nicole Spencer is responsible for the day-to-day operation of the 700,000-square foot office tower. Leading a team of 30, her responsibilities include management of the building's $20 million budget and oversight of capital improvement projects. Client satisfaction, tenant retention, and service innovations are hallmarks of Nicole's management style.

Nicole is a licensed attorney and real estate broker with more than eight years of experience managing Class A office properties in Chicago's central business district. In addition to her property responsibilities, she is a member of the Jones Lang LaSalle Chicago market's regional hiring committee and the Jones Lang LaSalle Americas diversity council. Within the Chicago civic community, Nicole is chair of the Building Owners and Managers Association of Chicago diversity committee, and a board member of the Chicago Loop Alliance.

Nicole earned her doctor of jurisprudence from Northwestern University and her bachelor's degree in political science from Bryn Mawr College.

Raised in St. Thomas, U.S. Virgin Islands and Washington, D.C., Nicole enjoys Chicago's rich cultural and social diversity.

Nicole A. B. Spencer
Vice President & General Manager
Jones Lang LaSalle

Rita Taylor-Nash has been employed for nearly 25 years with Health Care Service Corporation (HCSC), doing business as Blue Cross and Blue Shield of Illinois, Texas, New Mexico, and Oklahoma. She has held management positions in various areas of human resources including equal opportunity, affirmative action, and employment.

In her current position as director of corporate diversity, she has developed and implemented the company's diversity initiative. Through her leadership, HCSC has received several major and national diversity recognitions, including the 2005 Corporate Diversity Award from the Chicago Council on Urban Affairs, DiversityInc's Top 50 companies for diversity, Top 10 companies for Latinos, and Top 10 companies for African Americans.

She completed a transitional year at Yale University before completing a bachelor's in sociology at the University of Chicago. Rita also completed her master's degree at the University of Michigan.

Rita Taylor-Nash
Director of Corporate Diversity
Health Care Service Corporation

Celebrating African-American Achievements

Chicago's
CORPORATE BRASS

Chareice White is corporate director of community relations for Majestic Star and Fitzgeralds Casino Hotel. She is responsible for corporate and local sponsorship, charitable and in-kind donations, and corporate community related events. She also oversees special events for Don H. Barden, chairman and chief executive officer of the first and only African-American-owned-and-operated national casino company. The company consists of five casinos including Majestic Star Casino and Majestic Star II, which are located in Gary, Indiana and service Chicago.

Under the direction of White, the company has donated millions of dollars to various organizations. Very active in the community, she is an integral board member for the Boys & Girls Club of Northwest Indiana; the American Heart Association; the Northwest Indiana Sickle Cell Foundation; the Gary Chamber of Commerce; the National Black Public Relations Society; and the National Coalition of Black Meeting Planners. White is a board member of the Lake County Convention and Visitors Bureau and a member of The Links, Inc.

She is the key developer and organizer of the Majestic Star Student Program (M.S.S.P.) and the Majestic Star Community Ambassadors.

Chareice White
Corporate Director
Community Relations
Majestic Star and
Fitzgeralds Casino Hotel

Kenneth Wilson is vice president/general manager of OnSite, Cardinal Health's service business. In this position, he manages 500 people who provide instrument repair and management services to the hospital and surgery center markets. Half of the employees working in the OnSite business are service technicians who maintain, repair, and clean complex laparoscopic instrumentation used in minimally invasive surgical procedures. These technicians work beside the surgeon during the procedure to ensure the right instrument is available for the specific clinical need.

In addition to his current role as leader of the OnSite business, Wilson has been a leading sales executive for divisions of Cardinal during his 18-year career at the company.

He received a bachelor of arts degree in economics and social studies from Davidson College.

Wilson and his wife, Candace, are blessed with four sons and one daughter, and they reside in Libertyville, Illinois.

Kenneth W. Wilson
Vice President/General Manager
OnSite Services
Cardinal Health

Changing the Face of Real Estate

Real estate is our business. But our business is about more than buildings and investments. It's about real people from diverse backgrounds working together to transform the future of real estate services and money management. Because our work takes us into different cultures and communities around the world every day, we know firsthand that there is strength in unique experiences and diverse perspectives.

That's why we've made diversity a global priority—one that will further enrich our performance, our communities and the lives of our people. By cultivating a dynamic workplace in every one of our offices around the world, we ensure that differences among our people are not only celebrated, but also woven into the fabric of our firm. From our Diversity Council and Employee Resource Groups to our community involvement and the benefits we provide our people, we're changing the face of real estate to reflect the real world in which we live and work.

www.joneslanglasalle.com
diversity.council@am.jll.com

©2006 Jones Lang LaSalle IP, Inc. All rights reserved.

JONES LANG LASALLE

EXPERIENCE: A WORLD OF DIFFERENCE.

Chicago's
COUNSELORS AT LAW

"The law is a noble profession and a tough business. One can do good in the law and do well at the same time."

JOHNNIE L. COCHRAN, JR., 1937-2005

Chicago's
COUNSELORS AT LAW

Celebrating African-American Achievements

Warren Ballentine
Attorney at Law
Law Offices of Warren Ballentine

Vanita M. Banks
Counsel
Allstate Insurance Company

Born and raised on Chicago's South Side, lawyer and radio personality (WGCI 107.5 FM) Warren Ballentine's goal in life is to be a servant leader. He fulfills this goal everyday in his hometown.

Warren attended Chicago State University. While working at a steel mill, he took weekend courses and double majored in psychology and criminal law. Upon graduating from Chicago State University, Warren's love for law took him to Ohio Northern University School of Law. He took every course he could that revolved around family, entertainment, and criminal law. That passion led him to become the servant leader he is today.

Warren is an accredited motivational speaker for children and is heavily involved in community renewal. His aspiring will to succeed is birthed from a foundation passed on to him from his mother, grandmother, and aunt. These three women are responsible for instilling in Warren his moral values and belief in self. Warren's quote to live by is simply, "An injustice anywhere is an injustice everywhere."

Vanita Banks is counsel with Allstate Insurance Company, where she specializes in complex insurance, employment, and class action litigation. Banks advises management and business clients regarding proactive and preventive law measures, and has extensive experience in managing risk exposure, outside counsel, and litigation expenses. She is a frequent panelist on corporate substantive law and diversity programs.

Banks is vice president of the National Bar Association (NBA), the oldest and largest national bar association of African-American lawyers, judges, law professors, and law students in the world. She also serves as co-chair of the NBA Hurricane Katrina Task Force, and is a member of the National Bar Institute, the NBA foundation.

Banks earned a master of laws degree in taxation from DePaul College of Law in Chicago; a juris doctorate degree from Valparaiso University School of Law; and a bachelor of arts degree in political science from Purdue University.

Her professional and community service affiliations include the American Bar Association, Cook County Bar Association, Black Women Lawyers Association of Chicago, North Shore Labor Counsel, The Links, Inc., and Alpha Kappa Sorority, Inc.

Celebrating African-American Achievements

Chicago's
COUNSELORS AT LAW

Sharon R. Barner
Partner, Attorney at Law
Foley & Lardner LLP

Sharon R. Barner is a partner in Foley & Lardner LLP's Chicago office, and a member of the firm's management committee. She also serves as chair of the firm's intellectual property department, and was the former chair of the intellectual property litigation practice group.

With more than 20 years of experience as an intellectual property litigator, Sharon focuses on patent infringement litigation. She has successfully handled many "bet the company" cases, including: representing Pioneer Hi-Bred in genetically engineered corn seed litigation; obtaining a $2.6 million award in *Rockwell Graphics v. Dev, Inc.*; and representing Hughes Aircraft Co., in a 10-month trial against the United States involving infringement of satellite stabilizing technology, resulting in a $154 million damage award.

In 2003, she was named one of "America's Top Black Lawyers" by *Black Enterprise* magazine, an "Intellectual Property Superstar" by the MCCA and AIPLA, and a "Illinois Superstar" in 2004 and 2005.

Sharon received her law degree from the University of Michigan and a bachelor of science degree from Syracuse University.

Peter C.B. Bynoe
Partner, Attorney at Law
DLA Piper Rudnick Gray Cary

Peter C.B. Bynoe is a senior partner in the Chicago office of DLA Piper, a global law firm with more than 3,000 attorneys. Bynoe serves on the firm's executive committee. He is chairman of the firm's diversity committee and a member of the Chicago office hiring committee. He also serves as chairman of Telemat Ltd., a project management and financial services firm that he founded in 1982.

Bynoe is a director of Rewards Network and Covanta Holding Corporation. He is also a trustee of Rush University Medical Center and the Core Center for Infectious Disease Prevention.

In 2005, *Fortune* named him to its Fortune Diversity 500 list of the most influential African Americans, Latinos, and Asian Americans. Bynoe has been designated an Illinois Super Lawyer in 2005 and 2006. Before joining DLA Piper, he oversaw the development of U.S. Cellular Field; advised the Atlanta committee for the 1996 Olympic Games on the development of Olympic Stadium and its conversion to Turner Field; and owned the NBA's Denver Nuggets from 1989 to 1992.

Chicago's COUNSELORS AT LAW

Celebrating African-American Achievements

Demetrius E. Carney
Partner, Attorney at Law
Perkins Coie LLP

Demetrius E. Carney, attorney at law, is a partner of Perkins Coie LLP. Carney's practice is devoted to structuring relationships between local government agencies and private sector clients.

In an effort to create private/public partnerships, he helps to stimulate urban economic development through private activity bond financing structures (tax exempt and taxable), structured financings (debt and equity), and real estate and sales tax incentive abatements. He also counsel's private equity firms/funds with their urban markets investment initiatives, while providing strategic counseling to portfolio companies seeking growth capital from venture capital and equity markets.

A few of Carney's professional and civic activities include the Cook County Bar Association, the American Bar Association, and the National Bar Association. He is also a member of The Alliance of Business Leaders and Entrepreneurs, Inc., and The Economic Club of Chicago. Additionally, he serves as the president of the Chicago Police Board and several other organizations, foundations, and councils.

Earning a bachelor's degree from Loyola University in 1969, Carney received his juris doctorate degree from DePaul University College of Law in 1974.

Darren C. Collier
Of Counsel
Barnes & Thornburg LLP

Darren Collier is of counsel in the Chicago office of Barnes & Thornburg LLP. He concentrates his practice in the governmental services and finance department. Collier regularly counsels and assists clients with financing transactions, and has served as bond counsel for a variety of state entities.

Prior to joining Barnes & Thornburg LLP, Collier served as special assistant to the Illinois attorney general. He also participated in state lobbying efforts for the Illinois Housing Development Authority. In that position, he managed state and federal affairs for the organization including, the oversight of contract lobbyists in the state capitol and Washington, D.C.

Collier has developed position papers, talking points, and educational material for legislators and state executives. In addition, he served as the liaison for the organization to the governor's office.

Celebrating African-American Achievements

Chicago's
COUNSELORS AT LAW

Kevin B. Duckworth
Partner, Attorney at Law
Jenner & Block

Jeanne M. Gills
Partner, Attorney at Law
Foley & Lardner LLP

Kevin B. Duckworth is a partner at Jenner & Block's Chicago office.

Duckworth focuses his practice in complex civil commercial litigation, defending pharmaceutical, farm and construction equipment manufacturers, and consumer goods companies. In addition to the civil tort and employment matters, he has a successful municipal finance practice. He currently represents municipalities on bond issues and transactional matters.

Trying multiple cases in federal and state courts in Illinois, Michigan, Virginia, and Indiana, Duckworth has litigated matters in Nevada, Arizona, Florida, and Wisconsin. He has handled class action matters, trade infringement, and environmental matters for automotive, consumer package goods, and petroleum companies. In addition, Duckworth has extensive MDL experience.

A member of The National Football League Players Association Workers Compensation Panel, Duckworth is a member of the American, National, Illinois, and Chicago Bar Associations, Defense Research Institute, and various sections and committees of the ABA.

Duckworth received his undergraduate degree from Fisk University in 1981 and his juris doctorate from North Carolina Central University in 1985.

Jeanne M. Gills is a partner in Foley & Lardner LLP's Chicago office. She is a vice chair of Foley's national intellectual property litigation practice group, which is ranked among the top ten for IP litigation and in the top five for patent litigation. Her trial experience includes such "bet the company" cases as *DeKalb v. Pioneer*, a patent case concerning genetically engineered corn where more than $500 million was at stake. She also serves as co-team leader of the firm's trademark and copyright litigation team.

In 2003, AIPLA and MCCA named her one of the Top Minority IP Partners, and in 2005 and 2006, she was voted by her peers as an Illinois Super Lawyer.

A member of several Foley committees, Jeanne is chair of the African-American Attorneys Affinity Group. She is also a board member of the Evening Associates of the Art Institute of Chicago.

She holds an electrical engineering degree, with honors, from Michigan State University and a juris doctor degree from the University of Chicago Law School. In addition, Jeanne is a registered USPTO patent attorney.

Chicago's COUNSELORS AT LAW
Celebrating African-American Achievements

Martin P. Greene
Co-Founder &
Co-Managing Partner
Greene and Letts

Martin P. Greene is founder and co-managing partner of Greene and Letts, a nationally respected law firm he founded with Eileen M. Letts in 1990. Greene's primary practice is in labor, employment law, and other civil litigation. He represents such clients as: Sara Lee, Eastman Kodak, ITW, Northwestern Memorial Hospital, University of Illinois, and The University of Chicago, where he received his juris doctorate in 1977.

Greene serves on the board of visitors for the University of Illinois at Chicago, where he is a 1974 alum, and is vice president of the National Minority Law Group. He has served on transition teams for Mayor Harold Washington and President Ronald Reagan, where he worked under the direction of the late Jewel S. LaFontant in preparing a study on the U.S. Commission on Civil Rights.

Raised on Chicago's West side, Greene graduated from St. Ignatius College Prep. He is a member of the American, National, and Cook County Bar Associations.

Greene is a frequent speaker on labor and employment matters and on the need for greater diversity in business and education.

Bonita L. Hatchett, Esq.
Partner, Attorney at Law
Bell, Boyd & Lloyd LLC

Bonita L. Hatchett is a partner at Bell, Boyd & Lloyd LLC, one of Chicago's oldest law firms. As a member of the employee benefits practice, Hatchett advises employers on the laws that govern tax-favored employee benefit plans. Hatchett also represents employers in connection with regulatory audits, corporate transactions, and provides fiduciary advice. She serves on several firm committees.

Hatchett has leadership roles in several charitable organizations. In her spare time, she enjoys playing golf, hosting social events, and mentoring youth. She has published several law related articles in her area of practice. In 2004, the Law Bulletin Publishing Company named Hatchett a "Leading Lawyer in Employee Benefits Law."

Receiving her undergraduate degree from the University of Michigan, Hatchett holds a juris doctorate from Rutgers University Law School. She also earned a master's of law degree, along with a certificate in employee benefits law, from the Georgetown University Law Center. Hatchett is licensed to practice in Illinois and New Jersey.

Celebrating African-American Achievements

Chicago's
COUNSELORS AT LAW

Patricia Brown Holmes
Partner, Attorney at Law
Schiff Hardin LLP

A former state trial judge, Patricia Brown Holmes is now equity partner at Schiff Hardin LLP. She represents state and local agencies, corporations, and individuals in high profile general litigation matters, internal investigations, and compliance and white-collar criminal issues. A veteran trial and appellate lawyer, she honed her skills as chief assistant corporation counsel for the City of Chicago, assistant U.S. attorney for the Northern District of Illinois, and assistant state's attorney for Cook County. She also has extensive experience teaching and lecturing in the legal community.

Holmes is a leader in numerous professional and service organizations, including the Black Women Lawyers Association (BWLA), the Seventh Circuit Bar Association, Chicago Inn of Court, The Economics Club of Chicago, and Just the Beginning Foundation, Inc. A Leadership Greater Chicago fellow, she has received numerous awards, including the prestigious BWLA Visionary Award and the Seaberry Award for Service to the Legal Community.

Holmes, a member of Delta Sigma Theta Sorority, Inc., received both her undergraduate and law degrees from the University of Illinois at Urbana-Champaign. She is married to Michael Holmes and has three children.

Alan S. King
Partner, Attorney at Law
Gardner Carton & Douglas, LLP

Alan S. King is vice chair of Gardner Carton & Douglas LLP's human resource law department, and co-chair of its labor and employment practice group. His practice is concentrated in the area of employment litigation and counseling. King has extensive experience on behalf of both private and public employers in virtually all types of employment-related litigation. He is a frequent lecturer to bar associations and employer groups, with recent topics including the Americans with Disabilities Act, workplace harassment, violence in the workplace, employee handbooks, and at-will employment issues.

King is a member of Mayor Richard Daley's 21st Century Leadership Council, and serves on the board of directors of the Leadership Council for Metropolitan Open Communities, the Ounce of Prevention Fund, and the Chicago Public Schools' Children First Fund.

King was named to Law Bulletin Publishing Company's prestigious list of "40 Illinois Attorneys Under 40 to Watch" in 2003. In 2004, he was named a "Leading Lawyer" in management employment by the Leading Lawyers Network, and in 2005 he was selected as an Illinois "Super Lawyer" by *Chicago* magazine.

Chicago's
COUNSELORS AT LAW

Celebrating African-American Achievements

Eileen M. Letts
Co-Founder &
Co-Managing Partner
Greene and Letts

Eileen M. Letts is founder and co-managing partner of Greene and Letts, a nationally-respected law firm she founded with Martin P. Greene in 1990. The primary focus of Letts' practice involves defending a wide range of personal injury cases for corporations and governmental entities. A few cases include: Wal-Mart; Travelers, State Farm, Liberty Mutual, and General Casualty insurance companies; City of Chicago; and Daimler Chrysler Financial.

Letts maintains a prominent role in the development of the legal profession by serving on numerous committees for the American, National, Cook County, and Chicago Bar Associations. She is a member of Black Women Lawyers Association, The Economic Club of Chicago, and is past president of The Chicago Bar Foundation, which provides financial support to pro bono legal service organizations. She also served on the transition team for Mayor Harold Washington.

A 1975 graduate of The Ohio State University, Letts graduated from Chicago-Kent College of Law in 1978. A member of New Faith Baptist Church and Alpha Kappa Alpha Sorority, Inc., Letts is a frequent speaker and contributor on diversity and professional development.

Samuel Mendenhall
Partner, Attorney at Law
Winston & Strawn LLP

Samuel Mendenhall is a partner in the Chicago office of the international law firm of Winston & Strawn LLP. He concentrates his practice in commercial litigation, insurance coverage litigation, and product liability defense. Mendenhall's clients include Fortune 500 companies, governmental entities, and nonprofit agencies.

Prior to joining Winston & Strawn, Mendenhall served in the United States Army, where he graduated first in his training class. He was awarded the Army Achievement Medal for his leadership abilities and the Good Conduct Medal for exemplary conduct and discipline.

Mendenhall founded the Giveback Foundation, a nonprofit organization devoted to providing college scholarships, mentoring, and internship opportunities to inner-city high school students. He is a member of The Economic Club of Chicago, a fellow of Leadership Greater Chicago, and serves on the board of visitors of his alma mater, the University of Illinois College of Law. He was chosen as an Illinois Super Lawyer for 2005 and 2006 and was selected by the Law Bulletin Publishing Company for its 2001 edition of 40 Illinois Attorneys Under 40 to Watch.

Mendenhall is married and has two children.

Celebrating African-American Achievements

Chicago's
COUNSELORS AT LAW

Leslie D. Minier
Partner, Attorney at Law
Katten Muchin Rosenman LLP

Stephen S. Mitchell
Partner, Attorney at Law
Harris, Mitchell & Dinizulu, LLC

Leslie D. Minier is a partner in the Katten Muchin Rosenman LLP corporate practice. She concentrates on the areas of mergers and acquisitions, private equity, and general corporate matters, representing clients in a wide variety of industries. She is a member of the recruiting committee and co-chair of the firm's diversity committee.

Minier is a member of the executive committee of the Chicago Bar Association's Alliance for Women, The Economic Club of Chicago, the Illinois State Bar Association, the American Bar Association, the National Black MBA Association, Inc., and the Black Women Lawyers Association of Greater Chicago. She also serves as a member of the board of directors of the Joffrey Ballet.

Minier received her juris doctor degree in 1994 from Northwestern University School of Law. In addition, she received a master's degree in management from Northwestern University J.L. Kellogg Graduate School of Management in 1994; a master of science degree in electrical engineering from Georgia Institute of Technology in 1988; and a bachelor of science degree in electrical engineering from Tuskegee University in 1987.

Stephen S. Mitchell practices personal injury and medical malpractice law. He serves on the board of directors for the Cook County Bar Association, and is a hearing officer for the Illinois Supreme Court Attorney Registration and Disciplinary Commission.

Mitchell graduated from Florida A&M University with a bachelor of science degree in business economics, magna cum laude, along with a master's in public finance. In addition, Mitchell received his doctorate of law degree from the University of Wisconsin, where he was a member of the *Wisconsin Law Review* and the Wisconsin Moot Court board.

A former member of the board of directors for the Legal Assistance Foundation, Mitchell was selected as one of "40 Illinois Attorneys Under 40 To Watch in 2006." He is a member of Kappa Alpha Psi Fraternity, Inc., and the H.E. Daniels Lodge #532.

An art collector, Mitchell is on the board of directors of Diasporal Rhythms, an association of collectors. He is also an owner of Gallery Guichard, a prominent art gallery in Chicago that specializes in art of the Diaspora.

Chicago's COUNSELORS AT LAW

Celebrating African-American Achievements

Adrienne Banks Pitts
Partner, Attorney at Law
Winston & Strawn LLP

Adrienne B. Pitts, a litigation partner in the Chicago office of Winston & Strawn, concentrates her practice in commercial antitrust cases and white-collar criminal matters. She has tried several white-collar criminal matters in federal court. Pitts is one of the lawyers defending former Governor George H. Ryan in his federal corruption trial. She has also counseled clients through several federal grand jury investigations.

Pitts is a 2005 graduate of Leadership Greater Chicago. She is vice chair of the board of directors for Lawndale Educational and Regional Network (L.E.A.R.N.), a charter school in North Lawndale. The former chairperson of the Chicago Committee on Minorities in Large Law Firms, Pitts serves on its board of directors and executive committee.

Pitts received a bachelor's degree in economics from the University of Pennsylvania in 1990, and a juris doctorate with honors from Boston University School of Law in 1995. She is also a member of Alpha Kappa Alpha Sorority, Inc.

She is married with two children.

Tracie R. Porter
Principle, Attorney at Law
Law Offices of Tracie R. Porter, LLC

Tracie R. Porter is the principle of the Law Offices of Tracie R. Porter, LLC. Her practice concentrates on a broad variety of real estate law matters, including transactional and litigation cases, corporate law, and probate proceedings. She has handled a broad range of transactions from a $4,000 vacant lot purchase, to a $15.3 million commercial acquisition. Her real estate litigation practice includes investors, developers, and individuals.

Porter is an adjunct professor at IIT Chicago-Kent College of Law teaching business related law courses. At the John Marshall School of Law, she teaches commercial real estate law and legal drafting courses.

Porter is affiliated with the American Bar Association, the Chicago Bar Association, The Cook County Bar Association, the Illinois Real Estate Lawyers Association, and the Black Women Lawyers Association. She was published in the *Chicago Bar Association Journal,* and has been quoted and featured in various news media, including the real estate section of the *Chicago Tribune* and the *Citizen Newspaper*. She has been seen on several television programs discussing topics related to real estate.

Celebrating African-American Achievements

Chicago's
COUNSELORS AT LAW

Stephen H. Pugh
President
Pugh, Jones, Johnson & Quandt, P.C.

Stephen Pugh is a graduate of Loyola University Chicago School of Law and a Woodrow Wilson fellow. Previously, he was a law clerk to the Honorable James B. Parsons, U.S. District of Illinois; special trial attorney in the honors program for the U.S. Department of Justice; and partner with Chapman and Cutler.

Since founding Pugh, Jones, Johnson & Quandt, Pugh has practiced real estate litigation, director and officer liability cases, general and complex commercial litigation, and has represented local government entities. He tried the first civil RICO jury trial in the Northern District of Illinois, and is currently a hearing officer for the Chicago Board of Education in contractor debarment proceedings. A member of the bar of the U.S. Supreme Court, Pugh has extensive trial experience and has argued before the U.S. Circuit Courts of Appeals and the Illinois Supreme Court.

Pugh has authored several articles and has received numerous awards, including the prestigious Francis J. Rooney/St. Thomas Moore Award from Loyola University School of Law. He serves on many boards including Columbia College Chicago and the Emergency Fund.

Timothy Ray
Partner, Attorney at Law
Neal, Gerber & Eisenberg LLP

Timothy Ray is a partner within Chicago-based law firm Neal, Gerber & Eisenberg LLP's litigation practice group, where he concentrates on complex commercial litigation. He is admitted to practice in Illinois and before the U.S. District Court for the Northern District of Illinois and the U.S. Court of Appeals for the Seventh Circuit. Similarly, Tim has tried more than 30 jury trials to verdict in both federal and state courts.

Tim, who obtained his juris doctorate from The University of Iowa College of Law, is a member of his firm's hiring and diversity committees and co-chairs its minority initiative group. He is AV® peer review rated by Martindale-Hubbell (the highest possible rating).

Named one of 40 Attorneys Under 40 to Watch in 2004, Tim is a member of the following: the Federal Trial Bar; the Illinois Supreme Court Planning and Oversight Committee for a Judicial Performance Evaluation Program; the ISBA and Chicago Bar Association Joint Task Force for Funding Judicial Campaigns; the Cook County Bar Association board of directors; and the Chicago Committee of Minorities in Large Law Firms.

THE INAUGURAL EDITION   *Who's Who In Black Chicago*®

Chicago's
COUNSELORS AT LAW

Celebrating African-American Achievements

Gail Saracco
Partner, Attorney at Law
Mayer, Brown, Rowe & Maw LLP

Juan R. Thomas
Founder
The Thomas Group

Gail Saracco is a partner at the law firm of Mayer, Brown, Rowe & Maw LLP in Chicago. She was the international law firm's first black female attorney partner. Gail is a partner in the corporate group where she advises sponsors in structuring and negotiating private equity funds and represents investors in connection with their investments in private equity funds. Her practice also includes the representation of corporations in mergers and acquisitions. Gail is a member of the firm's committee on diversity and inclusion and the pro bono committee.

Gail was a 2003 Leadership Greater Chicago fellow and currently serves on the board of directors of the Leadership Fellows Association. She is also a member of the board of trustees of the Lawyers Committee for Civil Rights Under Law.

Gail is a 1987 graduate of Yale University and a 1990 cum laude graduate of The University of Michigan Law School, where she was a member of the *Michigan Law Review*.

A native of Jamaica, she currently resides in River Forest with her husband and two daughters.

Juan R. Thomas is founder of The Thomas Group. Thomas practices in the areas of labor and employment, real estate, and governmental relations on behalf of the firm's clients.

In April of 2005, he was elected Aurora Township clerk becoming the first African American to win a township-wide office in Aurora, Illinois, the second-largest city in Illinois. In 1995, Thomas became the youngest person ever elected to the West Aurora School Board, and he became the first African American ever reelected to the board in 1999.

Thomas has been featured in *Ebony* and the *Chicago Sun-Times* as a leader to watch in the 21st century. His civic affiliations include numerous local, state, and national organizations. He currently serves as chairman of the board of directors of the African-American Chamber of Commerce serving suburban Chicago counties.

Thomas graduated from Morehouse College and earned his law degree and his master's degree in educational policy from the University of Illinois. He is currently completing a master's degree in religious studies at The University of Chicago and attends Trinity United Church of Christ.

Celebrating African-American Achievements

Chicago's
COUNSELORS AT LAW

Ernest W. Torain, Jr.
Shareholder, Attorney at Law
Vedder, Price, Kaufman & Kammholz, P.C.

Ernie Torain attended Dartmouth College where he was a three-year starter on the football team and was named All-Ivy (second team) in his senior year. At Dartmouth, Torain was a member of the Beta Theta Pi Fraternity and the Dragon Senior Honor Society. After graduating from Dartmouth in 1987 with a bachelor of arts degree in economics, Torain attended The University of Michigan Law School, graduating in 1991. While at Michigan, he founded the Sports Law Society, which brought speakers to campus to discuss legal issues in sports.

Torain joined Vedder Price in the capital markets and the finance and transactions practice groups as a shareholder in Chicago in 2004. Torain represents both companies and investment banks with respect to corporate finance transactions, including public offerings, PIPEs, private placements, and related corporate securities matters. He has broad experience in managing the SEC registration or private placement process.

Torain is a member of the American Bar Association, the Chicago Bar Association, The Economic Club of Chicago, and he sits on the board of the Golden Apple Foundation. He lives in Evanston with his wife and two sons.

Everett S. Ward
Partner, Attorney at Law
Jenner & Block LLP

Everett S. Ward is a partner in Jenner & Block's Chicago office, and is a member of the real estate practice group. Ward has practiced law in the areas of commercial real estate and financing since 1986. He has significant experience with complex and sophisticated transactions, as well as day-to-day client counseling.

Ward is a member of the American Bar Association's section of real property, probate and trust law, and a member of the Real Estate Executives Council. He is also a member of the American College of Real Estate Lawyers.

Ward is a member of The Economic Club of Chicago and serves on the board of directors of the Heartland Alliance For Human Needs & Human Rights. He is a graduate of Princeton University (1983), and Harvard Law School (1986).

Chicago's
COUNSELORS AT LAW

Celebrating African-American Achievements

Allison L. Wood
Principal, Attorney at Law
Bellows & Bellows, P.C.

Allison L. Wood is a principal with the firm Bellows & Bellows, P.C. where she specializes in commercial and employment litigation. She has extensive trial experience representing corporate clients in various industries including pharmaceuticals, electronics, manufacturing, and transportation. Wood also counsels executives and senior level managers relative to employment disputes, and negotiates severance and compensation agreements. Prior to entering private practice, Wood was of counsel at Peoples Energy Corporation, and began her career as an assistant public defender where she tried numerous jury trials.

For more than a decade, Wood has been an adjunct faculty member at DePaul University College of Law teaching pre-trial and trial courses. She has published numerous articles on trial practice, and is often invited to teach in trial programs throughout the city.

Wood is a past treasurer of the Cook County Bar Association, past hearing chair for the Attorney Registration and Disciplinary Commission, and past chair of the board for a social service agency, Centers for New Horizons.

Wood received her law degree from DePaul University College of Law.

Work with the best.

At CDW, we take great pride in the work we do — and it shows. For the eighth consecutive year, CDW has been named one of Fortune's 100 Best Companies to Work For.

Visit us at CDW.com

FORTUNE® 100 BEST COMPANIES TO WORK FOR

CDW®
The Right Technology. Right Away.™
CDW.com • 800.800.4CDW

Chicago's
MEDIA PROFESSIONALS

"It's not what the dream is but what the dream does."

JOHN H. JOHNSON, 1918-2005
ENTREPRENEUR

Chicago's MEDIA PROFESSIONALS

Celebrating African-American Achievements

Derrick K. Baker
Columnist & Contributing Editor
N'DIGO Magapaper

Since 1992, Derrick K. Baker has written popular opinion columns published by *N'DIGO* magapaper, and distributed weekly by Knight Ridder News Service, to more than 400 newspapers nationwide. With more than 625,000 readers, *N'DIGO* is the nation's largest African-American weekly publication, offering readers a new view on contemporary culture.

An award-winning speech and annual report writer, Baker has appeared on local radio and television talk shows, including *Chicago Tonight*, and as a guest in several "table talks" and seminars. He is principal of DKB & Associates, a full-service public relations and marketing communications consultancy serving an array of corporate, nonprofit, municipal and small business clients. He has served as director of marketing for the Chicago Park District, and in employee communications at the Kemper National Insurance Companies.

The immediate past president of the Rotary Club of Chicago Southeast, Baker is a member of the International Association of Business Communicators and the Chicago Assembly.

Earning a master's degree from Roosevelt University, Baker received his bachelor's degree in journalism from Drake University.

Ken Bedford
Photojournalist
ABC-TV7

Ken Bedford has been a photojournalist for ABC-TV7 in Chicago for more than 30 years. He has won many prestigious awards including the Emmy and the coveted Peter Lisagor Award for photography in news and documentaries. Bedford has worked with media giants Oprah Winfrey, Peter Jennings, Max Robinson, and talk show host Phil Donahue, just to name a few.

Active in the community, Bedford produces fundraisers for organizations including Open Book, an after school reading skills program for inner-city youth, and the American Cancer Society. He also produces celebrity and news segments for hall of fame radio personality Herb Kent.

Since the death of his wife, Anaia, in April of 2004, Bedford has devoted much of his time to raising breast cancer awareness among African-American and other minority women. He formed a not-for-profit foundation named in his wife's memory, ABCAP, Inc. (Anaia's Breast Cancer Awareness Program).

Celebrating African-American Achievements

Chicago's
MEDIA PROFESSIONALS

Deborah O. Brown was born in 1973 into a family that stressed loyalty to kin, community, church, and country.

Brown graduated from Lewis University in May of 1995 after a stellar academic career. Upon graduation, she was armed with a degree that would open the door to a career at WGN-TV, where she is currently segment producer for the morning news.

A member of Delta Sigma Theta Sorority, Inc. and Rotary International, Brown works tirelessly in the community. She sits on the boards of Africa International House, the Chicago Film Festival, and is board president of the Women's Resource Assistance Program (WRAP). She is also a jeweler with Pro-Gems Jewelers and a print model, and was featured in *Barbershop 2* and *Roll Bounce*.

Brown is a member of St. Mark Missionary Baptist Church in Harvey, Illinois. This is where she worships and thanks God for his blessings. She recently started an AIDS ministry at the church. Brown hopes to continue her Emmy-nominated career in broadcasting as well as further develop her skills as a mentor and role model for others in the community.

Deborah Olivia Brown
Segment Producer, Morning News
WGN-TV

Delmarie L. Cobb owns and operates The Publicity Works, a Chicago-based public affairs, political consulting, and media relations firm. She is president of Deleco Communications, Inc., which produced the award-winning, national television newsmagazine, *Street Life*.

A practicing journalist for almost two decades, Cobb started as a television news reporter on network-affiliated stations throughout the country. Returning to Chicago, she became a WVON radio talk show host, a television producer, and print media columnist.

In 1996, she became the first African-American press secretary to the Democratic National Convention, and in 1988 served as national traveling press secretary for presidential candidate Jesse Jackson. She has advised and/or served as communications director for several candidates from national and statewide, to county and aldermanic races. In 1995, she developed the South Suburban Airport issue for U.S. Representative Jesse Jackson, Jr.'s campaign.

Delmarie L. Cobb
Owner & President
The Publicity Works
Deleco Communications, Inc.

Chicago's MEDIA PROFESSIONALS

Celebrating African-American Achievements

Richard Deal is an on-air personality for Soul 106.3 WSRB "The Best Mix of R&B" on Crawford Broadcasting. Before radio, Richard was an intern at NBC5 for *The Jenny Jones Show* during the 1996-1997 season. He got his start in radio in 1998 at Clear Channel's WGCI AM and FM stations under the leadership of Elroy Smith as "Shawn Knight."

In March of 2001, Jay Alan saw fit for Richard to join WPWX Power 92. Richard had been part of the Power 92 family for four years when Mr. Alan promoted him to join Soul 106.3 for the morning drive segment in February of 2005. Currently, Richard is still employed at Crawford Broadcasting as associate producer for *The Michael Baisden Show: Love, Lust, & Lies*.

Richard Deal is a graduate of Kennedy-King College and attends The Apostolic Church of God under the leadership of Bishop Arthur M. Brazier. He is a part of the Masonic Order at The M.W. St. John's Grand Lodge & O.E.S. chapter in Chicago. Richard is also the proud father of twin boys, Jacob and Jacolby.

Richard M. Deal
On-Air Personality
Soul 106.3 WSRB
Crawford Broadcasting

Marsha J. Eaglin, a proud Chicagoan, enjoys working for Christian Community Health Center, a faith-based, nonprofit organization founded in 1993. Eaglin joined the staff after serving on its board of directors, when there was a need to get health news/information to an underserved community.

For nearly 20 years, Eaglin has worked in media and is an award-winning news manager having received the Edward R. Murrow Award. She has worked for CBS/Network News Service and several FOX-TV stations. Additionally, Eaglin has worked for RainbowPUSH and WTTW/PBS in various communications positions.

Eaglin loves community service, particularly focusing on the Roseland neighborhood of Chicago. She works with youth enrichment programs, skill development in journalism, desktop publishing, and production. She also provides ministry to children each Sunday.

Eaglin serves on the board of Bethany Christian Services, and is a former board member of the National Association of Black Journalist and NABJ-Chicago.

A graduate of St. Xavier University as the first African-American media fellow, Eaglin is president of Proviso East High School, class of 1981.

She is the mother of two wonderful children.

Marsha J. Eaglin
Health News Producer &
Director of Media Communications
Christian Community Health Center

Celebrating African-American Achievements

Chicago's
MEDIA PROFESSIONALS

Evelyn Holmes is a general assignment reporter for ABC7 News. She joined the station in May of 2003 from Chicagoland Television News (CLTV), where she served as a weekday morning news anchor.

Holmes has worked in Chicago broadcasting for the past 13 years. She started at CLTV as a traffic reporter in June of 1996, and while there, she served as a weathercaster, general assignment reporter, and fill-in news anchor, as well as weekend news anchor.

Before moving to television, Holmes was a part of both the *Bob Collins* and the *Spike O'Dell Shows* on WGN Radio. Recently, she has served as a fill-in show host on WVON-AM radio.

Holmes is a Chicago native and a graduate of Northwestern University. She is a member of the Chicago Association of Black Journalists and the National Association of Black Journalists.

Holmes lives in the city and is involved in numerous charitable and community projects.

Evelyn Holmes
General Assignment Reporter
WLS-TV ABC7

Theresa Fambro Hooks ("Teesee") is a columnist/journalist for the *Chicago Defender*, a newspaper serving the African-American community. A 45-year veteran in her field, she pens a daily column, "Teesee's Town," reporting on arts, theatre, and the comings and goings of business, community, and social leaders. She covers special events in a regular feature, "Seen on the Scene," for which she takes photos. Previously, she was a *Defender* public relations vice president and president of Chicago Defender Charities, Inc.

Theresa's previous professional positions include regional community relations manager, Coors Beer; marketing/communications director, Parker House Sausage Co.; special assistant to the president for public information/community services, Olive-Harvey College; and community/public affairs manager, Philco-Ford Job Corps Center. She was also president of Theresa Fambro Hooks & Associates, a public relations, communications, and marketing firm.

Some of her many honors include Phenomenal Woman, V-103 FM; Lifetime Achievement, Black Public Relations Society; Russ Ewing Legacy Award of Excellence from the Chicago Association of Black Journalists; Phenomenal Woman, Alpha Phi Alpha Fraternity, Inc.; Woman Making History, National Council of Negro Women; and Outstanding Media Woman, Chicago Urban League.

Theresa Fambro Hooks ("Teesee")
Columnist/Journalist
Chicago Defender

THE INAUGURAL EDITION *Who's Who In Black Chicago*®

Chicago's
MEDIA PROFESSIONALS

Celebrating African-American Achievements

Leah Hope is an award-winning reporter for ABC7 Chicago. Prior to joining the station in 1997, Hope worked as an anchor/reporter at the ABC affiliate in Portland.

Hope's work covering important issues in the African-American community has been honored on both national and local levels. She has been recognized for journalistic excellence with two prestigious awards from the National Association of Black Journalists (NABJ) and two awards from NABJ's Chicago chapter.

Hope received an Emmy for the primetime special *9/11/02 The New Homeland*. She garnered an American Women in Radio and Television award for a program that explored women in science and technology. The Society of Professional Journalists honored Hope with four Peter Lisagor awards for breaking news coverage.

She is a member of the Investigative Reporters and Editors Association, the National Association of Black Journalists, American Women in Radio and Television, and the National Academy of Television Arts and Sciences, among others.

Hope is a graduate of New York's Syracuse University. She is the great-granddaughter of John Hope, the first African-American president of Morehouse College in Atlanta.

Leah Hope
Reporter
WLS-TV ABC7

As director of promotions, Larry Howard manages the development and execution of all event marketing, promotions, and community affairs for WGCI-FM 107.5.

At the age of 30, Howard has conquered the radio/communications industry. For the last ten years, he has worked for some of the country's leading radio stations and record labels, including WJLB, WJZZ, and WNIC in Detroit. He also worked for Universal/Motown Records.

Howard was nominated for Promotion/Marketing Director of the Year by *Billboard* magazine in 2001. Most recently, he was nominated for Promotions/Marketing Director of the Year by *R&R* (Radio & Records) in 2005.

A Detroit native, Howard gradated from Clark Atlanta University where he received a bachelor's degree in mass communications. He is also a member of Restoration Fellowship Church International. Howard is single and the youngest of three children of Larry and Carol Howard.

Larry Howard, Jr.
Promotions Director
WGCI-FM 107.5

Celebrating African-American Achievements

Chicago's
MEDIA PROFESSIONALS

Gregory J. Huskisson is a Chicago-based writer, editor, and media consultant. Before going independent, Huskisson was an editorial consultant for Crusader Newspapers in Chicago, vice president of news and community affairs for Freedom Media Group in Columbus, Ohio, and an executive consultant for Equal Access Media in Los Angeles, California.

Huskisson rejoined Black Press USA in 2003. After developing his craft at media conglomerate Knight-Ridder, Inc., Huskisson spent more than 15 years as a reporter, editor, and an executive at the *Detroit Free Press* newspaper and Knight-Ridder's corporate headquarters.

The Chicago native has also served as an executive-on-loan to the NAACP, is a contributing author in the best-selling book, *Chicken Soup for the African American Soul*, and is an executive producer of the critically acclaimed documentary, *Sister, I'm Sorry – An Apology to Our African American Queens*.

Huskisson has a master's degree from the Medill School of Journalism at Northwestern University, and a bachelor's degree from Morehouse College. He is a member of the National Association of Black Journalists, the National Association of Minority Media Executives, and many other civic organizations.

Gregory J. Huskisson
Writer, Editor &
Media Consultant

Cheryle Robinson Jackson is deputy chief of staff, communications for Illinois Governor Rod R. Blagojevich. As such, she serves as primary spokesperson, develops message strategy, oversees press relations in the governor's office, and coordinates communications and messages among 28 agencies.

Prior to joining the Blagojevich administration, Jackson was named Amtrak's regional vice president of communications and government affairs in January of 2000 and then served as national director of state government relations beginning in October of 2002. She was responsible for Amtrak's state and local government affairs nationally and for serving as spokesperson in 41 states. Jackson joined Amtrak after holding the position of vice president of communications for National Public Radio (NPR) in Washington, D.C. At NPR, she served as national spokesperson and oversaw the network's national marketing, advertising, and public affairs operation.

Jackson is a native of Chicago and graduated from Northwestern University in 1988. She and her husband, Charles, reside in Chicago's South Side.

Cheryle Robinson Jackson
Deputy Chief of Staff,
Communications
Office of Governor Rod R. Blagojevich

Chicago's MEDIA PROFESSIONALS

Celebrating African-American Achievements

Maureen Jenkins is a lifestyle reporter for the *Chicago Sun-Times*, where she writes about relationships, popular culture, and dining trends. She also contributes to the Food, Travel, and Weekend sections of the paper as well. She recently spent seven months in Florence, Italy, where she wrote freelance pieces for *Chicago Sun-Times*, *Black Enterprise,* and *Working Mother*.

Previously, Maureen was an award-winning writer for *Boeing Frontiers*, a monthly employee magazine published by Chicago-based Boeing, writing about global growth strategy for employees and external stakeholders. Maureen also worked in public relations for Sears and Golin/Harris Communications, where she helped handle marketing and public relation initiatives for the agency's national McDonald's account. Additionally, Maureen has worked as a reporter at the Rockford (Ill.) *Register Star* and *The Oregonian* in Portland, Oregon.

In 1999, she earned a master's degree from Garrett-Evangelical Theological Seminary, and covered religion at the *Charlotte Observer* and *Arizona Republic*.

An avid traveler, she belongs to the Chicago Council on Foreign Relations Young Professionals, Chicago Sister Cities Milan (Italy) Committee, Alliance Française de Chicago, and Delta Sigma Theta Sorority, Inc.

Maureen Jenkins
Lifestyle Reporter
Chicago Sun-Times

Lisa Lenoir is the travel and society editor for the *Chicago Sun-Times*. She writes travel features and manages freelancers and staffers who submit stories to the weekly Sunday Travel section. Prior to her appointment as travel editor in 2004, she was the newspaper's fashion editor.

Attending Indiana University, Lisa graduated in 1989 with a bachelor of arts degree in journalism and a minor in graphic design.

She has served in many organizations including the African-American Leadership Advisory Committee for the Art Institute of Chicago, Alpha Kappa Alpha Sorority, Inc., the North American Travel Journalists Association, and the Association for Women Journalists.

Her awards include the Chicago Association of Black Journalists, the Award of Excellence in Commentary in 1998, the 2003 Peter Lisagor Journalism Award in Features (team project), and the 2002-2003 Lowell Thomas Silver Award for Sun-Times Travel Section (team project).

In addition to her media work, Lisa teaches fashion journalism and writing for managers at Columbia College Chicago and creates handmade greeting cards for private clients.

Lisa Lenoir
Travel and Society Editor
Chicago Sun-Times

Celebrating African-American Achievements

Chicago's
MEDIA PROFESSIONALS

A nationally syndicated columnist with Creators Syndicate and the author of *Speak, Brother! A Black Man's View of America*, Roland Martin is executive editor of the *Chicago Defender*. He is also a commentator for TV One Cable Network and host of *The Roland S. Martin Show* on WVON-AM in Chicago.

A provocative and insightful analyst, Martin has appeared numerous times on national television and radio, and he hosts a weekly segment on *The Fifth Quarter*, a daily sports show on WOL-AM/XM Satellite Radio.

He has won more than 20 professional awards for journalistic excellence, including a regional Edward R. Murrow Award from the Radio Television News Directors, and the top sports reporting award from the National Association of Black Journalists.

Martin is a member of the National Association of Black Journalists, Alpha Phi Alpha Fraternity, Inc., and the American Society of Newspaper Editors.

He earned a bachelor's degree in journalism from Texas A&M University. He is married to Rev. Jacquie Hood Martin, author of *Fulfilled! The Art and Joy of Balanced Living*. They reside in Chicago and the Dallas suburb of Cedar Hill.

Roland S. Martin
Executive Editor
Chicago Defender

Crazy Howard McGee can be heard weekdays on WGCI-107.5 FM from 5:00 a.m. to 10:00 a.m. Crazy Howard McGee is a typical story of being in the right place at the right time. McGee, a Chicago native has literally gone from rags to riches on WGCI-107.5 FM.

McGee first started at WGCI-107.5 FM as a weekend personality, and then moved to middays before taking the afternoon drive slot in 1996. As a result, the station garnered the highest ratings in recent station history during McGee's two-year stint on the afternoon drive.

Crazy Howard McGee
Radio Personality
WGCI-107.5 FM

Chicago's
MEDIA PROFESSIONALS

Celebrating African-American Achievements

Sharon K. McGhee is an award-winning radio journalist and current talk show host on WVON 1450-AM's *The Talk of Chicago*.

By all accounts, talk radio is a format made for Sharon, a self-proclaimed news and information junkie equipped with a strong opinion. As host of *First Light* from 5 a.m. until 6 a.m., Monday through Friday, Sharon brings her world views, intelligence, and wit to her Windy City audience. She is also the writer and director of the *Pocket Book Monologues*, a nationwide stage production that address African-American female sexuality, premiering in 2006 in Chicago.

Sharon has been recognized by the Chicago Council of Negro Women for her commitment to raise self-esteem among African-American girls. Her professional affiliations include the National Association of Black Journalist.

An international traveler, Sharon has visited Africa, South America, Europe, and the Caribbean Islands.

Sharon K. McGhee
Radio Journalist
WVON 1450-AM

Mary Mitchell is an editorial board member and columnist for the *Chicago Sun-Times*. Her column appears Sundays, Tuesdays, and Thursdays.

Mitchell is the recipient of numerous journalism awards, including the prestigious Award of Excellence from the National Association of Black Journalists, the Studs Terkel Award from the Community Media Workshop, and the Peter Lisagor Award from the Chicago Headliner Club. Likewise, she is the recipient of the Phenomenal Woman Award by the Expo for Today's Black Woman and the Humanitarian Award from the 100 Black Men of Chicago. In 2004, *Crain's Chicago Business* honored Mitchell as one of the 100 Most Influential Women in Chicago.

Named "courageous" and "compassionate" by readers who trust her, Mitchell gives them a voice on issues ranging from police misconduct to the tragedy of black-on-black violence.

Mitchell earned a bachelor's in journalism at Columbia College Chicago. She is the mother of four children, the grandmother of three, and resides in Maywood, Illinois.

Mary Mitchell
Editorial Board Member &
Columnist
Chicago Sun-Times

Celebrating African-American Achievements

Chicago's
MEDIA PROFESSIONALS

Julieanna L. Richardson, public historian and founder/executive director of The HistoryMakers, has a unique and diverse background in theatre, television production, and the cable television industry.

Richardson is a magna cum laude graduate of Brandeis University, where she double-majored in theatre arts and American studies. After conducting oral histories on the Harlem Renaissance and Langston Hughes, she attended Harvard Law School.

After graduation, Richardson worked as a corporate lawyer prior to serving as the cable administrator for the City of Chicago Office of Cable Communications in the early 1980s. There, she established the Chicago Cable Commission, the city's regulatory body. Richardson went on to found Shop Chicago, a regionally-based home shopping channel. She was driven to start The HistoryMakers out of a strong desire to make a difference and to leave a living legacy.

Currently, Richardson serves on the board of directors of Lawyers for the Creative Arts, The HistoryMakers, and the Chicago Convention and Tourism Bureau.

Julieanna L. Richardson
Founder & Executive Director
The HistoryMakers

Zelda Robinson is a southern girl with a northern flair. Many know her from V103's *Troi Tyler Show* with *N'Spirational Conversations*, Gospel 1390AM, or CLTV Traffic. She is a writer, author, publisher, radio/TV personality, and media consultant.

Additionally, Robinson is CEO of Zelda Robinson Communications, an international speaker/training consulting company that specializes in career/personal development and youth training. She also hosts information seminars on How To Get Free Grant Money.

She has spoken around the world from London, England to East and South Africa. Her memberships include, the American Society of Training & Development, and the National Speakers Association. She is also vice president of broadcast for the Chicago Association of Black Journalists. Robinson has been featured on local and international news.

An author of several books and many business training manuals, Robinson is the producer and host of *Shelomith* television show on channel 19. She has taken her ministry out of the studio and into the community, changing lives, sharing words of wisdom, and assisting in the transfer of wealth.

Zelda Robinson
Chief Executive Officer
Zelda Robinson Communications

Chicago's
MEDIA PROFESSIONALS

Celebrating African-American Achievements

Charles Thomas joined ABC7 News in September of 1991 as a general assignment reporter after working for several years as a Midwest correspondent for ABC News in the Chicago and St. Louis Bureaus. He has worked as a professional journalist since 1973, shortly after his graduation from the University of Missouri's School of Journalism.

While working at the network, he traveled throughout the region, to all 50 states and to every continent. Chicago was always the most exciting and intriguing city for him, personally and professionally. When ABC7 offered him a staff position covering Chicago on a daily basis, it was a dream come true.

Thomas has covered a wide range of news stories for ABC7 in virtually every area of interest in Chicago. He has also traveled extensively to add the Chicago perspective to stories of national interest, including the O.J. Simpson trials, the Oklahoma City bombing, the Rodney King trials and civil disorder, major airline crashes, natural disasters, and many other assignments. He has also reported for ABC7 from Europe and Asia.

Charles Thomas
General Assignment Reporter
WLS-TV ABC7

Jim Tilmon always wanted to be a pilot. After college, he served eight years in the Army Corps of Engineers flying helicopters and fixed wing aircraft, leaving with the rank of captain. The third black pilot hired by American Airlines, and the fifth in the U.S., he was based in Chicago flying the DC-6, DC-7, BAC-111, and Boeing 727.

Tilmon has over 30 years' television experience hosting his live magazine format show, *Our People*, the first show of, for, and by black people in this nation seen on WTTW. He hosts "Tilmon Tempo" and serves as weather anchor and aviation reporter on WMAQ-TV, NBC-Chicago, and for CBS2 Chicago. Tilmon is also an expert analyst for cable news stations.

His accomplishments include a Chicago Emmy, a National Emmy nomination, Illinois AP and UPI awards, and the Silver Circle Award. Tilmon has been appointed to the Illinois Secretary of State's Veterans Advisory Council, named a DuSable Museum of African American History "Trailblazer" History Maker, and has been inducted into the Chicago Senior Citizens Hall of Fame.

James A. "Jim" Tilmon, Sr.
Chief Executive Officer
The Tilmon Group

Celebrating African-American Achievements

Chicago's MEDIA PROFESSIONALS

La Donna Tittle is producer, writer, and host of her own television show on Cable Access Network, *The La Donna Tittle TV/Radio Show*, featuring "Cookin' Wit' Tittle." She can be heard on the Web satellite radio broadcasts of WGCR-FM, and is an on-air talent and mentor at Kennedy-King College Radio, WKKC.

As a professional model, she launched her radio career with WBEE 1570 in 1970. Chicago's number one disc jockey in 1973 with WBMX. Tittle went on to join WJPC, Johnson Publishing Company in 1978. In 1983, she received radio's highest honor—Arbitron's highest ratings for Midday's—the Black Radio Exclusive Air Personality Award.

Her versatile career includes noteworthy theatrical performances with ETA, the Gospel Repertory Theater Company, and Goodman, Steppenwolf, and Touchstone Theaters. She also appeared in many national television commercials.

Tittle graduated from Dunbar Vocational High School, where she is a teacher, mentor, and an inductee of the Alumni Hall of Fame, and earned a bachelor's degree from Chicago State University. She is currently pursuing a master's degree at the Art Institute of Chicago, with plans to pursue a Ph.D. thereafter.

La Donna Tittle
Producer & Host
The La Donna Tittle TV/Radio Show

Dorothy Tucker has served as a reporter for CBS 2 since 1984. Currently, she reports for the station's 5:00 p.m. and 10:00 p.m. weekday newscasts. Tucker also serves as the station's consumer reporter, covering issues and trends to help viewers save money and avoid scams.

She joined CBS 2 from KDKA-TV in Pittsburgh, Pennsylvania. Prior to that, Tucker worked at KWGN-TV in Denver, Colorado and WREG-TV in Memphis, Tennessee. Tucker began her broadcasting career in Peoria, Illinois at WMBD-TV.

A few of her many awards include eight local Emmys, the Chicago Association of Black Journalists annual award, and a national UPI Spot News Award.

She is on the board of the National Association of Black Journalist of Chicago, and was co-chair of their Katrina fundraiser. Tucker also serves on the Project 30 Foundation for Whitney Young High School.

She graduated with honors from Northwestern University with a bachelor of science degree in communications. Tucker is currently a member of Northwestern University's Council of One Hundred.

Tucker, a native Chicagoan, lives in Hyde Park and is the mother of three.

Dorothy Tucker
Reporter
CBS 2

THE INAUGURAL EDITION *Who's Who In Black Chicago*

Chicago's
MEDIA PROFESSIONALS

Celebrating African-American Achievements

David "D-Nice" Walker is an air personality on Saturday mornings from 6 a.m. to 10 a.m. on WSRB-FM, Soul 106.3, and is executive producer of the ABC nationally syndicated, *The Michael Baisden Show*. As executive producer, David oversees all local creative and production aspects of the show, providing overall station production support. While on the air Saturday mornings, his entertaining "In The Mix Reports" keeps Chicagoland in the know about their favorite celebrities.

Walker is a member of the National Association of Black Journalists, and the National Association of Black Journalists Chicago Chapter. He is also a prominent member of the TV ministry at Embassies of Christ Church in Gary, Indiana.

With his lovely supporting wife, Towanna, by his side, Walker has made guest appearances on local cable television shows. He also produces and hosts *In The Mix Magazine*, a music video magazine show which airs throughout Northwest Indiana, Chicago, and surrounding suburbs.

To keep us positive and grounded, D-Nice ends his show every week by saying, "Anytime's a good time, whatever you do, keep God first."

David "D-Nice" Walker
Air Personality &
Executive Producer
WSRB-FM (Soul 106.3)

Milana L. Walter is director of station relations for NBC5 Chicago, an owned and operated NBC Universal broadcast station in the nation's number three market. She positions NBC5 in cause-related partnerships that match the station's initiatives and diverse demographics in Chicagoland. Her duties include working closely with news and marketing/promotions.

Milana is executive producer for the NBC5 Jefferson Awards for public service and the webcast NBC5/Telemundo Homework Hotline Finals.

Under her leadership, NBC5 partnered with Tavis Smiley and Tom Joyner for the Soul Success Tribute to John Johnson; the Homework Hotline has flourished to help more than 5,000 students with math and science; and the Angel Tree program with The Salvation Army has distributed more than 40,000 gifts. She also helped initiate a community webcast and Web presence, and created an NBC5 advisory committee for AIDS/HIV.

Milana is a published author, screenwriter, and award-winning television/video producer. She loves movies, music, cats and dogs, the French and Italian Riviera, and golfing.

A Chicago native, she has lived in New York, Los Angeles, and Miami and is a graduate of Tennessee State University and Southern University Law Center.

Milana L. Walter
Director, Station Relations
NBC5 Chicago

Chicago's
ACADEMIA

"Do you lead your students to the water and make them drink or do you try harder to make them thirsty?"

CARTER G. WOODSON, 1875-1950
HISTORIAN AND EDUCATOR

Chicago's ACADEMIA
Celebrating African-American Achievements

Dr. Olufemi Adeniji is a third-year principal of the School of Technology in Chicago. Born in Nigeria, he migrated to Britain in the early 1970s. After a short period of schooling, Adeniji worked with the Nigeria High Commission in London as an administrative clerk. He maintained the Nigerian-British diplomatic affairs files; created the data bank for the Nigerian students in London's and Liverpool's metropolitan school systems; and coordinated students' activities with school administrators in Liverpool, England.

Adeniji moved to Dallas, Texas in the late 1970s where he obtained a bachelor's degree from Bishop College and a doctorate from the University of North Texas. During the 1989-1990 school year, he received the New York City Rookie Teacher of the Year Award for his excellence, passion, and dedication to the education of all students. Adeniji also served as an adjunct professor at the College of New Rochelle before working with Chicago Public Schools. He is a proud African American.

Dr. Olufemi Adeniji
Principal
School of Technology

Affiliated with The University of Chicago since 1977, Danielle Allen, Ph.D., is a scholar whose intellectual scope spans the fields of the classics, philosophy, and political theory. Dean of the division of humanities at the University, Allen is the author of two books. The books are: *The World of Prometheus*, which examines the theory and practice of punishment in classical Athens, and *Talking to Strangers: anxieties of citizenship since Brown v. Board of Education* (September 2004), which combines brief readings of philosophers and political theorists with personal reflections on race politics in Chicago.

Danielle Allen received a bachelor of arts degree (1993) from Princeton; a master of arts degree (1998) and a doctor of philosophy degree (2001) from Harvard; and a master of philosophy degree (1994) and a doctor of philosophy degree (1996) from Cambridge.

She has written numerous articles on topics ranging from ancient poetry to Plato to bees to Ralph Ellison and September 11th. Allen is a 2001 recipient of a MacArthur Foundation fellowship.

Danielle Allen, Ph.D.
Dean, Division of Humanities
The University of Chicago

Celebrating African-American Achievements

Chicago's
ACADEMIA

Alise D. Barrymore serves as dean of university ministries and campus pastor at North Park University, where she oversees weekly chapel presentations; provides pastoral counseling; and contributes to the academic life of the campus through adjunct lectures.

Rev. Alise, as she is known, graduated from Yale University with a bachelor of arts in African and African-American studies. While completing her master of divinity degree from McCormick Theological Seminary, she received the Jesse Haley Award for Imagination in Preaching and the Arthur A. Hays Fellowship in Church History. In 2004, she was named one of the Twenty to Watch in *The African American Pulpit* magazine, a journal that later invited her to serve on its advisory board.

A speaker at national and local conferences hosted by denominations as diverse as Roman Catholic and Pentecostal, she has contributed to *What Can Happen When We Pray* and the *Women of Color Devotional Bible*. When not fulfilling her commitments as one of the founding pastors of The Emmaus Community, a postmodern worship community, she serves her neighbors through her sorority, Delta Sigma Theta Sorority, Inc.

Alise D. Barrymore
Dean, University Ministries
North Park University

Sharonda T. Benson is a faculty member at Kennedy King College in Chicago, Illinois. As a chemistry professor teaching organic chemistry and general chemistry, Benson actively supports and leads students to high academic achievement and success.

Founder of a student-based organization on campus entitled, Project Discovery, Benson inspires students to focus on careers in the sciences that are underrepresented by minorities. To increase minority representation in the science field, Benson integrates seminars, career workshops, shadowing projects, science related field trips, and research opportunities into the curriculum.

Benson is a member of Alpha Kappa Alpha Sorority, Inc., the National Organization of Black Chemists and Chemical Engineers, the American Chemical Society, and the U.S. Bowling Congress. She also volunteers by coaching bowling to high school students.

She received a bachelor of science degree in chemistry in 1997 from Norfolk State University, and a master's degree specializing in organometallic chemistry. Benson has co-published two articles in the *Journal of Organic Chemistry* and *Tetrahedron Letters*.

Benson is currently pursuing a doctorate degree in education in the area of educational leadership at Argosy University.

Sharonda T. Benson
Chemistry Professor
City Colleges of Chicago

Chicago's ACADEMIA
Celebrating African-American Achievements

Emmett Bradbury, III, Ph.D., is associate professor of philosophy and acting chair of African American studies at Chicago State University. He works in the areas of moral philosophy and African-American social, political, and philosophical thought.

In 2000, Bradbury was selected for entry into *Who's Who Among American Teachers*. He holds a bachelor's degree in philosophy from the University of Illinois at Chicago, and a master of arts degree in liberal studies and a doctor of philosophy degree in philosophy, both from Northwestern University in Evanston. Bradbury is a member of the American Philosophical Association and Kappa Alpha Psi Fraternity, Inc.

Emmett L. Bradbury III, Ph.D.
Acting Chair
African American Studies
Chicago State University

Rev. Lee H. Butler, Jr., Ph.D., is an associate professor of theology and psychology at Chicago Theological Seminary. He is the author of *A Loving Home: Caring for African American Marriage and Families* (2000) and *Liberating Our Dignity, Saving Our Souls* (2006). He is also an article contributor to many books and professional journals. A former director of the master of divinity program, his teaching and research interests are in the areas of pastoral theology and the practice of ministry, focusing on such topics as African-American religion, theology, spirituality, and sexuality.

His professional development includes experience in pastoral ministry, chaplaincy, pastoral counseling, ecumenics, and denominational and seminary administration. He received a bachelor's degree from Bucknell University; a master of divinity degree from Eastern Baptist Theological Seminary; a master of theology from Princeton Theological Seminary; and master of philosophy and doctor of philosophy degrees from Drew University.

He married Mary Anita Robinson Butler in 1989. They are currently being re-educated about life by their daughter, Adia Mary Robinson Butler, (*Adia* is Kiswahili meaning "God's gift") who was born in October of 2000.

Rev. Lee H. Butler, Jr., Ph.D.
Associate Professor
Theology & Psychology
Chicago Theological Seminary

Celebrating African-American Achievements

Chicago's
ACADEMIA

Dr. Madie Cannamoré has taught in Chicago Public Schools for more than 40 years. She has served on the board of directors for the Support Center of Chicago, and she designs and sells award-winning customized jewelry through CUZ-2, her home-based jewelry business. Cannamoré is a circle member of the Chicago Girl Scouts and a supporter of the Black Ensemble Theater.

Cannamoré is affiliated with many organizations and has received many awards, including Outstanding Woman of the Year from the American Association of Women in Community Colleges in 2005; Alumnae of the Year from Chicago State University in 2002; the Kathy Osterman Award; the Marcus Garvey Empowerment Award; and Distinguished Professor in 2001. A member of the Illinois Community College Trustee Association in 2003, she was featured in *Who's Who Among Educators* in 2000, 2005, and 2006. Cannamoré was named Educator of the Year by Phi Delta Kappa, and was inducted into Englewood High School's Premiere Hall of Fame.

She also participated in a grant program at Chicago State University and wrote two modules for middle school students/teachers for CDPU credit in 2004.

Dr. Madie M. Davis Cannamoré
Professor
Chicago City Colleges

Addie L. Davis is associate professor of mathematics at Olive-Harvey College, one of the City Colleges of Chicago, where she engages and encourages students to overcome their "math anxieties." She is the senior faculty advisor for the Lambda Iota chapter of Phi Theta Kappa, the international honor society of two-year colleges. Addie participates in numerous community activities and annual cancer walks in both the city and the suburbs.

Addie is Olive-Harvey's 2003-2004 distinguished professor. She also received the 2003-2004 Phenomenal Woman Award from the American Association of Women in Community Colleges (AAWCC) and the 2005 Paragon Award for her outstanding achievements in Phi Theta Kappa. She is repeatedly featured in *Who's Who Among America's Teachers* and *Who's Who of American Women*. A member of Little Mountain of Hope Ministry, Addie serves as chair of the women's ministry in an evangelical capacity. She has spoken on many occasions, both personally and professionally.

As an educator, Addie's personal motto is, "Once a teacher; always a student." To further her educational goals, she is actively pursuing her Ph.D. in education at Capella University.

Addie L. Davis
Associate Professor
Mathematics Department
Olive-Harvey College

Chicago's ACADEMIA

Celebrating African-American Achievements

Born and raised in Zimbabwe, Africa, Caleb Dube, Ph.D., obtained his bachelor of arts honors and master of philosophy degrees from the University of Zimbabwe. He was awarded a Fulbright scholarship to attend graduate school in the U.S., and he graduated with a doctorate of philosophy in cultural anthropology from Northwestern University in Evanston. From the fall of 2002 through the spring of 2006, Dube was assistant professor in the department of sociology at DePaul University. Beginning in the fall of 2006, he will be assistant professor of cultural anthropology in the department of sociology at Regis University in Denver, Colorado.

Dube's work involves teaching undergraduate students and conducting research in the community. His area of academic specialization is cultural anthropology, particularly the arts and culture. Dube's current research is on changes in Chicago's Bronzeville neighborhood, misperceptions of teenage motherhood, and music making as an occupation.

He serves on the board of directors of the African American Arts Alliance of Chicago. Additionally, some of his articles have appeared in the *International Dictionary of Black Composers* and the *Encyclopedia of African Folklore*.

Caleb Dube, Ph.D.
Assistant Professor
Department of Sociology
DePaul University

Donna M. Grant is a Ph.D. student and adjunct faculty in computer science at DePaul University. Her teaching areas include project management, systems analysis, and systems design. She also conducts research in women and information technology (IT).

Prior to pursuing a Ph.D., Grant spent 22 years in the IT industry. She previously worked as a director of process improvement for the Joint Commission on Accreditation of Healthcare Organizations, and was the director of information technology at Ameritech.

Grant is the recipient of the Graduate Assistance in Areas of National Need, and the Illinois Graduate Incentive Program fellowships. As a doctoral student, Grant has been accepted as a member of the Upsilon Pi Epsilon International Computer Science Honors Society, and the Honors Society of Phi Kappa Phi. Grant was a founding officer for the DePaul Chapter of the National Society of Black Engineers, and developed a technology summer camp, Girls with Engineering Mindz.

Earning a bachelor of science in mathematics from Northwestern University, Grant also received an MBA in finance with an additional master's in information systems from DePaul University.

Donna M. Grant
Adjunct Faculty, Computer Science
DePaul University

Celebrating African-American Achievements

Chicago's ACADEMIA

Yvonne Harris is the chair of the biology and biotechnology department at Truman College and is responsible for its day-to-day operations. She directs the activities of the biotechnology program and tissue culture facility, which are unique among two-year colleges in Illinois.

Yvonne has partnered, designed, developed, and implemented a number of grant-funded programs in partnership with industry and four-year institutions that focus on increasing the presence of minorities in research. She was co-creator, curriculum director, and project manager of the Illinois Regional Bioinformatics Program that resulted in a $6 million Department of Labor H1B matching fund grant, a first for Chicago. Yvonne also moderated the WYCC broadcasted Town Hall Meeting on stem cells, and is chair of the Minority Outreach Initiative in Chicago for the BIO2006 conference. She has received various awards, including Woman of the Year.

Receiving her doctorate degree from Northern Illinois University in molecular biology, Yvonne was a post-doctorate fellow at The University of Chicago and the University of Illinois at Chicago.

Yvonne Harris, Ph.D.
Chairperson
Department of Biology and Biotechnology
Truman College

Dwight N. Hopkins earned a bachelor's degree from Harvard University; master of divinity, master of philosophy, and doctor of philosophy degrees from Union Theological Seminary; and a doctor of philosophy degree from the University of Cape Town (South Africa).

He has written numerous books which include *Being Human: Races, Culture, and Religion*; *Heart and Head: Black Theology Past, Present, and Future*; *Black Theology in the U.S.A. and South Africa: Politics, Culture, and Liberation*; *Religions/Globalizations: Theories and Cases*; and *Shoes that Fit Our Feet: Sources for a Constructive Black Theology*.

Hopkins also penned *Introducing Black Theology of Liberation*; *Global Voices for Gender Justice*; *Cut Loose Your Stammering Tongue: Black Theology in the Slave Narratives*; *Loving the Body: Black Religious Studies and the Erotic*; and *Black Faith & Public Talk: Critical Essays in Honor of James H. Cone's Black Theology and Black Power*.

His other titles are *Changing Conversations: Religious Reflection and Cultural Analysis*; *Down, Up & Over: Slave Religion and Black Theology*; *Liberation Theologies, Post-Modernity and the Americas*; and *We Are One Voice: Essays on Black Theology in South Africa and the USA*.

Dwight N. Hopkins
Professor of Theology
The University of Chicago
Divinity School

Chicago's ACADEMIA

Celebrating African-American Achievements

Beverly D. Burton Letcher R.N., M.S.
Assistant Professor of Nursing
Malcolm X College

Beverly D. Burton Letcher graduated from North Park University in 1971 as the first African-American nursing graduate. Letcher was the first African-American, and youngest director of Nursing and Health Programs of the Chicago Chapter American Red Cross from 1975-1981.

Letcher joined Malcolm X College in 1983. She has served the college on numerous committees, and co-chaired the college governance sub-committee on resources. Letcher was elected chairperson of nursing in 1994 and 1998. In 2004, she attained the rank of assistant professor of nursing. She became the first nursing educator from City Colleges to receive certification as a nurse educator (CNE) by the National League for Nursing (2005).

Letcher is a member of National Black Nurses Association, Sigma Theta Tau International Honor Society of Nursing, Chi Eta Phi Sorority of Nursing, and the National League for Nursing. She enjoys volunteering in her community as a tutor for Delta Adult Learning and at The Bottomless Closet.

She is the proud wife of Mr. Thomas Letcher, and is the mother of two children, Kimberly and Keith.

Tracey Lewis-Elligan, Ph.D.
Assistant Professor
Department of Sociology
DePaul University

Tracey Lewis-Elligan, Ph.D., is an assistant professor in the department of sociology at DePaul University, the largest Catholic university in the United States. As a college professor, Lewis-Elligan is responsible for teaching and conducting research on health disparities and outcomes with a particular focus on African Americans and underserved communities. Her current research project is an exploratory study of African-American teen girls, investigating issues of body image and eating disorders.

Lewis-Elligan has been awarded grants from the W.K. Kellogg Community Health Scholars' Program and DePaul University to investigate health disparities and outcomes of African-American youth and their families. She has published several articles related to this work that have appeared in academic journals such as *Developmental Psychology* and various books.

Lewis-Elligan received a bachelor of arts degree in psychology in 1991 from Hampton University; a master of arts degree in psychology in 1995 from The New School for Social Research; and a doctorate of philosophy in child and family studies in 2001 from Syracuse University.

Celebrating African-American Achievements

Chicago's
ACADEMIA

June M. McKoy, M.D., J.D., is an assistant professor of medicine and preventive medicine at Northwestern University Feinberg School of Medicine in Chicago, and an appointed member of the Robert H. Lurie Comprehensive Cancer Center. McKoy is board certified in internal medicine and geriatric medicine. In this position, she provides clinical care to elderly patients, mentors medical students and fellows, and pursues National Cancer Institute-funded clinical cancer research. She also chairs the medical school's executive diversity committee.

McKoy received her medical degree from Southern Illinois University School of Medicine, a master's degree in public health from the University of Illinois (Delta Omega inductee), and a juris doctor degree from DePaul University College of Law. In 2005, she received a master's degree in law with honors from Northwestern University School of Law. She is a licensed Illinois attorney and a 2005 Leadership Greater Chicago fellow.

McKoy volunteers for the American Cancer Society and is the 2006 recipient of the Harold Washington Professional Achievement Award from Roosevelt University. A Jamaican immigrant, she enjoys writing poetry and traveling.

June M. McKoy, M.D., J.D.
Assistant Professor
Northwestern University
Feinberg School of Medicine

Patricia Mell joined the faculty of The John Marshall Law School as its 11th dean in 2003. She is the second African-American woman in the United States to lead a non-HBCU law school.

Before John Marshall, Mell had a distinguished career as an assistant attorney general and corporations counsel in the state of Ohio. As a faculty member and academic dean with 22 years in the legal academy, Mell has written several scholarly articles and made presentations in a number of national and international venues. Her areas of expertise are criminal law, the legal aspects of e-commerce, corporations, agency, and partnership. She also has an interest in computers and privacy, and her article on national security under the USA Patriot Act appeared recently in the *Denver Law Review*.

Mell has won numerous awards including being named one of the 100 Most Influential Women in Chicago by *Crain's Chicago Business* in 2004. Her co-authored textbook on criminal law is being published by Carolina Academic Press. She is the current editor of the American Bar Association Criminal Justice Section's sentencing publication, *Criminal Justice* magazine.

Patricia Mell
Faculty Member
The John Marshall Law School

Chicago's ACADEMIA

Celebrating African-American Achievements

Salikoko S. Mufwene is the Frank J. McLoraine distinguished service professor of linguistics at The University of Chicago. He also serves on the committee on evolutionary biology, and the department of comparative human development.

Earning his Ph.D. in linguistics with distinction from The University of Chicago, Mufwene taught at the University of the West Indies and at the University of Georgia. He joined The University of Chicago in 1992, chairing its department of linguistics. Mufwene also served as "Professeur Invité" at the Université de Lyon III, the Collège de France (in Paris), and at the Université de Paris III. He was a visiting professor at the National University of Singapore and at Harvard University.

He is the author of *The Ecology of Language Evolution* (Cambridge UP, 2001) and of *Créoles, écologie sociale, évolution linguistique* (l'Harmattan, 2005), and is the editor of *Africanisms in Afro-American Language Varieties* (U of Georgia Press, 1993). Mufwene is lead editor of several publications, has authored over 200 essays on creoles and African languages, and is the series editor of the *Cambridge Approaches to Language Contact*.

Salikoko S. Mufwene
Professor
Department of Linguistics
The University of Chicago

Caleb A. Olaleye is a professor of mathematics at South Suburban College (SSC) in South Holland, Illinois. As a member of the NSF Alliance for Minority participation, Caleb serves as mentor to many students.

Under the International/Intercultural committee at SSC, Caleb helps in the selection of students for the ICCB study abroad program. Caleb is a multiple year honoree of *Who's Who Among America's Teachers*.

Caleb hails from Abeokuta, Ogun State, Nigeria. He received a bachelor of science degree in engineering from the University of Illinois at Chicago. He also holds a master of science degree in mathematics and a master of arts degree in education from Chicago State University.

A parishioner at Saint Jude's Catholic Church in South Holland, Illinois, Caleb is a frequent visitor of the Holy Hill Cathedral Church of Hubertus, Wisconsin. His hobbies include playing the piano, listening to soft music, and watching sports games.

Married to Ade-Mosun Olaleye (Destiny), Caleb is father to Goodness (Angel), Victoria (Pride), Victor (Heroe), and Godwin (Joy). His favorite quote is, "The fear of God is the beginning of wisdom."

Caleb A. Olaleye
Professor of Mathematics
South Suburban College

Celebrating African-American Achievements

Chicago's ACADEMIA

Gina Miranda Samuels, Ph.D., is an assistant professor in the School of Social Service Administration at The University of Chicago. Her research and publications explore racial/ethnic/cultural identity development among trans-racial adoptees, family and social support networks among foster youth aging out of care, and interpretive research methods.

Samuels has practiced social work in the areas of child welfare and child protective services, juvenile probation, and Africentric school-based tutoring programs. Currently, she serves as a research expert on the Illinois Adoption Advisory Council and is an affiliated board member of MAVIN Foundation, a national organization addressing the needs and concerns of multiracial populations and trans-racial adoptees in the U.S.

At The University of Chicago, Samuels is a faculty affiliate of the Center for the Study of Race Politics and Culture and a faculty associate at the Chapin Hall Center for Children.

Samuels received a bachelor of science degree in social work from the University of Wisconsin-Oshkosh. She then earned her master of science in social work degree and doctorate of philosophy degree in social welfare both at the University of Wisconsin-Madison.

Gina Miranda Samuels, Ph.D.
Assistant Professor
School of Social Service Administration
The University of Chicago

Natatia M. Trotter-Gordon is director of business and industry services at Kennedy-King College, one of the city colleges of Chicago. As director, she is responsible for being a liaison for local businesses, as well as offering customized contract training to businesses as a way to increase employee competency on the job.

The business and industry department's best program has been the Entrepreneurship Certificate Program. This service assists aspiring individuals who would like to open a business and/or maintain their current businesses. Natatia has partnered with several community agencies to sponsor students for this program.

Natatia is an executive board member of Georgia Doty Health Education Fund, chief financial officer of Great Black Music Project, and a member of Alpha Kappa Alpha Sorority, Inc.

She received her bachelor's degree in chemistry from Spelman College in 1991, a bachelor's in biology from the National College of Chiropractic in 1995, and a master's degree in chemistry from the University of Illinois at Chicago in 1999.

Natatia M. Trotter-Gordon
Director of Business and Industry Services
Kennedy-King College

Chicago's ACADEMIA

Celebrating African-American Achievements

Dexter R. Voisin, Ph.D., L.C.S.W., is an associate professor with tenure in the School of Social Service Administration at The University of Chicago. His research projects involve the use of quantitative and qualitative approaches to understanding the pathways that illuminate the relationship between exposure to violence and HIV sexual risk behaviors among adolescents, and international HIV prevention in the Caribbean. Voisin has secured several prestigious grants, authored numerous articles, and presented his research to both national and international audiences.

Voisin is currently a consulting editor for several major academic journals. He is a faculty associate with the Chapin Hall Center for Children and the Center for the Study of Race, Politics, and Culture at The University of Chicago. Voisin is a research affiliate with Emory University School of Public Health, and a visiting research scholar at the Center for AIDS Prevention Studies at the University of California-San Francisco.

Voisin received his bachelor's in psychology, cum laude, from St. Andrews College, a master's in social work from the University of Michigan, and a master's of philosophy and Ph.D. from Columbia University.

Dexter R. Voisin, Ph.D., L.C.S.W.
Associate Professor
School of Social Service Administration
The University of Chicago

Sandra Walls has served as principal of Martin Luther King School since 1999. She began her teaching career in the Chicago Public Schools and taught several years before receiving her master of arts degree from Chicago State University in educational administration in 1993.

Prior to her current position, Sandra worked as an assistant principal in Chicago for two years before accepting a principal position with the West Harvey Dixmoor School District at Washington Elementary School in 1995. She also worked as a principal in School District 365U in Bolingbrook, Illinois.

Sandra was nominated for the Golden Apple Award in 1987; the Milken Award in 2001; and the Administrator of the Year Award in 2002, sponsored by the Illinois State Board Education. She also received a Creative Teacher Award from the William Penn School in 1989, and an Outstanding Teacher Service Award in 1992.

Married, Sandra is a mother of two, a proud grandmother of seven, and enjoys spending time with her family. She also loves to read and is a member of Mount Zion Baptist Church.

Sandra F. Walls
Principal
Martin Luther King School

Celebrating African-American Achievements

Chicago's
ACADEMIA

Ken Warren has taught at The University of Chicago since 1991 in the department of English and the committee on African and African-American studies. He has published two books, *Black and White Strangers: Race and American Literary Realism* (Chicago 1993), and *So Black and Blue: Ralph Ellison and the Occasion of Criticism* (Chicago 2003), along with numerous articles.

In 2005, he was awarded the Llewellyn John & Harriet Manchester Quantrell Award for Excellence in Undergraduate Teaching. Prior to coming to Chicago, he was assistant professor of English at Northwestern University in Evanston, Illinois.

He holds a bachelor's in history and literature from Harvard College and a Ph.D. in English and American literature from Stanford University.

He has served on the local school councils at William H. Ray Elementary School and Kenwood Academy High School in Chicago. He is married to Maria M. Warren, and together they have four adult children, Lenora, Mercedes, Marcus, and Gregory.

Kenneth W. Warren
Deputy Provost for Research & Minority Issues
The University of Chicago

Order Additional Copies

$34.95 Plus $7.00 S/H
Great Gift Idea
All Orders Shipped in 24hrs.
All Credit Cars Accepted

Call Today!
(614) 481-7300

Please call for inquiries for
bulk purchases
for minority youth groups,
schools, churches, civic
or professional organizations

THE INAUGURAL EDITION *Who's Who In Black Chicago*

WHO'S WHO PUBLISHING CO., LLC

Celebrating African-American Achievements

ACROSS THE NATION

- Who's Who In Black Columbus
- Who's Who In Black Cleveland
- Who's Who In Black Atlanta
- Who's Who In Black Cincinnati
- Who's Who In Black St. Louis
- Who's Who In Black Indianapolis
- Who's Who In Black Birmingham
- Black Judges in America

Visit Us Online @
www.whoswhopublishing.com
or call (614) 481-7300

Chicago's
SPIRITUAL LEADERS

"And I will give you shepherds according to My heart, who will feed you with knowledge and understanding."

JEREMIAH 3:15 NKJV

Chicago's SPIRITUAL LEADERS

Celebrating African-American Achievements

Dennis Rayford Bell was born on July 9, 1923 in Mississippi. In April of 1949, he first heard the gospel of Jesus Christ and began a new life.

Bell is a firm believer of education being the road to true freedom and success. Attending LaSalle University (Chicago), he completed his high school requirements. He also received a bachelor's degree in religious studies from Southwestern College (Oklahoma). At American Bible College (Florida), Bell was a straight "A" student pursuing his master's in theology. In August of 1979, he received his doctorate of theology and philosophy from Toledo Bible College. Bell is the first in the school's history to achieve two doctorate degrees in one year.

As senior pastor of Christ Temple Apostolic Faith Church for 48 years, his motto is "I'm apostolic across the fence, behind the barn, and everywhere." Bell's life has been one of serving the church and community. He is also a chaplain for the Chicago Police Department. His primary joy is sharing the life and saving grace of Jesus Christ with others.

Bishop D. Rayford Bell
Senior Pastor
Christ Temple Apostolic
Faith Church, Inc.

Pastor John Leland Belser, Sr. is a native of Maywood, Illinois. Belser has earned two bachelor degrees, a master of arts degree, and two teacher certificates with the State of Illinois.

Belser served as a public school educator for 18 years prior to becoming a pastor. He was honored by *Who's Who Among American High School Teachers* for four consecutive years, 2001 – 2005, and received the Most Inspirational Teacher Award from Western Illinois University.

Belser became the eighth pastor of the First Baptist Church of Melrose Park in 2002. He also serves as CEO of the H. McNelty School, a private nonprofit school operated by First Baptist Church for grades pre-school through eight.

Happily married to the former Kimberly Cherisse Ivy of Chicago, Belser and his wife are the proud parents of four children.

John Leland Belser, Sr.
Pastor
First Baptist Church of Melrose Park

Celebrating African-American Achievements

Chicago's
SPIRITUAL LEADERS

Apostle Columbus F. Bland is the founder and pastor of the Glory To Glory Family Christian Center. He has been married for 40 years to Katie Bland. Bland is the father of three, and a grandfather of five. Born in Charleston, Mississippi, Bland is one of 15 children. Because his family was very poor he had to forego a formal education to help support his family.

His life has been transformed by the power of God from an alcoholic and a gambler, to a new man of peace, integrity, and holiness. He has ministered in the Cook County correctional system for more than 14 years. His evangelistic ministry has traveled throughout the United States including Hawaii and the Bahamas.

Bland is a man that loves and obeys God. He has shared his home with several and disciples many to Christ. After prevailing with principalities and winning over depression, he is an effective marriage and family counselor. Bland is a role model to many men who find him to be approachable and down to earth.

Columbus F. Bland
Founder & Pastor
Glory To Glory Family Christian Center

Minister Epluribus Cornelius Cunningham received his calling to preach the gospel in November of 1989 at the age of 19. He was licensed to preach in 1990 under the ministry of pastor Napoleon Davis of the Christ First Baptist Church of Harvey, Illinois, where he served as an associate minister and minister of music for seven years.

Cunningham joined the staff of Salem Baptist Church of Chicago in 1998 under the leadership of Rev. James T. Meeks, senior pastor. He currently serves as pastor of K²B (Kid's Kingdom Building) Children's Ministry.

Cunningham has been instrumental in helping hundreds of children and adults to find faith, hope, and purpose through a relationship with Jesus Christ. His main goal in ministering to children is to help them to become active, productive, and kingdom-minded students and citizens in today's society. Cunningham accomplishes this goal each week as he leads Salem's Children Church, of more than 700 children, in what both parents and children consider being an exuberant and captivating time of praise, worship, and Bible study.

Minister Epluribus C. Cunningham
Children's Pastor
Salem Baptist Church of Chicago

Chicago's SPIRITUAL LEADERS

Celebrating African-American Achievements

Rev. Alexis L. Felder is founder of Triumphant Living Ministries International, which helps women and men to discover their true identity and access their authority in Jesus Christ. As minister of ministry operations at New Faith Baptist Church International, Felder is completing her first book entitled: "Preparing to Hear His Voice." Her sermons were featured in *The African American Pulpit's* Fall 2005 edition, where she was recognized as an emerging voice among women preachers.

Felder graduated with honors from Garrett-Evangelical Theological Seminary at Northwestern University in Evanston with a master of theological studies degree in New Testament. Currently, she is pursuing a doctor of ministry degree in preaching at McCormick Theological Seminary.

She is married to Rev. Dr. Trunell D. Felder, senior pastor of New Faith Baptist Church International in Matteson, Illinois, a thriving worship center with five additional churches in Ghana, West Africa. Felder and their son, Andrew, collaborate with Dr. Felder in ministry as he leads a flock of 6,000 members in the south suburbs of Chicago.

Rev. Alexis L. Felder
Founder
Triumphant Living Ministries International

Dr. Trunell D. Felder was born in Los Angeles, California, and reared in Detroit, Michigan. He earned a bachelor of arts degree in marketing from Michigan State University in East Lansing, Michigan. In 1990, he matriculated to Candler School of Theology at Emory University in Atlanta, Georgia. He received his master of divinity with a concentration in pastoral care in May of 1993.

In 2000, Felder graduated summa cum laude from the Interdenominational Theological Center (ITC) in Atlanta, Georgia with a doctor of ministry degree. His dissertation, entitled "An Inward – Outward Journey: A Paradigm for the Spiritual Formation of the African American Male Disciple," addresses the challenges and provides solutions for the spiritual formation of Christian African-American men in the church.

Presently, Felder is the senior pastor of New Faith Baptist Church International in Matteson, Illinois, a thriving worship center with 6,000 members and five churches in Ghana, West Africa.

Felder is married to the love of his life, the former Rev. Alexis L. Brinkley of Milwaukee, Wisconsin, and they have one son, Andrew.

Dr. Trunell D. Felder
Senior Pastor
New Faith Baptist Church International

Celebrating African-American Achievements

Chicago's
SPIRITUAL LEADERS

Rev. Dr. William H. Foster, Jr. is pastor of Providence Missionary Baptist Church (PMBC) located in Chicago. The congregation consists of more than 1,200 members. Some of Foster's goals are to meet the needs of people, to win souls to Christ, and to feed his flock the word of God. His principal commitment is the spiritual growth and development of people.

He has continued to move PMBC forward implementing several new ministries and capital improvements, including a youth church service; a computer technology center; the Providence Employment Resource Ministry; a marriage ministry; an early morning worship service; and a transitional housing facility.

Foster received his bachelor of science degree in business from Montana State University and his MBA degree from The University of Chicago. He received a master's degree in religion from Trinity Evangelical Divinity Seminary and a doctorate degree in ministry from United Theological Seminary.

Dr. Foster was drafted by the Chicago Bulls in 1980, and played for the Montana Golden Nuggets in the CBA. He has been featured in several publications, including *Dollars & Sense* and *Crain's Chicago Business*.

Rev. Dr. William H. Foster, Jr.
Pastor
Providence Missionary Baptist Church

The Reverend Dr. Glenn A. Harris, Jr. is an associate minister of Bread of Life Missionary Baptist Church. A native of Chicago, Harris was born the second child of two to Angelique and Glenn Harris, Sr.

Harris graduated from the public schools of District 63 and District 207 education systems. He also attended Columbia College in Chicago for oral communications in public speaking. Harris then went on to pursue pasturing his own church that began in October of 1999. After being ordained in the ministry in January of 1999, he received an honorary doctrine degree in theology for his merit on his thesis.

Later, wanting to learn from Universal Ministries School of Theology in Milford, Illinois, Harris received his associate of divinity in theology in August of 2004. In that same year, he also earned a diploma as a pharmacy technician from the Professional Career Development Institute in Atlanta, Georgia.

Receiving his bachelor's degree in biblical studies in 2006, Harris also holds a High Honors Achievement Award for a GPA of 7.0. He currently plans to pursue a master's degree.

Rev. Dr. Glenn A. Harris, Jr.
Associate Minister
Bread of Life Missionary Baptist Church

Chicago's
SPIRITUAL LEADERS

Celebrating African-American Achievements

Dr. Mildred C. Harris, pastor and educator is founder, president, and chief executive officer of God First Ministries (Chicago, Illinois), with chapters in Georgia, Indiana, Ohio, and New York. For 20 years, the ministry has sponsored the largest community breakfast in Chicago.

In 1999, Mayor Richard M. Daley appointed Harris commissioner for the Chicago Housing Authority (CHA) with a plan for transformation budget of $1.5 billion. She refurbished 57 sitting rooms in CHA senior buildings, raising more than $200,000.

Harris received the Dominick's Fresh Spirit Award for Chicago's leading women religious leaders, the 2005 NBC5 Chicago Jefferson Award, and the 2005 Mitsubishi Motors Unsung Heroine Award from the Mitsubishi Motors USA Foundation. She is listed in *Who's Who in the World*, and she sits on numerous Illinois state government boards.

Harris holds a bachelor of science degree from DePaul University and three master's degrees from Columbia University, New York City; Governors State University, Park Forest, Illinois; and Loyola University, Chicago, Illinois. She also holds a doctorate in ministry from the International Bible Institute Seminary in Plymouth, Florida.

Dr. Mildred C. Harris
President & Chief Executive Officer
God First Ministries

Chicago native Marshall Elijah Hatch, Sr. has been pastor of New Mount Pilgrim Missionary Baptist Church since 1993. His spiritual development began in Shiloh Missionary Baptist Church under the pastorate of his father, the late Reverend Elijah Hatch. In 1985, he was ordained and appointed pastor of Commonwealth Missionary Baptist Church in North Lawndale. In 1998, he was selected for one of the most highly coveted fellowships at Harvard Divinity School.

Throughout his ministry, Hatch has commenced numerous community outreach programs. His civic involvement spans more than two decades. He is the national director of religious affairs of the RainbowPUSH Coalition, and serves on the boards of the African American Leadership Partnership and the Westside Ministers AIDS Coalition.

Hatch holds doctorate and master's degrees in ministry and theological studies, respectively, from McCormick Theological Seminary in Chicago. He also holds a master's degree in government from Georgetown University and a bachelor's degree in political science from Western Illinois University.

Hatch is married to the former Priscilla Murchison, and they are the parents of four children, Joyce, Janelle, Marshall, and Maurice.

Rev. Marshall Elijah Hatch, Sr.
Pastor
New Mount Pilgrim
Missionary Baptist Church

Celebrating African-American Achievements

Chicago's
SPIRITUAL LEADERS

Charles Jenkins has firmly established himself as one of the most dynamic forces in the African-American community. As a community leader, counselor, and preacher, 30-year-old Jenkins is respected and revered for his innovative thinking, age-old wisdom, contemporary leadership, and business savvy. As pastor of the historic Fellowship Missionary Baptist Church (FMBC), Jenkins has more than doubled revenues, implemented cutting-edge programs, increased real estate holdings, and created an empowering environment for youth, while impacting nations for God. As a result of his unwavering commitment to adding value to others, more than 5,500 new parishioners have united with FMBC in merely five years.

A graduate of Moody Bible Institute, Jenkins earned a bachelor of science degree in Christian education. He is currently completing a master's degree at Trinity Evangelical Divinity School.

A man of balance, Jenkins is married to Tara Rawls-Jenkins and has two young daughters, Princess and Paris.

Charles Jenkins is a man that brings people together to ensure mobility and momentum for individuals, communities, and organizations. He is considered a yardstick for his generation.

Charles Jenkins
Pastor
Fellowship Missionary Baptist Church

Sheraine Lathon is senior pastor and administrator of Liberty Temple Full Gospel Church. Her fiery and cutting-edge message of godly order and holiness has caused thousands to turn their hearts toward God.

With 22 years of dedicated service, especially in church administration and finance, Lathon has progressed at Liberty Temple from member, to evangelist, to elder, to pastor, teacher, and prophet.

Lathon established an annual health fair for Chicago communities, offering free mammograms and screenings. She sponsors shelters throughout the city and feeds 1,500 disadvantaged families biannually. She also helps her overseer in the planting and nourishing of ministries all over the nation.

Lathon is an associate professor at Logos Ministerial Training Institute and Friends International University. Her areas of expertise are church history, homiletics, and hermeneutics. She holds a bachelor's degree and a master's degree in church administration and a doctorate in divinity. Her name appears in many Who's Who publications.

Pastor Lathon honors her husband, Willie, and her sons, Eric and Chris, for their prayers and encouragement in allowing her to pursue God's plan for her life.

Sheraine Lathon
Senior Pastor & Administrator
Liberty Temple Full Gospel Church

Chicago's
SPIRITUAL LEADERS

Celebrating African-American Achievements

Dr. Arnella Elizabeth Pierce
Founder & Pastor
Revelation International
Outreach Ministry

Dr. Arnella Elizabeth Pierce, founder of Revelation International Outreach Ministry, has been the pastor of this nondenominational ministry for 15 years. Through Pierce's pastoral leadership, teaching, and vision of an "alternative village," holistic programs have evolved. This includes Blessings to Go, a feed the homeless outreach, and Zoe, a motivational prison lecture program. Through The Bridge Project, Pierce conducts workshops essential for healing the soul and mind. A newly renovated three-story convent houses the ministry's offices, chapel, sanctuary, and soon to be health spa.

Pierce has authored several inspirational and healing books, in particular, *But You Say You Love Me,* and coming soon, "The Pregnant Man." As a playwright, Pierce also writes and directs plays for "soul revelation," including *Destiny's Decision.* Her next production is scheduled for the summer of 2006.

Pierce received a bachelor's degree in journalism from Columbia College, holds a master's degree in religious education, and received a doctorate in theology. Pierce also established Revelation Institute in 1998, where she is dean.

Rev. Dr. Albert "Al" Sampson
Pastor
Fernwood United Methodist Church

Rev. Dr. Albert Sampson will celebrate his 50th anniversary in the ministry, as well as his 31st pastoral anniversary of Fernwood United Methodist Church.

As presiding elder of the United Methodist Church South End Cooperative Parish, Sampson is leadership director of the United Methodist South End Cooperative E3 (Economics, Education and Evangelism) Initiative. He is also founder and president of the faith-based organized Farmers Agribusiness Resource Management (FARM), and the Neighborhood Social Entrepreneurs Society.

Sampson was one of only three ministers ordained by Dr. Martin Luther King, Jr. at Ebenezer Baptist Church in 1966. In addition, he was inducted into the Martin Luther King, Jr. board of preachers of Morehouse College.

A distinguished biblical scholar, Sampson is a theological consultant for *The Original African Heritage Study Bible.* President George W. Bush and Mr. Jim Towey, director of the White House Office of Faith-Based and Community Initiatives, recently invited Sampson to participate as a panelist in the 2nd White House National Conference on Faith-Based and Community Initiatives in Washington, D.C. Sampson presented his position paper, "Paradigm Shift Change for Social Strength 2006 and Beyond!"

Celebrating African-American Achievements

Chicago's SPIRITUAL LEADERS

Rev. Michael G. Sykes is associate pastor for visitation ministries at Trinity United Church of Christ, where Rev. Jeremiah A. Wright, Jr. is senior pastor. Sykes also holds the ecclesiastical office of cluster dean for the Chicago Metropolitan Association of the United Church of Christ, and he chairs the education committee of the Urban Clinical Pastoral Education Program.

In addition to his church duties, he serves as pastoral care coordinator at Michael Reese Hospital. In his capacity as head of pastoral care, Sykes is a member of the hospital's institutional review board, which provides oversight for medical research involving human subjects. Moreover, he occupies a seat on the institution's bio-medical ethics committee.

Sykes holds a master of divinity degree from Chicago Theological Seminary. Before entering seminary, he studied political science at the University of Illinois at Chicago and Bradley University in Peoria. Sykes' employment background also includes experience in the field of corporate marketing, where he held management positions with Citibank (assistant vice president) and Time Warner (marketing manager).

Rev. Michael G. Sykes
Associate Pastor
Trinity United Church of Christ

Bishop Larry D. Trotter was born and raised in Chicago, Illinois and grew up in one of its most disreputable housing projects. In 1981, he began to pastor The Sweet Holy Spirit Church, which now has a resident membership of more than 8,000 members.

Trotter's unique blend of encouragement and deliverance preaching, in congruence with his perceptible teaching and healing gifts, has afforded him the opportunity to minister in nearly all of the United States, and more than 18 countries worldwide. He has preached to more than 30,000 people in the New Orleans Superdome, and to more than 2 million people in Nigeria. He has also led mission trips to Ethiopia, Finland, Ghana, Zimbabwe, Greece, and India.

On December 30, 1993, Bishop Larry D. Trotter was consecrated to the sacred office of bishop, and on June 12, 2004, he was unanimously elected as the presiding prelate of the United Covenant Churches of Christ (UCCC). As the presiding prelate of the UCCC, Trotter presides over 21 bishops and 250 churches worldwide.

Bishop Larry D. Trotter
Pastor
The Sweet Holy Spirit Church

Chicago's SPIRITUAL LEADERS

Celebrating African-American Achievements

The Reverend Marvin E. Wiley, a native of Pine Bluff, Arkansas, is the pastor of the Rock of Ages Baptist Church located in Maywood, Illinois. He made history at the Rock of Ages Baptist Church in March of 1991, becoming its second pastor in 40 years.

The church has experienced spiritual, numerical, and financial growth under his dynamic leadership. Due to the phenomenal growth that Rock of Ages has experienced under the leadership of Wiley, a new multi-million dollar worship facility was constructed to the glory of God and service of mankind. Under his leadership, a 501(c)3 organization, Vision of Restoration, Inc. (VOR) was organized. VOR provides educational and economic development, mental/social services, and career development and enhancement for the community.

Under Wiley's innovative leadership, a new Spiritual Growth and Development Center, a four-level, multi-million dollar facility opened in 2004. The new 40,000 square foot edifice offers many additional resources for worship, education, and business.

Wiley's ability to teach and preach has carried him across the country for leadership, stewardship, and evangelistic services.

Rev. Marvin E. Wiley
Pastor
Rock of Ages Baptist Church

Rev. Ramah E. Wright is a graduate of Garrett Evangelical Theological Seminary in Evanston, Illinois, where she received a master of divinity degree. Currently, she serves as associate pastor for adolescents (teens) and women at Trinity United Church of Christ (UCC) in Chicago. "Rev. Ramah," as the congregation refers to her, has served as the co-convener of Trinity's annual women's conference, the facilitator of Bible classes for women and teens, and the coordinator of youth revivals, youth retreats, and the junior deacon training program.

A native of Chicago, Ramah was the first born to Leonard and Marjorie Bratton. She earned bachelor of science and master of science degrees in mathematics from Chicago State University, and taught high school mathematics for 19 years.

Ramah is married to the Rev. Dr. Jeremiah A. Wright, Jr. They are copartners in the ministry to more than 8,000 members of Trinity UCC. They are also the proud parents of five children, Janet, Jeri, Nikol, Nathan, and Jamila; and the proud grandparents of Jeremiah, Jazmin, and Steven Jr.

Rev. Ramah E. Wright
Associate Pastor
Adolescents & Women
Trinity United Church of Christ

Chicago's
COMMUNITY LEADERS

"Both tears and sweat are salty, but they render a different result. Tears will get you sympathy; sweat will get you change."

REV. JESSE L. JACKSON, SR.
MINISTER AND CIVIL RIGHTS ACTIVIST

Chicago's COMMUNITY LEADERS

Celebrating African-American Achievements

Patrice Ball-Reed
Deputy Attorney General
Child Support Enforcement
Office of the Illinois Attorney General

Patrice Ball-Reed graduated from Trinity College in Hartford, Connecticut with a bachelor of arts degree in economics (1980). Upon graduating from The John Marshall Law School, she began working as an associate in a small, general practice law firm.

Patrice learned to practice law in the private sector and moved on to the public sector. Her first position was as an assistant state's attorney for Cook County, where she served for 14 years. She spent seven years in the child support enforcement division, as a supervisor and senior trial attorney, and seven years in the real estate property tax unit, as a deputy supervisor. She then became the first African-American female to hold the position of deputy attorney general for child support enforcement at the Office of the Illinois Attorney General in April of 2003.

An attorney, wife, mother, and grandmother, Patrice has enjoyed her career. During her 20 years as an attorney, she has received numerous awards, held leadership positions, and participated in many organizations. She is a member of multiple bar associations and Delta Sigma Theta Sorority, Inc.

The Honorable Arthur L. Bennett
Trustee
Village of South Holland

Village of South Holland Trustee Arthur L. Bennett is chairman of park operations and programs. The first African American to hold an elected office in South Holland, he oversees 30 parks and a community center with recreational services and facilities. Bennett was actively involved in the development of the multimillion-dollar center. He also established an endowment fund committee to help defray some of the development cost expenses. The committee has had great success raising more than $500,000 in pledges and donations.

A widower before joining village government, Bennett retired from the Chicago Transit Authority, where he was the supervisor of more than 900 employees. He coordinated the implementation of lift-equipped bus service for mainline operations, and the establishment of the federally mandated Commercial Driver's License Program involving some 6,500 employees. He is respected for his ability to see the larger perspective on significant issues.

Bennett was the first African American to join the South Holland Lions Club, and he eventually became its president. He serves on the Academic Enrichment Foundation for District 205, and the village's public safety and community coordination committees.

Celebrating African-American Achievements

Chicago's
COMMUNITY LEADERS

Leslie Brown
Founder
Support Advocates for Women

Leslie Brown is a mother of six children and a servant of Jesus Christ. A battered woman and former prisoner, she served seven years at Dwight Correctional Center before Governor Jim Thompson granted her clemency in 1988.

Since her release, Brown founded Support Advocates for Women (SAW). SAW is an aftercare program for female ex-offenders that also provides free transportation for children to visit their incarcerated mothers. She teaches self-esteem classes in the Kankakee Minimum Security Unit and is involved in several prison ministry groups.

Brown also opened Leslie's Place, a transitional living facility for female ex-prisoners that can house approximately 30 women at its two locations. Since its inception in 1994, more than 500 women have lived at the facility, which has a 95% success rate of women not returning to prison.

Brown has appeared on several television and radio programs including *The Oprah Winfrey Show*, *Donahue*, *WGN News*, WGCI, and WVON. Recently designated one of the 100 Most Influential Chicago Women by *Crain's Chicago Business*, she was highlighted by Harry Porterfield of *ABC 7 News* as Someone You Should Know.

Marrice Coverson
Founder & President
Institute for Positive Living

Marrice Coverson is founder and president of the Institute for Positive Living (IPL) and the executive director of the IPL's Open Book Program. In this position, she heads up a range of citywide programs that promote literacy and the love of reading among African-American adolescents and their parents. Program participants are introduced to quality literature and get a chance to interact with award-winning authors, writers, and performing artists.

Marrice is a recipient of the Women of Excellence Black Pearl Award and the Community Leadership Award from the Illinois Institute of Technology. Her essay, "For the Love of Reading," appears in *Turn the Page and You Don't Stop* (2006).

Marrice holds a bachelor of arts degree in sociology from Mississippi Valley State University and a master of arts degree in public administration from Roosevelt University. Marrice is completing a master's degree in religious studies at Chicago Theological Seminary. She is also pastor of the Church of the Spirit and is the first African American since 1924 to hold a trustee position on the board of the National Spiritualist Association of Churches.

Chicago's COMMUNITY LEADERS

Celebrating African-American Achievements

Freida J. Curry
Director, Center for Urban Business
University of Illinois at Chicago

Geraldine de Haas
Founder & President
Jazz Unites, Inc.

Freida J. Curry is the director of the Center for Urban Business at the University of Illinois at Chicago. She has built a successful career in entrepreneurship training, business consulting, business loan preparation, public speaking, and marketing. Curry's passion is helping individuals achieve success by building strong business ventures; her niche is micro businesses. As an entrepreneur-development expert, she has worked with organizations that include the Department of Commerce and Economic Opportunity, the Women's Business Development Center, the Women's Self Employment Project, and the Small Business Administration.

Curry is also owner of Skills of Power, a company that sells health/nutrition products and Web sites. She is the previous owner of recording label I AM Records as well as Freida Curry & Associates, a marketing consulting and personal coaching firm. Some of her other positions have included vice president at Burrell Communications, director at the Women's Self Employment Project, and account director at Leo Burnett Advertising.

Curry received a master's degree from Northwestern University.

Founder and president of Jazz Unites, Inc. (JUI), Geraldine de Haas is "the First Lady of Chicago Jazz." She is a gifted jazz advocate, performer, and producer.

She first sang professionally in the 1950s with her brother and sister as Andy and the Bey Sisters. After an extended European tour, the popular trio performed in the U.S., making several recordings before disbanding in 1966.

In the 1970s, de Haas performed in Chicago theaters and jazz venues. When Duke Ellington died, she was inspired to begin the 1974 Ellington Tribute, the first non-classical, free concert in downtown parks, a precursor to all the music festivals now part of Chicago's attractions.

In 1981, she founded JUI to further jazz appreciation and the "real" jazz tradition on the South Side. In 1983, JUI presented the first South Shore JazzFest. The free weekend festival remains the South Side's largest and most popular musical event. It is the only African-American produced jazz festival in the nation.

De Haas is married to musician Edgar de Haas. Their children, Aisha and Darius, are both performance artists.

Celebrating African-American Achievements

Chicago's COMMUNITY LEADERS

Donna Dixon
Director of Senior Programs
Chicago Housing Authority

Donna Dixon, director of senior programs with the Chicago Housing Authority (CHA), manages programs for over 9,000 residents in 58 senior buildings. Donna, affectionately known by many seniors as "Miss Baby," is respected and admired as an advocate for senior rights, a problem solver, a counselor, and the ultimate professional. During her tenure with the Chicago Housing Authority, she has been responsible for the relocation of more than 8,000 residents during the $350 million rehabilitation of the senior buildings. Donna also plans and executes the annual CHA Senior Holiday Gala for 2,000 seniors.

Prior to her current position, Donna held positions such as director of volunteer services for the Department of Aging, day care facility director, and educator. She has a bachelor's in elementary education from Lewis University where she recently received the Black Student Union's Outstanding Alumni award.

A member of Delta Sigma Theta Sorority, Inc., Donna has been appointed to Mayor Daley's Senior Task Force, the Cook County State Attorney's Office African American Advisory Council, and is an active member of Faith United Methodist Church.

Hollis Dorrough, Jr.
Deputy Police Chief
Village of South Holland

Hollis Dorrough, Jr. is a college graduate of Calumet College of St. Joseph (Whiting, Indiana) with a degree in law enforcement management. He currently serves as deputy police chief for the Village of South Holland, Illinois. He has served in this capacity for four years.

After 32 years of service, Dorrough retired from the City of Chicago Police Department. His last position there was sergeant of police, serving on the security team for Mayor Richard M. Daley. Dorrough's years of police service included seven years as a supervising sergeant at the Chicago Police Training Academy where he was instrumental in creating the first domestic violence program, which is still being used today. He also received Governor Jim Edgar's award for working with numerous outside agencies that assisted abused women and children, the homeless, and residents of shelters.

Dorrough is looking forward to retirement and the chance to fulfill his dreams of writing music, singing, and teaching.

Chicago's COMMUNITY LEADERS
Celebrating African-American Achievements

Calvin L. Holmes
Executive Director
Chicago Community Loan Fund

Calvin Holmes is the executive director of the Chicago Community Loan Fund (CCLF), a certified community development financial institution. His company provides low-cost, flexible financing, technical assistance to community development organizations, and conducts neighborhood revitalization projects throughout metropolitan Chicago.

Holmes has worked for the loan fund for nearly 11 years, and in 1998, was promoted to his current executive director position. Under his leadership, CCLF's capitalization has more than quadrupled, from $3.7 million to more than $15 million in total capital.

In 2001, Holmes was honored as one of *Crain's Chicago Business* journal's 40 Under 40 young leaders, and was a 2002-2003 Leadership Greater Chicago fellow. He holds a master's degree in urban and regional planning, with a concentration in real estate development, from Cornell University. Holmes also received a bachelor's degree in African-American studies from Northwestern University.

Holmes currently serves on a number of non- and for-profit boards. Notably, he is a director of the Opportunity Finance Network, serves as secretary of the Interfaith Housing Development Corporation, and treasurer for both the Parkland Condominium Association and the Supportive Services Development Corporation.

Rev. Dr. Stanley Keeble
CEO & Founder
Chicago Gospel Music Heritage Museum

Rev. Dr. Stanley Keeble, a native Chicagoan, began his music career in the 1950s when he worked at Fellowship Baptist Church under pastor Clay Evans. During these years, he played the piano and organ, sang, and directed the radio choir of his church.

He has traveled across the country playing for some of the greatest artists of that era. A few of which include, Inez Andrews, Jessy Dixon, Marvin Yancy, and the choir of Operation. Keeble has traveled and sang in Europe, was a regular on the *Jubilee Showcase* television show, and organized a community choir, the Voices of Triumph.

He was the first to teach gospel music as an accredited course for the Chicago Public Schools, and taught gospel workshops in churches and schools across the country.

Keeble has played on numerous recordings and has recorded several CDs. Appearing at the Apollo in New York City, the House of Blues, and the Chicago Gospel Fest, he was also the musical director for the play, *Evolution of Gospel*.

Keeble is CEO and founder of the Chicago Gospel Music Heritage Museum.

Celebrating African-American Achievements

Chicago's COMMUNITY LEADERS

Gwendolyn Kenner-Johnson
Associate Director
Office of Family Support Services
Illinois Department of Human Services

Gwendolyn Kenner-Johnson is associate director of the Office of Family Support Services for the Illinois Department of Human Services. With a budget of more than $280 million dollars, she is responsible for the bureaus of homeless services and supportive housing, refugee and immigrant services, and Title XX social services.

Kenner-Johnson's experience includes the management and administration of social services programs in Illinois and California, as well as national consulting, speaking, and lecturing engagements. She holds a degree in psychology from Spelman College in Atlanta and a master of education degree from Northeastern Illinois University in Chicago. Additionally, she has been quoted in several trade publications including *Ebony*.

Kenner-Johnson has received awards from the YMCA, UNCF, the Spelman Alumnae Association, the Lake Shore Links, and Chicago Public Schools. She is married to Martin G. Johnson, a retired executive; mother to Michele Jolivette, a college professor; and grandmother to Teal and Aubrey. She is immediate past president of The Links, Inc., Lake Shore chapter; a member of Delta Sigma Theta Sorority, Inc.; and a member of the sanctuary choir of Trinity United Church of Christ.

Linda F. Murrain
Executive Director
Goodwill Industries of
Metropolitan Chicago, Inc.

Linda Murrain is executive director of Goodwill Industries of Metropolitan Chicago, Inc., a nonprofit human services agency. In this position, she is responsible for providing vocational, rehabilitative skill development and work opportunities for people with barriers to employment. She is the first African American to hold this position.

Committed to the growth and development of today's youth, Linda spends countless hours working with children ages two to 19 through Jack and Jill of America, Inc., where she is mid-western regional director. In 2002, she was recognized as the Distinguished Mother of the Year in her chapter. Due to her community involvement, Linda received the Distinguished Woman Award in 2003, 2004, and 2005 from the Society of Mannequins. She also received the Excellence in Communications Award from President Bill Clinton in 1999.

Linda attended Fisk University and received a bachelor of science degree from Chicago State University. She has been certified in leadership from the Center for Creative Leadership.

A resident of Chicago, Linda is the wife of Carl Murrain and is the proud mother of one son, Maurice.

THE INAUGURAL EDITION *Who's Who In Black Chicago*

Chicago's COMMUNITY LEADERS

Celebrating African-American Achievements

David A. Northern, Sr.
Deputy Director
Lake County Housing Authority

Dr. Jean Oden
Co-Founder
Special Education Teachers Organization

David A. Northern, Sr. is the deputy director of the Lake County Housing Authority. As deputy director, David assists with administration and oversight. He helps to ensure compliance with HUD regulations of agencies with annual resources of roughly $27 million, with an inventory of 3,809 plus properties/housing vouchers.

David's educational background includes a master's degree from Indiana University Northwest, and a bachelor's degree in accounting from Ball State University. Dedicated to giving back to the community, his civic affiliations include serving as vice president of housing for the Illinois Chapter of NAHRO, and executive council member at large for the Alumni Association of Indiana University.

Having received numerous honors for giving himself to the community, David was awarded The Graduate of the Last Decade Award 2004 from Ball State University. Likewise, he was profiled in the *Ebony* magazine editorial, The Fast Track: "30 Leaders Who Are 30 And Under" in 2004. David enjoys life with his wife and two kids.

Jean Oden's teaching goals were achieved when she was assigned to a first grade classroom at Herzl Elementary School in 1959. Since then, she has strived to serve predominately black schools in poor neighborhoods in an effort to motivate and inspire.

Oden is co-founder of Special Education Teachers Organization, a service improving educational services to physically and mentally disabled students in Chicago. She also founded the Black Parents United for Education and Related Services, an organization for black parents fighting for educational inequities; and U.N.I.T.E., a social research organization noting educational services to social problems in the community.

Graduating from Chicago Teachers College with a bachelor's degree in education, Oden received her master's degree from Chicago State University. She also holds a doctorate degree from National-Louis University.

Among her numerous affiliations, Jean is the secretary of Chicago Southside NAACP, a mayoral appointee to the African-American Advisory Council, and a member of the Chicago League of Women Voters. Her various endeavors, from community levels to the state, national, and international levels, have placed an African-American voice in key public policy decision-making.

Celebrating African-American Achievements

Chicago's COMMUNITY LEADERS

Aurie A. Pennick
Executive Director & Treasurer
Field Foundation of Illinois

Aurie Pennick is the executive director and treasurer of the Field Foundation of Illinois where she oversees approximately $60 million in foundation assets. Pennick is an attorney with many years of experience in the civic and philanthropic sector.

She has been the recipient of numerous awards and appointments which include: the Chicago Police Board; the official U.S. Delegation for the 1996 Habitat II Global Conference on Cities in Istanbul, Turkey; the Aspen Institute Fellowship in 2002; and the Chicago Commission on Human Relations 2003 Human Relations Award.

Earning both a bachelor's and a master's degree in administration of criminal justice from the University of Illinois at Chicago, Pennick received a law degree from John Marshall Law School. She serves on the board of the Field Museum, the Rosalind Franklin University of Medicine and Science, the Funders Network, and the Chicago Network. She also serves on the advisory board of the *Illinois Issues* magazine.

Pennick has two very talented daughters.

Lisa M. Rollins
Senior Director, Development &
Communications, Metropolitan Division
The Salvation Army

Lisa M. Rollins is senior director of development and communications of The Salvation Army (TSA) Metropolitan Division, headquartered in Chicago. She directs all fundraising efforts including philanthropic, corporate, civic, and governmental giving. She is the first woman to hold the position.

As chief fundraiser on behalf of TSA, Lisa manages a variety of programs and campaigns, and oversees all aspects of development and communications. An expert in fundraising for nonprofit organizations, she is a part of a new vanguard of professionals bringing innovative ideas, strategies, and systems to the development field.

Lisa holds a bachelor of science degree in biology education from Bethune-Cookman College and a master of business administration degree from Hampton University in Hampton, Virginia. She is a member of the National Academy of Volunteerism and Alpha Kappa Alpha Sorority, Inc. She has received numerous awards and honors and is a recent Black Pearl Award recipient.

A native of Brunswick, Maine, Lisa lives in Matteson, Illinois with her husband, Larry, and three children.

Chicago's COMMUNITY LEADERS

Celebrating African-American Achievements

Furmin D. Sessoms
Deputy Public Defender
Law Office of the
Cook County Public Defender

Furmin D. Sessoms is the deputy public defender for the Law Office of the Cook County Public Defender, which employs 827 people, of whom 504 are attorneys. With an annual budget of $52 million, the Law Office handles nearly 400,000 cases per year in the second-largest unified court system in the country. Sessoms is responsible for the finance, administration, investigations, and community affairs divisions.

Sessoms previously worked in civil litigation and has consulted in community relations and governmental affairs. He served as executive director of the Chicago Southside branch of the NAACP. He is a graduate of the University of California, Berkeley and the Georgetown University Law Center.

Sessoms is as a member of the editorial board of the National Bar Association's *NBA Magazine*, the advisory board of the Chicago United Negro College Fund, Alpha Phi Alpha Fraternity, Inc., the Chicago Assembly, and is a life member of the NAACP. He received the 2001 Cook County Bar Association's Harold Washington Award for Service to the Community, and the 1996 President's Award from the Chicago Southside NAACP.

Drema Lee Woldman
National Area III Director
Top Ladies of Distinction, Inc.

Drema Lee Woldman is the Area III director of Top Ladies of Distinction, Inc., a national 501(c)(3) community-service based organization founded in 1964 comprised of 60,000+ members and more than 140 chapters. She oversees chapters and programs of service in nine states.

She has received the Black Eagle Heritage Award and the Great Lakes Region Trailblazer Award for outstanding community and volunteer service. Woldman has appeared on WGN's *People to People* and in *Good Housekeeping* with former First Lady, Hillary Rodham Clinton.

In her profession, she is a manager at a top five worldwide law firm and is a licensed Realtor®. Woldman received a bachelor of social work degree from West Virginia State University. She is a life member of Alpha Kappa Alpha Sorority, Inc. and the National Council of Negro Women. She is also a member of The Links, Inc., NAACP, and Toastmasters International.

A native West Virginian, Drema is the wife of Barry, the proud mother of Nichole, and the doting grandmother of Journee.

Chicago's

ENTREPRENEURS

"You are as good as you desire to be, but never perfect, though you strive to be. You look for that chord you never find, but in the process you find other chords along the way."

RAMSEY LEWIS
JAZZ MUSICIAN

Chicago's ENTREPRENEURS

Celebrating African-American Achievements

Jocelyn H. Adams is the owner of Jocelyn H. Adams State Farm Insurance and Financial Services. Her full-service insurance and financial service agency provides clients with the information they need to make informed decisions regarding their financial futures.

While working as a marketing manager for the National Black MBA Association, Inc. (NBNBAA), Jocelyn received a law degree from Loyola University School of Law in 2002. She also earned her MBA in marketing and strategic decision making from Loyola Graduate School of Business in 2003. Prior to opening her own agency, Jocelyn worked for retail giant, The Home Depot, Inc, in a leadership development program.

Jocelyn is a lifetime member of the NBMBAA. She has been a guest speaker for several high school classes, entrepreneurial conferences, and homebuyer expos.

She is married to real estate professional Mani Adams. Jocelyn is the proud mother of two beautiful boys, Mani Jr. and Jaeson Patrick, and loves to travel.

Jocelyn H. Adams
Owner
Jocelyn H. Adams State Farm
Insurance & Financial Services

Sheila L. Agnew is an established entrepreneur with extensive experience in event marketing, promotions, trade show and exhibit management, and meeting and convention planning. She is also known for her outstanding creativity in providing clients with unique decorative event settings.

With the exceptional ability to manage projects, develop community, educational, and entertainment programs with professional delivery, her work has taken her to cities across the country. Likewise, Sheila's event designs have been recognized in national trade magazines.

Her company, S&S Productions, Ltd., provides full-service event production and planning with concentration on corporate and entertainment events and has offices in Chicago and Columbus, Ohio.

Sheila earned a bachelor's degree in business administration from Chicago State University. Some of her honors include, Harlan High School Outstanding Alumni, Parkway Community House "Business Woman of the Year," Revlon Professional Set Design, Kizzy Award for Entrepreneurship, and a finalist in the 1999 *Heart & Soul* magazine reader model fitness search.

A mentor to many in various programs for women and youth, Shelia plans to debut as an author in 2006.

Sheila L. Agnew
Owner
S&S Productions, Ltd.

Celebrating African-American Achievements

Chicago's ENTREPRENEURS

Sharon C. Allen is the founder and marketing and sales director of Resolutions International, Inc., a small market research, grant writing, and business service agency. She is also an adjunct instructor at Columbia College, where she teaches a variety of junior and senior level business courses.

A passionate member of the GLM Mentoring Program, Sharon is parliamentarian and past president of the Lambda Nu Omega Graduate Chapter of Alpha Kappa Alpha Sorority, Inc. She is a member of the National MBA association, the American Management Association, the National Association of Women Business Owners (NAWBO), and the RainbowPUSH Coalition. Sharon made history in 1990, as she was the youngest Lake County Urban League board chair at the age of 25.

Her community service awards include StreetWise Volunteer of the Year, AKA Sorority Sister of the Year, and she was featured in *Who's Who in Professional Management* in 1998 and 2005.

An honors graduate of Jackson State University, Sharon holds an MBA degree from Roosevelt University.

Sharon is the mother of 11-year-old daughter, Imani, whom she considers her pride and joy.

Sharon C. Allen
Founder
Resolutions International, Inc.

Tracey Alston is the founder of Danielle Ashley Communications, a full-service integrated marketing, advertising, and public relations agency established in 1994. As chief executive officer, Alston has an extraordinary talent for developing advertising and marketing programs that positively impact her clients' bottom line. Her services are especially sought after for political campaigns.

Alston is a passionate believer in community involvement and grassroots outreach. She is a board member of Jack and Jill of America, Inc., South Suburban Chicago chapter, and a dedicated member of the League of Women Voters. By combining her two loves, business and people, Alston has created a company that puts her in touch with both.

She received a bachelor of arts degree in communications from Columbia College of Chicago. With 14 years of radio management experience, Alston became the youngest female radio station owner (WBEE-AM Chicago) in the United States. For two consecutive years, Danielle Ashley Communications has been recognized as one of the fastest-growing urban businesses in the nation by *Inc.* magazine's Inner City 100. Alston is the loving mother of three girls.

Tracey Alston
President & Chief Executive Officer
Danielle Ashley Communications

Chicago's ENTREPRENEURS

Celebrating African-American Achievements

Calvin Ashford, Jr. is principal and design director of Gilmore-Ashford-Powers Design. Ashford has been honored as one of the top interior designers in the country. He is listed in *Who's Who In Interior Design*. Gilmore-Ashford-Powers Design provides a wide range of services for residential and commercial designs.

Ashford has clients located in Chicago, New York, Palm Springs, and throughout the U.S., Great Britain, and Canada.

Among his many awards, Ashford has received the Pioneer Award in Design by the Organization of Black Designers, the J.B. Industry Internationally Design Award, the Steward Award for creative design, and the Chicago Design Source Excellence Award. Similarly, Ashford and his work has been profiled in many publications including: *Architectural Digest, Interior Designs, London Design & Interior, Apartment Life, The New York Times, Ebony, Chicago Defender, Chicago Tribune,* and *Chicago Sun-Times*.

Receiving a bachelor of arts degree from Columbia University, Ashford holds a doctorate from the University of Michigan.

His design philosophy is to focus on designing environments that adapt to people, rather than people adapting to the design.

Calvin Ashford, Jr.
Principal & Design Director
Gilmore-Ashford-Powers Design

Mark and Marlon Austin, self-taught designers, have always had a love for art and well-tailored suits. Being very good artists and impeccable dressers, they decided to combine the two and make a go in the fashion industry. Mark and Marlon began designing neckwear and soon opened up their first boutique. While sourcing abroad for the best quality made goods for their boutique, Marlon was approached with an opportunity to begin work in Europe. Later on, they began to rep a line of custom made men and women's business suits made in Switzerland.

Mark and Marlon still personally design for some of the world's foremost celebrities, athletes, and businessmen. In 2003, they shifted gears from solely working with a private client base and focused more of their attention on marketing their brand of Bespoke and ready to wear clothing to the wholesale trade.

The design company has grown considerably and is now in its 12th year. Bespoke Apparel Group has showrooms in Chicago and St. Louis. Likewise, Mark and Marlon reside in both cities.

Mark and Marlon Austin
Designers & Owners
Bespoke Apparel Group LLC

Celebrating African-American Achievements

Chicago's
ENTREPRENEURS

Phyllis D. Banks is president of P. Banks Communications, Inc., a full-service marketing communications, and public relations entity servicing a broad client mix of Fortune 500 corporations, nonprofit organizations, and governmental agencies. Banks conceptualizes, develops, and implements marketing communications programs to meet client needs.

She has received numerous awards and honors including, the prestigious Publicity Club of Chicago (PCC), Golden Trumpet Award, three PCC Silver Trumpets, and an International Association of Business Communicators Spectra Award. She began her career as a newspaper reporter for the *Fort Wayne News Sentinel* where she shared a Pulitzer Prize awarded to the editorial staff for local reporting excellence.

Banks is a member of Trinity United Church of Christ. In addition, she is a member of the Black Public Relations Society and the Chicago Association of Black Journalists. Likewise, she is an advisory board member of Open Book, and a volunteer for several nonprofit organizations.

Banks has a bachelor of arts degree in forensics from Indiana University.

Phyllis D. Banks
President
P. Banks Communications, Inc.

Barbara Ann Bates, the Chicago-based CEO and president of Bates Designs, is a savvy fashion smart entrepreneur who designs and creates garments with an affinity to texture.

The urban alternative to the traditional couture, Bates Designs not surprisingly attracts people from all walks of life. Bates' mark of quality has caught the eye of many high profile clients such as: Oprah Winfrey, Michael Jordan, Mary Ann Childers, Lisa Siracusa, Robin Robinson, Scottie Pippen, Steve Harvey, Whitney Houston, the Winans family, and many more.

Established in September of 1986, Bates Designs continues to experience growth. Barbara believes that building a successful business is like constructing a quality garment. Each requires hard work sparked with creativity, respect for valuable resources, the knowledge of how best to use them, unwavering attention to detail, and a clear vision of what the market not only wants, but also what it needs.

Barbara Bates
CEO & President
Bates Designs

Chicago's ENTREPRENEURS

Celebrating African-American Achievements

From publisher and lecturer, relationship expert and life coach to internationally known speaker and best-selling author, Bonita Bennett is widely known for her literary skill and sage advice. For more than 23 years, she has been the voice of wisdom, compassion, and inspiration to thousands of singles through *Being Single Magazine,* which she founded in 1982. She is also president of HarBon Publishing and is a popular radio personality.

In 1990, she released her bestselling book *How to Catch and Keep the Man of Your Dreams.* Her latest novel, *The Coming of Dawn* was released in March of 2005.

Bennett has been profiled in some of the nation's major newspapers, including *Chicago Tribune, Chicago Sun-Times, The Washington Post*, and the *New York Post*. She also had her own radio show on several major stations in the Chicagoland area, and was syndicated nationally and internationally by SJS Entertainment/New York.

Bennett is thoroughly committed to two community projects. Three years ago, she founded the Cook County Jail Re-Hab Project to help rehabilitate female inmates. Five years ago, she began Girl Talk, a monthly interactive community workshop for women.

Bonita L. Bennett
President & Chief Executive Officer
HarBon Publishing

Robert Blackwell, Jr. is the founder and president of Electronic Knowledge Interchange, Inc. (EKI). EKI is an e-Solutions application, development, and implementation company specializing in intranet, extranet, workflow, and Web-based supply chain management and other e-commerce solutions. EKI serves some of the largest companies in the U.S., as well as the City of Chicago and the State of Illinois.

Blackwell founded Killerspin L.L.C. in 2001. Since that time, Killerspin has become the leading American table tennis retailer and top table tennis event producer in the world. In addition to table tennis equipment, apparel, DVDs, and televised events, the company dominates American table tennis. Its endorsed players have achieved numerous titles including winning every spot on the U.S. Men's Table Tennis Team.

Serving in numerous affiliations, a few of Blackwell's board memberships include: U.S. Bank (Chicago Region), The Mayor's Council of Technology Advisors, After School Matters, and The Metropolitan Planning Commission. Likewise, he is a board member of The Belle Center, the Chicagoland Entrepreneurial Center, and the Federation of International Table Tennis Manufacturers.

Robert Blackwell, Jr.
Founder & President
Electronic Knowledge Interchange, Inc.

Celebrating African-American Achievements

Chicago's
ENTREPRENEURS

Roslyn C. Chapman is president of The Chapman Edge, a manufacturers' representative company based in Chicago, Illinois. The Chapman Edge specializes in selling manufacturers' products to drug and discount retail chain outlets at the national account level. Roslyn runs the overall operations of the business and oversees client relationship management.

Prior to starting her business in 2000, Roslyn held various national account sales roles with Alberto Culver and Johnson Products. She received a bachelor of arts degree in psychology from Hampton University in 1978. She credits her personal and professional mentors as playing a major role in her career development and business success.

Roslyn is involved with various trade organizations, including the NACDS, ECRM, AHBAI, and GMDC, and she is often quoted in industry publications.

A travel enthusiast, she is often called on by her friends as a personal concierge for dining and fun vacation destination recommendations. She enjoys worshiping at several churches and is a member of Trinity United Church of Christ. Her sorority of choice 28 years ago is Delta Sigma Theta Sorority, Inc.

Roslyn C. Chapman
Chief Executive Officer
The Chapman Edge

Gwen C. Duncan-James founded Duncan & Associates in 1972, providing accounting services to other local entrepreneurs and individuals. Two years later, Gwen founded Duncan Nurses Registry, Inc., which quickly grew to be the largest African-American nurses' registry in the Chicago area. In 1980, she reorganized her company and formed Gareda Diversified Business Services, Inc.

Through the years, Gareda has provided services ranging from cable television installation to hospital staffing. Today, Gareda proudly reigns as a premier healthcare agency boasting an employee base of more than 1,100 professional nurses, therapists, homemakers, and respite care workers.

Gwen has spent her entire career as a successful entrepreneur. Against the odds, she became one of the first and most successful African-American providers of supplementary staffing in the Chicago area. By daring to venture into uncharted waters, Gwen has bolstered her business savvy, as evidenced by the company's consistent growth.

Throughout her illustrious career, Gwen has received numerous awards for her extraordinary success, including awards in 2004 and 2005 as a finalist for the prestigious Ernst & Young Entrepreneur of the Year.

Gwen C. Duncan-James
President & Chief Executive Officer
Gareda Diversified
Business Services, Inc.

Chicago's ENTREPRENEURS

Celebrating African-American Achievements

Dan Duster is president of 3D Development Group, LLC, a corporate training company that focuses on life enhancement and productivity improvement. Founded in 2001, its core programs are effective communication skills, goal setting and life balance, and customer service and sales training.

Duster's family has had a positive influence in the Chicago area for decades, going back to his great-grandmother, Ida B. Wells. He educates people concerning her legacy, as well as the struggles and triumphs of other leaders in African-American history. A community activist, Duster is a board member and advisor to several organizations.

He received his bachelor of science degree from the University of Illinois in 1991, where he was very involved on campus.

Duster has spoken to audiences across the nation through his workshops and keynote speeches. He has authored several books and motivational CDs, and has appeared in *The Washington Post*, on *CNN.com*, and dozens of other publications and radio stations. In 2006, he was nominated to the White House for his volunteerism and impact on the community.

Dan Duster
President
3D Development Group

Jylla Moore Foster is an executive coach, trainer, speaker, and consultant. Her areas of expertise include team effectiveness, communication, behavior styles, managing change, business innovation, and diversity. Foster is the author of the award-winning book, *DUE NORTH! Strengthen Your Leadership Assets*.

A former IBM sales vice president, she was the first executive director for the Information Technology Senior Management Forum (ITSMF). She also served as international president of Zeta Phi Beta Sorority, Inc. Foster is a graduate of Corporate Coach University, a licensed facilitator for The Coaching Clinic®, an award-winning distributor of Inscape Publishing's DiSC® assessments, and a certified Retirement/Transition Coach.

Jylla received her MBA from Indiana University and a bachelor of science degree in mathematics, magna cum laude, from Livingstone College where she has also been recognized with an honorary doctorate degree. She is currently pursuing a Ph.D. in organizational development at Benedictine University.

A native of Salisbury, North Carolina, Jylla is the proud mother of a daughter, Anjylla.

Jylla Moore Foster
President & CEO
Crystal Stairs, Inc.

Celebrating African-American Achievements

Chicago's ENTREPRENEURS

Roosevelt Haywood, III is chief executive officer and president of Haywood and Fleming Associates (HFA), a risk consulting, risk management, and insurance procurement firm he established in 1984. The firm provides expertise and service to a number of large and complex entities in the private and public sectors. HFA also serves small businesses as well as high net worth individuals.

Haywood has more than 30 years of experience in the insurance industry and has served the profession in a number of capacities. He has been chairman of the National African American Insurance Association and board governor of the Chartered Property and Casualty Underwriters (CPCU) Society. Currently, Haywood serves on the advisory board of the International Association of Black Actuaries, and on the emerging producers council of the St. Paul Travelers Insurance Company. He received his business degree from Indiana University in 1973.

Haywood has appeared in a number of industry trade publications such as *National Underwriter* and *Independent Agent*. Likewise, his firm has been featured as the Marketing Agency of the Month in *Rough Notes* magazine, the leading publication for the insurance industry.

Roosevelt Haywood, III
President & Chief Executive Officer
Haywood and Fleming Associates

James Hill, Jr. is chairman and chief executive officer of Hill, Taylor LLC, a CPA firm which he founded in 1972. The firm specializes in auditing employee benefit plans and nonprofit corporations.

Hill received a bachelor of science degree from Central State University, and an MBA from The University of Chicago.

He has served as a board member of various community and nonprofit organizations and is currently active in various professional organizations, a few of which include, principal of Chicago United, Economic Club of Chicago board member, and Illinois Institute of Technology life trustee. Likewise, he serves on the City of Chicago economic advisory board.

A member of the AICPA, Illinois CPA Society, and the National Association of Black Accountants, Hill is also a National Association of Black MBA affiliate. Having received numerous awards and honors from both his professional and community work, Hill holds the Alumnus of the Year award by The University of Chicago, the Outstanding Young Man of America award, a certificate of appreciation award by the comptroller of the State of Illinois, along with many others.

James Hill, Jr.
Chairman & CEO
Hill, Taylor LLC

Chicago's ENTREPRENEURS

Celebrating African-American Achievements

Amy Hilliard is founder and chief executive officer of The ComfortCake Company, makers of "pound cake so good it feels like a hug." A graduate of Howard University and the Harvard Business School, Hilliard started her company from scratch in 2001 with United Airlines as its first customer. ComfortCake® is sold in more than 1,500 retail stores, through its Web site, and delivers four million servings yearly to Chicago Public Schools. ComfortCake and the new Sugarless Sweetness® diabetic line have been featured on CNN, the Food Network, and Home Shopping Network.

Hilliard also owns The Hilliard Group, a marketing and product development firm. Her corporate experience includes L'Oréal/Soft Sheen, Pillsbury, Gillette, and Burrell Communications Group. The first African American on the National Association of the Specialty Food Trade's board, Hilliard also sits on PepsiCo's African-American advisory board and the diversity council of Premier Auto Group.

A nationally recognized speaker profiled in publications including *Entrepreneur*, *Essence*, *Chicago Tribune*, *BusinessWeek*, *Black Enterprise*, and *Ebony*, Hilliard is the author of *Tap Into Your Juice-Find Your Gifts, Lose Your Fears and Build Your Dreams*.

Amy S. Hilliard
Founder & Chief Executive Officer
The ComfortCake Company

Louis Jones formed Louis Jones Enterprises, Inc. (LJE) in 1984 to provide professional construction management, architecture, and engineering services.

During his 30-year career, Jones managed large construction projects and programs such as the reconstruction of 56 San Francisco public schools for earthquake safety standards, and served as deputy director of construction-facilities for the O'Hare Airport Development Program. He was also responsible for Provident Hospital's reconstruction, Cook County's new Second District Circuit Court Complex, and the Chicago Public Schools Rehab Program.

Receiving a bachelor's degree in architecture from the University of Illinois at Chicago, Jones is a licensed architect and licensed general contractor.

Jones and his wife, Barbara Marie Davenport-Jones, MSW/LCSW, are the parents of adult children: Camiria, Eds./Ph.D., Lynnea, interior designer, and Langston, an animator and filmmaker.

The recipient of numerous awards and recognitions, Jones continues to serve his community as president of the Architecture, Construction, and Engineering Technical Charter High School, and a member of AIA, NOMA, and BCU. Jones also serves on the Illinois Capital Development board, the Illinois Employment Security advisory board, and the Governor's Transition Team.

Louis Jones, AIA
President & Chief Executive Officer
Louis Jones Enterprises, Inc.

Celebrating African-American Achievements

Chicago's
ENTREPRENEURS

Olivet Jones is a self-described "parallel entrepreneur." As founder and principal of The Felicity Group, Ltd., she provides high level consulting services in the area of organization development and diversity to executives of the most well known corporations in America. For more than 20 years, she has built her company to a level where she was featured as a subject matter expert on ABC's *20/20* television show.

"My passion for diversity and inclusion stems from my early experiences in the corporate world," she says. Born in North Carolina in the era of legal segregation, Jones personally witnessed the impact that strong communities had in the lives of individuals. "We didn't know we were poor. Everybody in my community had a second job or a small business of some kind. That's when I realized economic determination for our people was mission critical."

As an author, consultant, and coach, Jones works what she calls the "full spectrum," influencing corporations to institute approaches that fully engage people by supporting the personal and professional development of her individual clients.

Olivet Benbow Jones
Founder & Principal
The Felicity Group, Ltd.

Jerline Lambert is president and chief executive officer of Lambert's Realty, Inc., which she founded in 1968 and incorporated in 1977. Lambert's Realty is a family affair, with four of her five children joining the business and its ten other employees. Lambert is a broker, a certified real estate property manager, and a state certified real estate appraiser. She hails from Forrest City, Arkansas, and she earned a bachelor of arts degree from Northeastern University in Chicago.

Lambert has served on the national board of the RainbowPUSH Coalition, the Midwest Community Council, and the Cosmopolitan Chamber of Commerce. A past president of the Dearborn Real Estate Board, she was appointed to serve as federal district coordinator for Congressman Danny K. Davis, bringing to his attention various housing-related issues. Lambert was also appointed by Governor Jim Edger to serve as a member of his commission on mortgage practices.

Lambert has received many honors including the HistoryMakers, *Who's Who in Real Estate*, the Midwest Community Council's Distinguished Service in Business Award, and the Cosmopolitan Chamber's Eloise Johnson Award for Neighborhood Commitment and Service.

Jerline Lambert
President & Chief Executive Officer
Lambert's Realty, Inc.

Chicago's ENTREPRENEURS

Celebrating African-American Achievements

Cassandra R. Lee
Founder, President, and CEO
SSANEE, Inc.

Cassandra R. Lee, also known as the D.I.V.A. of Dialog™, is one of the most dynamic and electrifying inspirational speakers in the United States. As the founder, president, and CEO of SSANEE, Inc. (sawn-knee), an edutainment™ company, Cassandra provides entertaining theatrical shows and skill-building educational seminars. She offers a unique form of education and entertainment that leaves a long-lasting impression on her audiences. Her seminar topics include communication skills, financial empowerment, goal achievement, leadership, and self-esteem.

A former employee of the American Bar Association, Cassandra refined her skills in administration, management, planning, and training that has allowed her to transition into the public speaking arena. She studied English and speech communication at the University of Illinois at Urbana-Champaign. Cassandra also holds certifications in diversity training, women's issues, and public speaking.

Cassandra is a member of the National Association for Campus Activities, the Professional Woman Network, and Toastmasters International.

In her spare time, Cassandra loves to work out and believes that a healthy body is the key to longevity and peace of mind. She resides in Chicago, Illinois.

Thomas L. McLeary, CLU
President
Endow, Incorporated

Thomas L. McLeary, CLU, is president of Endow, Incorporated, a multi-line insurance services company that he co-founded in 1978. The firm specializes in insurance planning and benefit management for a client base that includes public entities, small and large private corporations, and individuals with large net worth.

McLeary is the first African American to be elected president of the Chicago and Illinois Associations of Life Underwriters. For his years of outstanding contributions, he received the Chicago Association's highest honor, The Distinguished Service Award. McLeary also received the Chicago chapter of CLU and ChFC's highest award, The Heubner Scholar, becoming one of only seven individuals to receive both awards. He served four years on the board of directors of the 80,000-member National Association of Insurance and Financial Advisors.

McLeary has chaired the 15,000-member Minority Business Committee of the National Minority Supplier Development Council (2003-2006). He also chaired the 1,300-member Minority Business Committee in Chicago for 18 years, and has served on the boards of many national and local organizations.

Tom resides in Chicago with his Bunnie and children, Tiffanie, Deanna, and Thomas.

Celebrating African-American Achievements

Chicago's
ENTREPRENEURS

Pepper Miller founded The Hunter-Miller Group, Inc. (HMG), a consumer research, trend analysis, and marketing strategy company, in 1985. Since then, she has been helping Fortune 500 companies understand how to effectively market their products and messages to the African-American market. Some of her corporate clients include: American Airlines, Allstate, Ford Motor Company, General Motors, General Mills, Proctor & Gamble, and the Chicago Symphony Orchestra.

In 2005, Pepper and co-author Herb Kemp, launched the landmark African-American marketing book, *What's Black About It? Insights to Increase Your Share of a Changing African-American Market* (Paramount Market Publishers).

Pepper served as co-research partner and consultant for the first segmentation study on African-American women commissioned by *Essence*: 2005 WOW II (Window on Our Women). Having established the Ruth C. Hunter Market Research Scholarship Fund through the N'DIGO Foundation, Pepper helped to expose and encourage African-American students to market research as a career option.

HMG and the Census 2000 Ad Team received the David Ogilvy Research Award for the Census 2000 Advertising Campaign. Additionally, Pepper has been a member of Trinity UCC since 1995.

Pepper Miller
Founder & President
The Hunter-Miller Group, Inc.

In 1989, Hoyett Owens founded I Like It Communications, Inc., a minority-owned and operated advertising/public relations agency specializing in consumer promotions. The firm's clients include TV One, Darden Restaurants, Quaker Oats, and Wm. Wrigley Jr. Owens' leadership is represented by his successful signature programs and creative, results-driven strategies.

Owens began his professional career with one of the nation's Fortune 500 jewelers. He tripled the region's annual sales, which exceeded $25 million, and was promoted to vice president of operations.

In 1983, Owens was recruited by WVON, a Chicago radio station. His entrepreneurial skills quickly led to his promotion to general manager. In that capacity, he changed the format to talk radio. In 1996, Owens purchased All Printing & Graphics, Inc., a full-service, commercial sheet-fed printing company that is now the largest African-American-owned printing company in the country.

Owens graduated from Jackson State University with a bachelor's degree in speech communications. He is on the board of directors of PII and is treasurer for ABLE. He also serves on panels and provides presentations to help other businesses pursue economic development and partnerships.

Hoyett W. Owens, Jr.
President and CEO
I Like It Communications, Inc.

Chicago's
ENTREPRENEURS

Celebrating African-American Achievements

Edward Prentice, III is chief executive officer and president of Centrax Corporation, an e-learning and e-marketing development firm founded in 1985. Centrax clients include Kraft, Ameriprise, Grainger, Lucent, Siemens, ABN AMRO, Fifth Third Bank, Wrigley, the American Medical Association, and Harley-Davidson to name a few. As the firm's chief executive, Edward works with a talented team and solid processes to create engaging programs that drive knowledge transfer. He is currently leveraging the strengths of the company to forge new ground in emerging fields such as video blogs (vlogs), mobile learning (m-learning), and 3D animation and visualization.

Edward is a board member of Entrenuity, an organization whose mission is to prepare young people for true success through experiential entrepreneurship and spiritual development training.

Edward also gives his heart and soul to his community. His long-term goals are to have the means to be a productive philanthropist, to give back to the community in all ways possible. Edward donates time and equipment to local area churches to enlighten disadvantaged youth on the power of the Internet.

Edward Prentice, III
President & Chief Executive Officer
Centrax Corporation

Pamela and Stanley Rakestraw co-founded SCR Medical Transportation, Inc. in July of 1986 to provide medical transportation to various healthcare and elderly populations.

What they lacked in resources, the Rakestraw's made up for with a few dedicated employees, lots of heart and drive. Now in its 18th year of operation, SCR services more than 700,000 clients annually and is one of the fastest-growing transportation companies in the country. Safety, caring, and respect are the values that govern more than the operations. SCR has never had an employee layoff and has an almost 20-year history of 95% on-time performance. Their fleet of 130 multi-service vehicles offers 24-hour dispatching.

Building families and community through their business is a priority to the Rakestraw's. They offer a full complement of company benefits to their workforce along with family-oriented, company-sponsored events. For example, one employee won a van in a one-dollar raffle.

The Rakestraw's are active in and support many charitable and community organizations.

**Pamela M. &
Stanley C. Rakestraw**
Co-Founders
SCR Medical Transportation, Inc.

Celebrating African-American Achievements

Chicago's ENTREPRENEURS

Eddie S. Read is the chief executive officer of United Services of Chicago, Inc., where he manages a staff of 15 employees. He implements and directs the company's Community Construction Orientation Program, and organized an employment placement and retention service for his economically disadvantaged clients. As a worker advocate, Read specializes in construction trades.

As founder and president of the United Independent Workers International Union, Read represents workers in all aspects of business. He is president of the Chicago Black United Communities and manages the various issues and initiatives facing the black community. Serving as an aide to activist Lu Palmer for 23 years, Read was also the campaign manager, consultant, and field director for several independent and progressive candidates.

A few of his outstanding awards and memberships include: the Cook County Bar Association; the Harold Washington Award; the South Austin Coalition Service Award; and the Midwest Community Council for Distinguished Community Service in Employment.

Married to Clarice Caul, Read is a father of five, and a grandfather of seven.

Eddie S. Read
Chief Executive Officer
United Services of Chicago, Inc.

Deborah M. Sawyer is an environmental scientist, certified hazardous materials manager, and president and CEO of Environmental Design International, Inc. (EDI). EDI is a full-service minority and woman-owned, licensed, and professional engineering firm specializing in hazardous waste management and civil engineering.

While completing a master's degree in petroleum microbiology, Sawyer managed a synthetic fuels laboratory. She joined the Ohio Environmental Protection Agency and URS Corporation as a program manager of the toxic and hazardous waste group. In six months, Sawyer booked $1 million in projects. Despite formidable obstacles in a male-dominated field, Sawyer founded EDI in 1991. Today, EDI has 65 employees, offices in three Midwestern states, and annual revenue exceeding $6 million.

Sawyer's recognitions include U.S. SBA's Minority Small Business Person of the Year at the national level in 1994; and from Bank of America, the National Association of Women Business Owners, Women of Color in Technology, and the Women's Business Development Center awards. Recently, EDI, as managing partner of a joint venture, was awarded a $70 million contract for construction inspection on the Dan Ryan Expressway Reconstruction.

Deborah M. Sawyer, CHMM
President & CEO
Environmental Design
International Inc.

Chicago's ENTREPRENEURS

Celebrating African-American Achievements

Charles R. Sherrell
President
Drums Horns & Voices, Inc.

Drums Horns & Voices, Inc. (DHV) is a privately-owned company dedicated exclusively to funding the support and development of African-American fine arts, including dance, theater, photography, sculpture, painting, literature, and real jazz music.

DHV operates under the leadership of its founder, Charles Sherrell, who owned and managed Chicago's only jazz music radio station, WBEE, for nearly 35 years. He brought jazz music to schools, colleges, and neighborhoods. Likewise, Sherrell established monthly seminars for jazz lovers, and provided clinics for young musicians to learn how to play the music pioneered by the art form's creators.

DHV annually introduces fine arts to hundreds of thousands of Chicagoans. It promotes plays and concerts, sponsors art shows, and financially supports forums and programs to promote photography and filming among African-American students and professionals.

Charles Sherrell is a lifetime member of the NAACP and Kappa Alpha Psi Fraternity, Inc. He is a romance language linguist, avid skier, scuba diver, and golfer.

He is married to Trutie Thigpen Sherrell, a retired college business education professor.

Erika and Monika Simmons
Designers
Double Stitch Clothing Line

Erika and Monika Simmons are the multi-talented twin designers of Double Stitch. What began as a holiday gift giving tradition, created a demand that rapidly expanded into a line of fun and flirtatious handmade designs that challenge the traditional concept of crochet.

Double Stitch was awarded the 2005 Fashion Group International's Rising Star award for the 5th Annual Style Makers and Rule Breakers awards gala. Erika and Monika's clothing line has been featured on several television shows and in various nationally distributed publications. A few of which include: NBC's *Fashion 5*, *WGN Morning Show*, ABC's *190 North*, *The New York Times*, *Time Out Chicago*, *Chicago Magazine*, *Chicago Sun-Times*, *Chicago Defender*, *N'DIGO* Magapaper, *Brides Noir*, and *Upscale* magazines.

While the twins have worked with celebrities like the fabulous Patti Labelle, they continue to stay focused on uplifting their community through self-esteem workshops and child entrepreneurship programs.

Erica and Monika's favorite quote is, "Pursue the things you love doing, and do them so well that people can't take their eyes off you. All other tangible rewards will come as a result"-Maya Angelou.

Who's Who In Black Chicago® THE INAUGURAL EDITION

Celebrating African-American Achievements

Chicago's ENTREPRENEURS

John D. Sterling is the founder and CEO of Synchronous Solutions, Inc., doing business as Synch-Solutions, Inc. Located in the heart of downtown Chicago, Synch-Solutions has quickly emerged as a premier management consulting and information technology firm. Since its beginnings in 1998, Synch-Solutions vastly expanded its network committed to understanding clients' complex business challenges. Synch-Solutions aligns client technology initiatives with business goals to deliver enterprise-wide results.

Guided by his mission to foster economic development and promote volunteerism throughout urban communities, Sterling is dedicated to numerous philanthropic endeavors. His efforts have touched myriad organizations, and continue to support causes such as the rebirth of New Orleans, the Research Foundation for Juvenile Diabetes, Uhlich Children's Advantage Network, and Girl Scouts of America, to name a few.

Whether in the office, field, or the community, Sterling carries a standard of excellence that is the foundation of the Synch-Solutions enterprise. With all of his accomplishments cemented together that enabled him to bridge uncharted waters, family values will always remain the cornerstone to Sterling's success.

John D. Sterling
Chief Executive Officer
Synch-Solutions, Inc.

Michael Sutton is president of Infrastructure Engineering, Inc. (IEI), a professional engineering consulting firm providing services in civil, structural, construction, traffic engineering, and program and transportation management. Sutton has 30 years of experience in the planning, design, and construction of highway, railroad, transit, airport, and related facilities. He has an extensive background in transportation projects, particularly mass transit facilities and highways.

Prior to acquiring IEI, Sutton held managerial responsibilities with various consulting engineering firms. Early in his career, he worked for the Illinois Department of Transportation, developing a solid foundation for the planning and implementation of public work projects.

Sutton holds memberships with the American Council of Engineering Companies, American Society of Civil Engineers, Chicagoland Chamber of Commerce, and the City Club of Chicago. He participates in the Consulting Engineers Council of Illinois, Illinois Road and Transportation Builders Association, Institute of Transportation Engineers, and the National Society of Black Engineers. Sutton is active in the RainbowPUSH Coalition, Black Contractors United, and the Alliance of Business Leaders and Entrepreneurs.

He received his bachelor's degree in civil engineering from Northwestern University.

Michael Sutton, P.E.
President
Infrastructure Engineering, Inc.

Chicago's ENTREPRENEURS

Celebrating African-American Achievements

Tiffany Taylor-Eastmond is the owner of Taylor Business Solutions, a virtual assistance firm that she founded in 2002, designed to provide off-site administrative support to small businesses that specializes in affordable income tax preparation. As a former personnel security specialist, Tiffany has an administrative background that measures more than 11 years, including eight years working as an assistant to U.S. government executives.

A full-time Realtor®, Tiffany is passionate in all that she does as her strong professional communication and negotiation skills make the difference for her clients.

Tiffany is an active member of Trinity United Church of Christ, the IT Ministry, and the Order of Eastern Star. Dedicated to giving back to the community, she serves as a mentor in Trinity's Intonjone Ministry, a program for girls ages eight to 18, intended to nurture and provide support as they experience life.

A native of Chicago, Tiffany is the wife of Marlon Eastmond, and the proud mother of two daughters, Nikayla and Aniyah.

Tiffany Taylor-Eastmond
Owner
Taylor Business Solutions

Patricia A. Walton is president of Walton's Urban Retreat, founded in 1995. Patricia has focused on providing an environment to experience peace, relaxation, gaining knowledge with skills, and stress management and prevention.

Patricia developed her spa skills at the world-renowned Elizabeth Arden Salon. Walton's Urban Retreat was born from her experience as an on-site therapist in the corporate community; it was the first of its kind in a Chicago mall.

Currently involved in a four-year research study to investigate the effects of massage on cancer patients within a hospice setting, Patricia has volunteered with Mercy Hospital in the neonatal unit. She is an active member of the American Massage Therapy Association.

Patricia has a bachelor of arts degree from Columbia College and is a nationally certified licensed massage therapist, a Reiki master, and a meditation instructor graduate of the Temple of Kriya Yoga. She also studied at the Chicago School of Massage Therapy. Additionally, she is trained in several massage modalities, including Palmer's method of seated massage.

Patricia enjoys interior decorating, music, dancing, and all things related to the healing arts.

Patricia A. Walton
President
Walton's Urban Retreat

Chicago's
PROFESSIONALS

"I have missed more than 9,000 shots in my career. I have lost almost 300 games. On 26 occasions I have been entrusted to take the winning shot... and missed. I have failed over and over and over again in my life. And thats precisely why I succeed."

**MICHAEL JORDAN
BASKETBALL STAR**

Chicago's PROFESSIONALS
Celebrating African-American Achievements

Sharron Banks
Administrative Services Manager
Flowers Communications Group, Inc.

Sharron Banks is the administrative services manager for Flowers Communications Group, Inc. (FCG), one of the largest African-American-owned public relations firms in the Midwest. Her first job after she graduated from college, Banks joined the agency in 1995 as a secretary. Over the years, she has held several positions, including account coordinator, senior account coordinator, and office administrator. In her role as account coordinator, Banks executed and facilitated local and national events and receptions for FCG's clients.

Banks is currently responsible for maintaining efficient office operations, including: recruiting, corporate purchasing, administrative and clerical supervision, the company's healthcare program and insurance and benefits package, as well as personnel orientation and training.

Banks attended historically black Wilberforce University in Ohio and earned an associate degree in business management and a bachelor's degree in business administration from Robert Morris College.

Ingrid E. Bridges
Administrative Assistant to Mayor Richard M. Daley
City of Chicago

As administrative assistant to the Honorable Mayor Richard M. Daley of Chicago, Ingrid E. Bridges serves as liaison to the entire ecumenical community. Pegged as a renaissance woman of religion, this journalist is sought out for her oratorical skills and her ability to create award-winning stories about the humanistic journey.

Formerly, Bridges was religion editor of the *Chicago Defender* for 15 years. There, she earned the Merit Award for best church page from the National Newspaper Publishers Association for upholding the highest standards of journalism. An author of the book *The Choices We Make - a days journey*, Bridges remains devoted to her ultimate calling, writing.

Born in Chicago, Bridges graduated from Columbia College with a bachelor of arts degree in journalism. She received an honorary doctorate of humanities from the Chicago Baptist Institute in 1998, and an honorary doctorate of humanities from GMOR Theological Institute of Northeastern Indiana in 2003.

Bridges loves cooking, jogging, and praising God as a member of Apostolic Church of God, where Bishop Arthur M. Brazier is pastor. She has one son, Brian Jr., a graduate of Florida A&M University.

M. Wayne Brittingham
Human Resource Leader
Hewitt Associates

Wayne Brittingham is human resource leader for the global consulting business at Hewitt Associates. As a member of the consulting leadership team, he is responsible for global human resource strategy and execution. He leads a team of highly experienced HR professionals who bring both general business and functional expertise to one of the leading HR consultancies in the world.

He previously consulted with clients on a wide range of issues related to human resource effectiveness, corporate restructuring and change, executive compensation, leadership, broad based compensation, and talent. Before Hewitt, Wayne worked for USAA, American Express, Fujitsu, and Office Depot as the vice president of human resources for the Business Services Group. At Nokia, Wayne was a member of the company's senior human resources management team for the Americas, leading the business group for the American region in recruitment and resourcing and workforce planning, representing $5.4 billion in revenue.

Wayne is a graduate of the New York Military Academy, and Johnson and Wales University School of Business. He received his MBA in international human resources and management from the University of Dallas.

Celebrating African-American Achievements

Chicago's PROFESSIONALS

Jonese L. Burnett received her master's degree in May of 2003 from Florida Agricultural and Mechanical University. Soon after, she joined Cintas Corporation on the distribution-production planning management team. Burnett now serves as a program manager for the national accounts sales division, where she manages a multi-million dollar portfolio. She has successfully completed several areas of training while recently becoming a Six Sigma Green Belt.

Born and raised in Chicago, Burnett has attended the Mt. Pisgah Missionary Baptist Church her entire life, where she is a member of the women's auxiliary and the youth ministry. Burnett serves as a board member, secretary, and director of communications for various associations, councils, and organizations throughout the Chicago area.

She gives back to her community as a mentor for students at Beasley Academic Center and Whitney Young Magnet High School. Burnett also serves on the fundraising committee for the Centers for New Horizons. In her spare time, she is constantly engaged in community service projects for children, breast cancer awareness, and battered women. Additionally, Burnett enjoys investing and rehabbing real estate, traveling, and shopping.

Jonese L. Burnett
Program Manager
National Accounts
Sales Division
Cintas Corporation

Jeffrey Carroll is senior account executive for Siemens Building Technologies. In this position, he delivers energy solutions to clients in the Chicagoland area. Jeffrey is a seasoned energy professional with 14 years of experience. His accomplishments include engineering, energy supply management, and consulting.

Jeffrey is a true energy professional, having earned certifications from the Association of Energy Engineers and the Gas Technology Institute. His experience in energy technologies includes power generation, energy product development, and demand side energy management. He is also co-founder of East Gate Energy Corp.

Receiving his bachelor of science degree in mechanical engineering from the Illinois Institute of Technology, Jeffrey is president of the Association of Professional Energy Consultants, and a member of Prince Hall Lodge No. 52 and Arabic Temple No. 44 Shriners.

He is a trustee at Park Manor Christian Church, Hales Franciscan High School, and a regular volunteer for the Chicago Cares charity.

A native of Chicago, Illinois, Jeffrey enjoys numerous hobbies.

Jeffrey Carroll
Senior Account Executive
Siemens Building
Technologies

Marcus A. Chapman is a senior sales executive for Lehigh Direct, a specialty direct mail printing company. As a member of Lehigh's national campaign executive sales team, Chapman is charged with targeting a variety of interactive direct mail tools, magazine inserts, and advertising opportunities championing their flagship ProCard™ product to Fortune 500 companies.

Chapman's experience in communications is diverse (publishing, telecommunications, and print), and he attributes his success to his at-home training, education, and belief in self. He believes that "the way you habitually think of yourself determines your success because of its prescriptive power. What you believe to be possible influences your hopes, aspirations, actions and the outcome of your plans."

A native of Dixmoor, Illinois, Marcus received a bachelor of arts degree in communications with a concentration in marketing from the University of Pennsylvania. While attending Pennsylvania, Marcus' activities included varsity football, Alpha Phi Alpha Fraternity, Inc., the Student Christian Association, and Say Yes to Education, a nonprofit mentoring program for at-risk inner-city students.

Marcus A. Chapman
Senior Sales Executive
Lehigh Direct

THE INAUGURAL EDITION *Who's Who In Black Chicago*®

Chicago's PROFESSIONALS
Celebrating African-American Achievements

Curtis L. Cooper is a senior account manager for Clear Channel Radio, Chicago. He represents seven radio stations reaching more than three million listeners/consumers. Curtis assists advertising agencies in increasing the market share of their myriad clients. In addition, he is responsible for generating non-traditional revenue and new business development.

Born and raised in Chicago, Curtis' marketing and sales career began in the corporate sales department at Great America. He later became an account manager for V-103 Chicago.

A graduate of the University of Illinois at Urbana-Champaign, Curtis played football there during the late 1970s. He is married and has a daughter named Courtney.

Curtis L. Cooper
Senior Account Manager
Clear Channel Radio,
Chicago

Kareem is a visually handicapped, seventh-year attorney at Winston & Strawn. He practices in the litigation department on various cases, including products liability, contract disputes, and other commercial litigation.

He received his bachelor's degree in advertising in 1995 from the University of Illinois. In 1999, Kareem graduated cum laude from the University of Illinois where he received his juris doctorate and MBA.

Several of Kareem's honors include, appearing in the November/December 2001 issue of *Ebony* magazine as one of 30 Leaders of the Future Under 30, and receiving Winston & Strawn's 1999-2000 Probono Commitment to Legal Service Award.

Dedicated to community service, Kareem serves as president of the board of directors for the Black Ensemble Theater, the largest black-run theater in Chicago. Additionally, Kareem facilitates a workshop for the Tavis Smiley Foundation's Youth to Leaders Program; and has served as the keynote speaker at Lincoln Challenge Academy, designed to aid children who have dropped out of high school. He has mentored a high school student through the LINK Unlimited program, and served as president of the Black Law Students' Association.

Kareem A. Dale
Attorney at Law
Winston & Strawn LLP

Melissa Donaldson is the inclusion practices manager for CDW, a Fortune 500 company, and a leading provider of technology products and services for business, government, and education.

In her current role, Donaldson serves as a strategic partner to all business units to create a diverse workforce, foster an inclusive work environment, and leverage diversity in order to drive CDW's successes. Additionally, Donaldson is responsible for developing strategic plans for diverse recruiting, inclusion training, and education and communication initiatives. She also oversees the development and operation of inclusion councils and affinity groups, and forging partnerships with external networks and organizations.

Donaldson joined CDW in 1999 and played a pivotal role in developing the company's inaugural leadership development program, earning CDW recognition as one of the "Top 50 Training Companies" by *Training* magazine.

Holding a bachelor of science degree in management science from Wright State University, she also received a master's degree in administration from Central Michigan University.

Donaldson is a member of the Chicagoland Chapter of the American Society of Training and Development, and the National Association of Female Executives.

Melissa Donaldson
Inclusion Practices Manager
CDW Corporation

Who's Who In Black Chicago® THE INAUGURAL EDITION

Celebrating African-American Achievements

Chicago's PROFESSIONALS

Pat joined International Truck and Engine Corporation as their supplier diversity manager in 1998. She is a consistent supporter of minority business development as shown by her 30-plus years of involvement with the Chicago Minority Business Development Council.

An immediate past chairman of the board of directors for Chicago Minority Business Development Council, Hanes maintains working relationships with several M/WBE business development councils. She is currently an executive board member for NMSDC.

Earning numerous awards and recognitions for her work in minority business development, Hanes is largely responsible for International Truck and Engine receiving the "Success Award" from the MBC/CMBDC for 2003.

Her accomplishments have been chronicled in the media including, *Minority Business News USA*, *Women and Minorities in Business*, *The Chicago Defender*, and many more.

An honors graduate, Hanes received her bachelor's in business administration from DePaul University. She also holds the lifetime certified purchasing managers title from the Institute for Supply Management.

Patricia Hanes
Manager, Corporate
Supplier Diversity
International Truck and
Engine Corporation

Sharon Hidalgo is a sales and account executive for Hewitt Associates, a global human resource consulting and outsourcing firm located in Lincolnshire, Illinois. Sharon is actively involved in corporate diversity initiatives at Hewitt Associates. She is a member of the Multi-Cultural Leadership Advisory Council, and the governance committee for the Minority Leadership Dialogue. Sharon is a "Champion" of the Women in Leadership at Hewitt, and serves as the co-business sponsor to the Latino and Hispanic Associates Network group at Hewitt.

She has held several successful senior management and marketing and operations positions at Marsh & McLennan and Xerox Corporation, respectively. Sharon sits on the executive board of Changing Worlds, a nonprofit organization whose mission is to foster inclusive communities through oral history, writing, and art programs. These programs are designed to improve student learning, affirm identity, and enhance cross-cultural understandings.

Sharon is a graduate of Indiana University, where she majored in speech pathology and audiology. She is a member of the National Association of African Americans in Human Resources, Alpha Kappa Alpha Sorority, Inc., and The Monarch Awards Foundation.

Sharon R. Hidalgo
Sales & Account Executive
Hewitt Associates

Lawrence N. Hill is an associate in the Chicago office of Gardner Carton & Douglas LLP and a member of the firm's litigation department. Hill focuses his practice on general and complex commercial litigation related to commercial disputes and investigative matters. His practice includes a range of litigation experience in matters relating to the resolution of business disputes including arbitrations, product liability defense, and complex federal litigation. In addition, he practices contract, copyright infringement, and tort defense actions in federal and state courts. Hill also has experience representing entities involved in investigations conducted by regulatory and law enforcement agencies.

A 2000 honors graduate of the Chicago-Kent College of Law, Hill received his bachelor of science degree from Roosevelt University in 1990.

Hill was appointed by the Illinois Supreme Court as a member of the Illinois Board of Admissions to the Bar. Additionally, he serves as a member of the board of trustees of Ancona School, and is a member of several committees of the Cook County Bar Association where he received its Presidential Award in 2003.

Lawrence N. Hill
Associate Attorney
Gardner Carton &
Douglas LLP

THE INAUGURAL EDITION *Who's Who In Black Chicago*

Chicago's PROFESSIONALS
Celebrating African-American Achievements

Dana Holmes
Communications Consultant
Hewitt Associates

Dana Holmes is communications consultant for Hewitt's corporate relations department. She is responsible for serving as business partner and advisor to senior leadership by implementing companywide communication strategies that support Hewitt's brand, leadership development, business continuity, and diversity and inclusion efforts.

She is a seasoned professional with more than 14 years of corporate communications experience, which spans the fashion, consumer packaged goods, health care, human resources, entertainment, and nonprofit industries. From 1994 to 1997, Dana held the post of fashion editor for the *Chicago Daily Defender*, the nation's most prestigious and oldest black daily newspaper founded in 1905.

In addition, Dana has held memberships with the Chicago Association of Black Journalists, Public Relations Society of America, the Illinois State University Black Colleagues Association, and Abbott Laboratories Women Leaders in Action Event Planning Committee. She is also member of the Kraft Foods African-American Council advisory board, Hewitt Associates Women in Leadership Governance Council, and Fashion Group International. Dana served on the board of directors for the Lake County Urban League, and is a member of the International Association of Business Communicators.

Claudine Jordan
Business Manager
The ComfortCake Company

The business manager of The ComfortCake Company, makers of "pound cake so good it feels like a hug," Claudine Jordan has been with the company since it launched in 2001 with United Airlines as its first customer. ComfortCake® is sold in more than 1,500 retail stores, through its Web site, and delivers four million servings yearly to Chicago Public Schools.

An administrative, customer service, and public relations expert, Jordan has worked as the key right hand of Amy S. Hilliard, founder and chief executive officer of ComfortCake for more than 12 years. This includes corporate stints at L'Oréal/Soft Sheen and Burrell Communications Group. A Chicago native, Jordan's public relations background also includes ten years with Burson-Marsteller on accounts such as Quaker Oats/Gatorade, McDonald's, Procter & Gamble, and G.D. Searle, just to name a few.

Also responsible for the company's numerous community relations efforts, Jordan is part of the ComfortCake team featured on CNN, the Food Network, Home Shopping Network, and the *Black Enterprise Report*.

Cynthia Jordan
Director of Events
Chicago Minority Business Development Council

As director of special events for the Chicago Minority Business Development Council (CMBDC), Cynthia oversees the execution of events, meetings, and programs throughout the year. She helps to ensure that the leading corporations and minority business enterprises that make up the council members, have an opportunity to meet and network for the purposes of global supplier diversity.

Under her leadership, the prestigious annual Chicago Business Opportunity Fair has become one of Chicago's premiere events. It showcases and recognizes the products and services of minority businesses for corporate buyers and government agencies.

Cynthia is also a principal consultant with Royal Affairs, an event planning and management company servicing fantasy weddings for clients that have included NBA players, to most recently, "A World of Possibilities" event with actor and activist Danny Glover.

She attended Graham College in Massachusetts and Boston University where she studied fashion merchandising and business. Cynthia is the proud mother of two children, Erika and Marcus.

Celebrating African-American Achievements

Chicago's
PROFESSIONALS

As client security relationship manager for Hewitt Associates, Tyrone Parker is responsible for ensuring client satisfaction with Hewitt's security program. He works with client information security personnel and various IS security groups to manage security risks. Tyrone conducts security audits as well as manages relationships with third party vendors to ensure compliance with security requirements.

His memberships include PUSH (People United to Save Humanity), the Leadership Team for black associates at Hewitt Associates, and a past board member and current executive vice president with the Black Data Processing Associates (BDPA). Tyrone is also a member of Omega Psi Phi Fraternity, Inc., and is active on many committees at Rock of Ages Baptist Church in Maywood, Illinois.

Presently, Tyrone is completing his graduate degree at Keller Graduate School of Business.

Tyrone Parker
Client Security
Relationship Manager
Hewitt Associates

Bruce C. Powell is a certified and licensed massage therapist. He received his certification from the Chicago School of Massage Therapy in 1995. In the same year, Bruce received his national certification for therapeutic massage and bodywork. He is also a member of the Associated Bodywork and Massage Professionals. His training in massage and his love for helping people are shown through his energy and enthusiastic style.

Bruce received special recognition from the Ronald McDonald Children's Charities for his volunteer work at their Chicago location. In the years 2000 and 2004, he was pictured in *Ebony* doing massage while working at Bettye O Day Spa. Bruce, an avid walker/runner and cyclist who also adopted a vegetarian/vegan diet, has lost a total of 150 pounds.

Bruce's experience and knowledge in massage, nutrition, and exercise has helped him to better serve, not only his clientele, but also his family and friends. He believes that health is the greatest of all human blessings, and to achieve total wellness, the mind, the body, and the spirit must be addressed. Bruce is operating in his gifts.

Bruce C. Powell
Massage Therapist
Bettye O Day Spa

Joy Sparks is an artist. She is an entertainer with many skills, of which she is a Screen Actor's Guild member and published writer.

Sparks graduated from Loyola University of Chicago with a bachelor's degree in English and philosophy. After graduating college, Joy was a social worker for abused children in the south suburbs of Chicago and Cincinnati, Ohio. Joy quickly learned one thing about herself, she loved the performing arts more. As a result, Sparks pursued acting and found continued success with the roles she plays on stage and on camera. She also teaches middle school and high school students a love for literature and an appreciation of the theatre.

Additionally, Joy has written several articles for papers around the Chicagoland area and has co-authored a book entitled *Bye-Bye Boardroom: Confessions From a New Breed of Stay-At-Home Moms*. In addition, she was featured and quoted in the January 2005 edition of *Glamour*. Her love of the arts keep her persistent in setting goals and always claiming and achieving new levels of success with God in the forefront.

Joy Sparks
Artist & Entertainer

Chicago's PROFESSIONALS
Celebrating African-American Achievements

Michelle Speller-Thurman is an associate in the Chicago office of Jenner & Block, LLP, a full-service law firm with more than 400 attorneys located in Chicago, Dallas, New York, and Washington, D.C. She is a member of Jenner's corporate, mergers and acquisitions, and corporate finance practices, and the firm's hiring committee and pro bono committee. Speller-Thurman's practice is concentrated on corporate finance, mergers and acquisitions, and general corporate matters.

Speller-Thurman currently serves as the co-chair of the Chicago Bar Association's career assistance committee. She is also a member of the Black Women Lawyers' Association and a member of the planning committee for the Cook County Bar Association Minority Law Student Job Fair.

Speller-Thurman graduated from Northwestern University School of Law in 1999 and received her bachelor of science degree in finance from the University of Illinois at Urbana-Champaign in 1991. She lives in Chicago with her husband, Cedric D. Thurman, and nine-year-old son, Alexander.

Michelle Speller-Thurman
Associate, Attorney at Law
Jenner & Block, LLP

As global senior operations manager for diversity at Hewitt Associates, Tyronne Stoudemire is responsible for the overall operation and optimization of a comprehensive suite of diversity programs. In partnership with the chief diversity officer, chief executive officer, and other senior leaders, Tyronne focuses on driving sustainable change through the implementation and management of key diversity programs across Hewitt's global landscape.

Tyronne is a member of the advisory board for Diversity Best Practices, a member of the National Black MBA Chicago chapter, and a board of trustees member of the Music Institute of Evanston, Illinois.

Receiving the Monarch Award for outstanding male, Tyronne was also awarded the People's Voice award for Most Inspirational African American in Lake County.

Tyronne Stoudemire
Global Senior Operations Manager
Hewitt Associates

Charmon Parker Williams, Ph.D., is a talent program manager supporting human resources strategy and executive talent management for Hewitt's human resources outsourcing business segment. She is the lead for Hewitt's affinity group for African-American associates and part of the Multicultural Leadership Dialogue.

Prior to Hewitt, Charmon was principal consultant for her own management consulting firm; vice president of the human resources and diversity practice for James H. Lowry and Associates; personnel officer at Harris Bank; personnel psychologist for the Office of Personnel Management; and adjunct professor at Northwestern's Kellogg School of Management.

Charmon has presented at several national conferences and is co-developer and co-facilitator for a seminar called "Creating Your Self Brand." A published writer in the areas of career management, leadership development, and diversity, she is a contributing writer for *Black MBA Magazine* and *Black IT Professional*. She is a board member with the Boys and Girls Club of Chicago.

Charmon has a master's degree and a doctorate of philosophy degree in industrial psychology from Illinois Institute of Technology, and a bachelor of arts degree in psychology from Syracuse University.

Charmon Parker Williams, Ph.D.
Talent Program Manager
Hewitt Associates

Celebrating African-American Achievements

BIOGRAPHICAL INDEX

Adams, Carol L.	146
Adams, Carolyn	86
Adams, Jocelyn H.	296
Adeniji, Olufemi	262
Agnew, Sheila L.	296
Allen, Danielle	262
Allen, Sharon C.	297
Alston, Tracey	297
Armstrong, Richard	135
Ashford, Jr., Calvin	298
Austin, Mark	298
Austin, Marlon	298
Baker, Derrick K.	248
Ballentine, Warren	234
Ball-Reed, Patrice	286
Banks, Patricia	146
Banks, Phyllis D.	299
Banks, Sharron	314
Banks, Vanita M.	234
Barner, Sharon R.	235
Barrow, Willie	147
Barrymore, Alise D.	263
Bates, Barbara	299
Bates, Yasmin	214
Batson, Phyllis	113
Bedford, Ken	248
Bell, D. Rayford	276
Bell, Fran J.	147
Bell, James	58
Belser, Sr., John Leland	276
Beneby, Doyle	115
Bennett, Arthur L.	286
Bennett, Bonita L.	300
Benson, Sharonda T.	263
Billinger, Monica Armstrong	214
Bishop, Patricia Martin	148
Blackwell, Pamela	148
Blackwell, Jr., Robert	300
Blackwell, Sr., Robert D.	149
Bland, Columbus F.	277
Bonaparte, Jr., William	149
Bonds, Ty	215
Bordelon, Richard L.	126
Bowles, Barbara L.	150
Boyd, Cynthia E.	150
Bradbury, III, Emmett L.	264
Bridges, Ingrid E.	314
Brittingham, M. Wayne	314
Brookins, Kevin B.	113
Brooks, Albertina Walker	151
Brooks, Marc	151
Brown, Deborah Olivia	249
Brown, Dorothy	152
Brown, Ellamae	119
Brown, F. Keith	152
Brown, Julian E.	215
Brown, Leslie	287
Brown, Morocco	209

Celebrating African-American Achievements

BIOGRAPHICAL INDEX

Brown, Yuri 139	Chapman, Roslyn C. 301
Burnett, Jonese L. 315	Chess, Eva 217
Burns, Jr., Jeff 153	Clark, Frank M. 112
Burrell, Tom.. 54	Clark, III, Frank M. 217
Burton, Cheryl 153	Cobb, Alfonso 218
Bush, Bernetta D. 154	Cobb, Delmarie L. 249
Butler, Jr., Calvin G. 154	Coker, Julie 46
Butler, Jr., Lee H. 264	Coleman, Sharon Johnson 156
Bynoe, Peter C. B. 235	Coleman, Jr., Charles 46
Byrd, Gill 206	Coley, Angela L. 218
Byrd, Sharon E. 155	Collier, Darren C. 236
Caldwell, Karen 119	Collins-Langston, Annazette R. 157
Campbell, Susan M. 216	Compton, James W. 157
Campbell, William C. 155	Coney, Lester 219
Cannamoré, Madie M. Davis.. 265	Cooke, Kevann M. 158
Carnette, Michael E. 102	Cooper, Curtis L. 316
Carney, Demetrius E. 236	Coverson, Marrice 287
Carothers, Isaac 156	Crutchfield, Lisa.. 115
Carpenter, Jerry 216	Cuff, Cecilia 47
Carroll, Jeffrey 315	Cunningham, Epluribus C. 277
Carson, Joyce L. 110	Cunningham, Joy Virginia 158
Carter, Warrick 66	Curry, Freida J. 288
Change, Lamont 120	Dale, Kareem A. 316
Chapman, Marcus A. 315	Dale, Robert J.. 159

322 *Who's Who In Black Chicago*® THE INAUGURAL EDITION

Celebrating African-American Achievements

BIOGRAPHICAL INDEX

Daly, Ronald 138	Eaglin, Marsha J. 250
Daniel, Elnora D. 92	Earles, R. Martin 161
Daniels-Halisi, Pamela 121	Eason-Watkins, Barbara 162
Davis, Addie L. 265	Ebie, Nyambi 162
Davis, Danny K. 159	Elligan, Don 163
Davis, Heather A. 219	Ervin, Tim 120
Davis, Michael D. 160	Essex, James 163
Davis, Milton O. 36	Evans, Timothy C. 164
Davis, Shani 160	Evans, Jr., Willard S. 220
Davis, William Quincy 161	Farrakhan, Louis 164
Deal, Richard M. 250	Felder, Alexis L. 278
Dee, Merri 74	Felder, Trunell D. 278
De Haas, Geraldine 288	Fenn, Janice 64
Delanois, J. Clark 126	Ferguson, Diana 134
Dickerson, Amina J. 220	Flowers, D. Michelle 60
Dixon, Donna 289	Flowers, Mary E. 165
Donaldson, Melissa 316	Ford, Lula M. 165
Dorcas, Dana 139	Foster, Jylla Moore 302
Dorrough, Jr., Hollis 289	Foster, Jr., William H. 279
Drake, Darryl 207	Freeman, Charles E. 166
Dube, Caleb..266	Freeman, Ernest V. 221
Duckworth, Kevin B. 237	Giles, Tracey Banks 141
Duncan-James, Gwen C. 301	Gills, Jeanne M. 237
Duster, Dan 302	Glanton, Richard H. 110

THE INAUGURAL EDITION **Who's Who In Black Chicago**® **323**

Celebrating African-American Achievements

BIOGRAPHICAL INDEX

Goodwin, Harold 207	Hinton, Gregory T. 169
Gordon, Sheila Y. 221	Hobson, Mellody 56
Graham-Hodo, Trina.. 140	Hodges, Raymond S. 169
Grant, Donna M. 266	Holland, Louis A. 170
Gray-Young, Deborah 222	Holmes, Calvin L. 290
Greene, Martin P. 238	Holmes, Dana 318
Gregg, Bobbie 222	Holmes, Evelyn 251
Guichard, Andre 90	Holmes, Patricia Brown 239
Hairston, Leslie A. 166	Hooker, John 112
Hanes, Patricia 317	Hooks, Theresa Fambro 251
Hardy, Kevin 127	Hope, Leah 252
Harris, Jr., Glenn A. 279	Hopkins, Dwight N. 267
Harris, Mildred C. 280	Horn, III, Charles 223
Harris, Yvonne 267	Hornsberry, Noel 140
Hart, Brett 135	Horton, Selina 121
Hartman, Hermene 167	Howard, Bobbie 210
Hatch, Sr., Marshall Elijah 280	Howard, Jr., Larry 252
Hatchett, Bonita L. 238	Howard, Robert 170
Hawkins, Ron 167	Hunter, Mattie 171
Haywood, III, Roosevelt 303	Huskisson, Gregory J. 253
Heard, Jacquelyn L. 168	Isaac, William 142
Hickman, Stephanie J. 114	Jackson, Cheryle Robinson 253
Hidalgo, Sharon R. 317	Jackson, Darrell B. 127
Higgins, Robert S. D. 168	Jackson, Don 171
Hill, Jr., James 303	Jackson, Sr., Jessie 172
Hill, Lawrence N. 317	Jackson, Richard D. 223
Hilliard, Amy S. 304	Jarrett, Valerie B. 172

Celebrating African-American Achievements

BIOGRAPHICAL INDEX

Jean-Baptiste, Lionel	173
Jenkins, Charles	281
Jenkins, Maureen	254
Jennetten, Amy	47
Johnson, Don	208
Johnson, John H.	37
Johnson, Karen F.	103
Johnson, S. Jermikko	82
Johnson, Jr., Oscar	122
Johnson, William A.	173
Jones, Elliott	224
Jones, Jr., Emil	174
Jones, Louis	304
Jones, Olivet Benbow	305
Jordan, Claudine	318
Jordan, Cynthia	318
Jordan, Karen	174
Jordan, Michael	175
Karim, Ayesha	141
Keeble, Stanley	290
Keith, Jeanette Newton	175
Kenner-Johnson, Gwendolyn	291
Kent, Herb	62
Kerr, Anedra	224
King, Alan S.	239
King, Paul D.	225
Lambert, Jerline	305
Lathon, Sheraine	281
LaVelle, Avis	176
Lee, Cassandra R.	306
Lenoir, Lisa	254
Letcher, Beverly D. Burton	268
Letts, Eileen M.	240
Lewis, Adorn L.	176
Lewis, J. Corey	177
Lewis-Elligan, Tracey	268
Lindsey, Connie L.	128
Lofton, George W.	115
Logan, Lyle	128
Lomax-Juzang, Doris	68
Long-Hill, LaTretta	225
Loud, III, Irwin C.	177
Lowry, James	76
Lumpkin, William L.	48
Lyle, Fredrenna M.	178
Madhubuti, Haki R.	178
Martin, Jerrold	111
Martin, Linda D.	103
Martin, Roland S.	255
Mason, Terry	179

Celebrating African-American Achievements

BIOGRAPHICAL INDEX

McCain, Anthony 226	Morris, Aldon 84
McClinton, Lena 226	Morris, Eugene 183
McElvane, Pamela A. 179	Morrow, Derrick 49
McGee, Howard 255	Moyo, Yvette J. 183
McGhee, Sharon K. 256	Mufwene, Salikoko S. 270
McGowan, Barbara J. 180	Muhammad, Ishmael R. 184
McKinney, Denise B. 104	Murrain, Linda F. 291
McKissack, Cheryl Mayberry 180	Nash, Bob 184
McKissack, Deryl 181	Nelson, Kerry L. 129
McKoy, June M. 269	Nesbitt, Martin H. 185
McLeary, Thomas L. 306	Northern, Sr., David A. 292
Medlin, Tony 210	Oden, Jean 292
Meeks, James T. 181	Olaleye, Caleb A. 270
Mell, Patricia 269	Oliver, Lawrence 105
Mendenhall, Samuel 240	Olopade, Olufunmilayo 185
Miller, Marquis D. 182	Orgain, Javette C. 186
Miller, Pepper 307	Owens, Jr., Hoyett W. 307
Miller, Jr., Willie 118	Palmore, Mary K. 186
Mims, Verett A. 104	Palmore, Roderick 134
Minier, Leslie D. 241	Parham, Richelle 227
Mitchell, Mary 256	Parker, Tyrone 319
Mitchell, Stephen S. 241	Payne, Allison 187
Mitts, Emma 182	Pearson-McNeil, Cheryl 227
Moncure, Roosevelt 48	Pennick, Aurie A. 293
Montgomery, James 80	Pierce, Arnella Elizabeth 282

Celebrating African-American Achievements
BIOGRAPHICAL INDEX

Pierce, Ozzie	105
Pitts, Adrienne Banks	242
Porter, Tracie R.	242
Porterfield, Harry	88
Powell, Bruce C.	319
Powell, Connie Davis	49
Preckwinkle, Toni	187
Prentice, III, Edward	308
Primo, III, Quintin E.	188
Pugh, Stephen H.	243
Rakestraw, Pamela	308
Rakestraw, Stanley	308
Rawls, Elliot	138
Ray, Timothy	243
Read, Eddie S.	309
Redmond, Wynona	228
Reid, Phillip B. J.	106
Rice, Judith C.	188
Rice, Linda Johnson	189
Richardson, Julieanna L.	257
Ringo, Wesley L.	129
Robinson, Zelda	257
Rogers, Desiree Glapion	189
Rogers, Jr., John W.	190
Rollins, Lisa M.	293
Rose, Jim	190
Rush, Bobby L.	191
Salter, Kwame S.	191
Sampson, Albert	282
Samuels, Gina Miranda	271
Sanders, Hosea	192
Sanders, Lauri M.	228
Saracco, Gail	244
Saunders, Warner	192
Sawyer, Deborah M.	309
Scott, Michael W.	193
Seabrook, III, Lemuel	229
Sessoms, Furmin D.	294
Sherrell, Charles R.	310
Simmons, Carlton	143
Simmons, Erika	310
Simmons, Monika	310
Smith, Barbara W.	130
Smith, Donna N.	118
Smith, Horace E.	193
Smith, James	229
Smith, Lovie	206
Smith, Marc A.	143
Smith, Stephanie B.	194
Sneed, Paula A.	194
Spann, Pervis	195
Spann-Cooper, Melody	195
Sparks, Joy	319
Speller-Thurman, Michelle	320
Spencer, Nicole A. B.	230
Spencer, Tim	208
Staples, Mavis	196
Starks, Dana V.	196
Sterling, John D.	311
Stewart, Darcel M.	106
Stoudemire, Tyrone	320
Strassner, Jr., Howard T.	197
Strickland, Eric	130
Stuttley, Michael W.	197
Sutton, Michael	311
Sykes, Michael G.	283
Sylk, Sam	198
Taylor-Eastmond, Tiffany	312
Taylor-Nash, Rita	230
Telman, Deborah H.	107
Thomas, Charles	258
Thomas, Juan R.	244
Thurman, Cedric D.	198
Tilmon, Sr., James A.	258
Tittle, LaDonna	259
Torain, Jr., Ernest W.	245
Trotter, Cortez	199
Trotter, Larry D.	283
Trotter-Gordon, Natatia M.	271
Tucker, Dorothy	259
Tucker, Joyce E.	102
Turks, Kevin	211
Tyler, Jason J.	199
Tzomes, Pete	70
Voisin, Dexter R.	272
Walker, David	260
Walls, Sandra F.	272
Walter, Milana L.	260
Walton, Patricia A.	312
Ward, Everett S.	245
Ward, Regina	122
Ward, Roxanne M.	200
Warren, Kenneth W.	273
Washington, Eddie	200
Washington, Gary S.	123
Washington, Harold	38
Webb, Sarah	123
West, Mary Beth Stone	201
Whitaker, Eric E.	201
White, Chareice	231
White, Jesse	202
Wiley, Marvin E.	284
Wilkins, Anthony E.	131
Wilks, Steven	209
Williams, Charmon Parker	320
Williams, Erika Madison	142
Williams, Jacinta	211
Williams, Rufus	202
Williams, Ruth	203
Wilson, Kenneth W.	231
Winfrey, Oprah	203
Witherspoon, Terry	50
Woldman, Drema Lee	294
Wood, Allison L.	246
Woodley, Arlynn R.	131
Woods, Jamila S.	50
Wright, Antoinette	78
Wright, Jr., Jeremiah	72
Wright, Ramah E.	284

Celebrating African-American Achievements

ADVERTISERS' INDEX

Abbott 97	International Truck and Engine Corporation 124
Aon 24	Jones Lang LaSalle 232
Blue Cross Blue Shield... 124	Kraft 94, 144
Boeing 25, 204	LaSalle Bank 51
CDW 98, 246	Motorola 41
Chicago Defender 108	National City 4
Cintas 30	N'DIGO 34
Columbia College Chicago... 26	Nicor Gas 98
Ernst & Young 132	Peoples Energy 31
Exelon 23	Powell Photography & Digital Imaging..................... 116
Flowers Communications Group 99	Rush University Medical Center 39
Harris.. 52	Sara Lee 42
Hewitt 32	Sirva 53
Houghton Mifflin 40	U.S. Cellular... 14, 136
Hyatt Regency Chicago............................... 7, 44-45, 95	Who's Who Publishing Co., LLC 33, 96, 98, 111,
Illinois Lottery 100	107, 212, 273, 274